GREAT ESSAYS BY NOBEL PRIZE WINNERS

Great Essays

EDITED BY LEO HAMALIAN AND EDMOND L. VOLPE

THE NOONDAY PRESS   NEW YORK
A DIVISION OF
FARRAR, STRAUS & CUDAHY

by Nobel Prize Winners

ACKNOWLEDGMENTS

The editors wish to express their thanks to the persons and publishers listed below for their kind cooperation in granting permission to reprint copyrighted material.

Oriental Singing, by Selma Lagerlöf. From *Harvest* by Selma Lagerlöf, translated by Florence and Naboth Hedir. Copyright 1934, 1935 by Doubleday & Company, Inc. Reprinted by permission.

Killing for Sport, by George Bernard Shaw. Reprinted by permission of the Public Trustee and The Society of Authors, London, England.

Chekhov, by Thomas Mann. Reprinted from *Last Essays* by Thomas Mann, translated by Richard and Clara Winston and Tania and James Stern, by permission of Alfred A. Knopf, Inc. Copyright 1958 by Alfred A. Knopf, Inc.

Castles in Spain by John Galsworthy. Reprinted from *Candelabra* by John Galsworthy, published by Charles Scribner's Sons.

The Death of Gide, by Roger Martin du Gard. From *Recollections of André Gide* by Roger Martin du Gard. Copyright 1953 by The Viking Press, Inc. and reprinted with their permission.

The Brothers Karamazov or The Downfall of Europe, by Herman Hesse. Translated by Harvey Gross. From: *Gesammelte Schriften, Band VII*, by Herman Hesse. Copyright 1957 by Suhrkamp Verlag, and reprinted by permission of the publisher.

Hamlet, by T. S. Eliot. From *Selected Essays 1917-1932* by T. S. Eliot, copyright, 1932 by Harcourt, Brace and Company, Inc. and reprinted with their permission.

Man Will Prevail by William Faulkner. Reprinted from *The Faulkner Reader*, published by Random House, Inc.

Rebellion and Art, by Albert Camus. Reprinted from the Vintage

Books Edition of *The Rebel* by Albert Camus, translated by Anthony Bower, by special arrangement with Alfred A. Knopf, Inc. Copyright 1956 by Alfred A. Knopf, Inc.

On Translating Shakespeare, by Boris Pasternak. Reprinted from *I Remember*, published by Pantheon Books, Inc., by permission of the publisher.

East and West, by Rabindranath Tagore. Reprinted from *Creative Unity*, by permission of the publisher, Macmillan & Company Ltd.

The Place of Music in General History, by Romain Rolland. Reprinted from *Musicians of Former Days* by Romain Rolland, by permission of the publisher, Routledge & Kegan Paul Ltd.

Why do we Laugh?, by Henri Bergson. From the book *Comedy*, copyright © 1956 by Wylie Sypher, which contains "Laughter" by Henri Bergson. Reprinted by permission of Doubleday & Company, Inc.

The Eagle and the Serpent, by Johannes V. Jensen. Reprinted from *The Long Journey*, Book 2, by Johannes V. Jensen, by permission of Alfred A. Knopf, Inc. Copyright 1923 by Alfred A. Knopf, Inc.

Marriage and Morals, by Bertrand Russell. From *Marriage and Morals* by Bertrand Russell. By permission of Liveright, Publishers, New York. Copyright: (R) 1956, Bertrand Russell.

The Renunciation of Thought, by Albert Schweitzer. Excerpts from *Out of My Life and Thought* by Albert Schweitzer. Copyright 1933, 1949, by Henry Holt and Company, Inc. Reprinted by permission of the publishers.

The Fundaments of Theoretical Physics, by Albert Einstein. Reprinted from *Out of My Later Years* by Albert Einstein by permission of the Estate of Albert Einstein.

Unity of Knowledge, by Niels Bohr. Reprinted by permission of The Trustees of Columbia University in the City of New York.

Brain Collaborates with Psyche, by Charles S. Sherrington. Reprinted from *Man on his Nature*, published by Cambridge University Press, by permission of the publisher.

Science as a Means of International Understanding, by Werner Karl Heisenberg. Reprinted from *Philosophical Problems in Nuclear Science*, by permission of the publisher, Pantheon Books, Inc.

The Social Evolution of Man, by Thomas Hunt Morgan. Reprinted from *Scientific Basis of Evolution* by Thomas Hunt Morgan. By permission of W. W. Norton & Company, Inc. Copyright 1932 by W. W. Norton & Company, Inc.

The Future of Understanding, by Erwin Schrödinger. From *Mind and Matter* by Erwin Schrödinger, published by the Cambridge University Press, and reprinted by permission of the publisher.

Scientist and Humanist, by Isidor Isaac Rabi. Reprinted by permission of the Trustees of Columbia University in the City of New York.

Science and Common Sense, by Percy Bridgman. Reprinted by permission of *The Scientific Monthly.*

The Culture of Man in the Atomic Age, by Nikolai Semenov. Reprinted from *Bulletin of the Atomic Scientists* (January, 1959); by permission of the editors of the *Bulletin of the Atomic Scientists.*

To Aram, Virginia, Agnes,
Stan and Joe

Contents

The distinction bestowed upon each of the authors in this collection stems from the last wishes of Alfred Bernhard Nobel, the Swedish scientist whose memory, more than sixty years after his death, can still provoke bitter controversy. His detractors paint an image of him as the irresponsible man who first played with dynamite, as a ruthless munitions-maker who amassed a fortune by peddling his deadly discovery to any buyer, as a "warmaker" whose guilt drove him to a desperate philanthropic gesture just before his death in San Remo, Italy, in 1896. Others believe that he should be remembered as a quiet, gentle, and studious man who dedicated his life to research in chemistry, engineering, and agriculture, who accidentally discovered dynamite while doing so, and who founded with the wealth he made from his discovery a fund designed to promote the arts and sciences and to perpetuate peace on earth. Despite these controversial views of the man, there has been no disagreement about the virtue and value of the awards he established.

In his will, Nobel provided that the major portion of his fortune should be utilized in the following manner: the capital was to be invested by his executors in reliable securities, from which the interest was to be distributed annually "in the form of prizes among those who have, within the respective twelve months successively elapsed, rendered the greatest service to mankind." He also stipulated that the interest should be divided into five equal portions (now about $40,000 each) to be awarded to the person making the most important contributions in physics, chemistry, medicine and physiology, literature, and international peace. The prizes for physics and chemistry were to be awarded by the Swedish Academy of Sciences, for physiology and medicine by the Carolinian Institution at Stockholm, for literature by the Academy at

Stockholm, for peace by a five-person committee elected by the Norwegian Storting or Parliament (Norway and Sweden, at that time, were united). After Nobel's death, the Nobel Foundation was formed, and from January 1, 1901, the "administration of the Nobel Foundation," elected by the representatives, undertook to manage the funds.

The groups involved clarified the somewhat turgid phrases of Nobel's will. Literature was interpreted to mean not only *belles-lettres* but also other works provided they had literary merit. Thus, over the years, while the Academy has preferred the imaginative artist, historians like Mommsen and Churchill and philosophers like Russell, Eucken, and Bergson have been honored. They also stipulated that while the prizes were to be awarded for the candidate's latest work, older achievements would be taken into consideration if their importance had become apparent within the twelve-month period. Hence, while a particular work or deed has usually been cited as the basis of the award, writers like T. S. Eliot, André Gide, and Ivan Bunin, scientists like Werner Karl Heisenberg and Nikolai Semenov have had a lifetime's endeavor rewarded in Stockholm. Furthermore, it was decided that the prize for each of the five groups could be divided or allotted jointly to two or more prize winners or withheld until the following year if no suitable candidate was found. As a result, the prize in literature was divided between Fréderic Mistral and Don Jose Echergaray in 1904, and between Karl Gjellerup and Henrik Pontoppidan in 1917; and it was withheld seven other years, all war years with the exception of 1935. In the sciences, where teamwork is important, the years of joint awards are too numerous to list, and it was chiefly during the years of the two world wars that they were withheld. The fact that the prize for peace was withheld a total of fourteen times many observers would interpret ominously.

All the distributing bodies named in the will have set up committees of three to five persons. In support of these committees, as well as for the purpose of examining the qualifications of the proposed candidates, the distributing bodies have also formed special scientific committees called Nobel Institutions: the Nobel Institution of the Swedish Academy; the Nobel Institution of Norway at Oslo, and the Nobel Institution for Physical Chemistry at

Stockholm. These committees, after careful deliberation, express their opinion about the candidates, but the final decisions are announced by the distributing bodies.

Nominations for awards can be made only by authorized persons: members of the distributing bodies, members of the Nobel Committees, former Nobel Prize winners, designated university and college faculties; and for the peace prize, members of governments or international organizations. Nominations must be submitted in writing and accompanied by the candidate's qualifications and publications.

The distributing bodies have scrupulously observed Nobel's request that "no consideration whatever is to be given to the nationality of the candidate"—except during the war years, when candidates of neutral countries were given preference (hence the preponderance of Scandinavian names during these periods). The winners represent 28 countries, mostly European, but China, India, Australia, Argentina, Chile, Canada, and the United States have been honored. After a slow start, the United States has sent 71 Americans to Stockholm in all fields; Great Britain and her Empire, 52; Germany, 49 (not including those who declined the award because of Hitler's decree that forbade Germans to accept it); and France, 32.

The breakdown of each category reveals some interesting sidelights. For one thing, the awards generally tend to support the popular stereotypes about national character. The Germans, reputed to be a precise people distinguished by their discipline of habit, and the English, always regarded as trail-blazers in the exploration of physical and biological phenomena, dominate the science list before World War II: in physics, 11 Germans and 11 Englishmen were elected; in chemistry, 16 Germans and 6 Englishmen; in medicine and physiology, 6 Germans and 6 Englishmen. After World War II, Americans completely eclipsed their colleagues in all three fields: 18 in medicine and physiology, 9 in physics, and 8 in chemistry (the English are runners-up in all three fields). The French, to whom the ages have attributed eloquence and elegance in letters, have won the literature prize 9 times. No doubt much to the surprise of those who believe the United States is the land of the philistine, American writers have taken the prize 6 times to tie the English for second place. In the field of peace, Americans again lead, 12 to 8 over the French. On the basis of the awards in peace, the Scandinavians maintain their reputation as peace-loving people with 8 awards, and on the basis of population, the Swiss with a total of 11 prizes have the best record. The call has gone to Russia only 6 times, perhaps an indication that her policy of cultural isolation has kept her artists and scientists from receiving the popular international recognition that otherwise might have crowned their endeavors.

Since the Nobel Foundation was created, about three hundred men and women have been summoned to Stockholm to be applauded by the world for their contributions to the advancement of humanity. This volume of essays presents the memorable thoughts of some of these distinguished people. In our preceding volume, *Great Short Stories by Nozel Prize Winners,* we were confined to one group of award winners, but in this collection we have been free to range over the vast body of literature produced by the winners in all five fields in which prizes are given. This literature, though sometimes technical and tedious, was far more often stimulating and exciting. Men who have achieved greatness in one area of human endeavor need not necessarily be sages in other areas of human experience, but we discovered that their opinions, no matter how far afield from their own calling, were almost always worth pondering. Hence, we have not hesitated to represent an award winner by an essay unrelated in theme to his field of special knowledge or achievement.

With so much excellent material to choose from, we strove for a collection that would display the greatness of mind and heart of each author and that would provide the reader with a wide variety of subject, style, and opinion. Not all the greatest writers and most radiant minds of our century can speak here—all were not elected to the award—but enough of them are present to provide the sort of stimulation men have always enjoyed in the company of extraordinary intellect and sensibility.

Leo Hamalian and Edmond L. Volpe
The City College of New York

LITERATURE

Rudyard Kipling

A MEETING WITH MARK TWAIN

RUDYARD KIPLING, *the English novelist, short-story writer, and poet, was born in 1865 in India, the land associated with much of his writing. Educated in England, at the age of eighteen he returned to India, where he soon became an expert journalist and the author of stories and poems much in demand. In 1889, he traveled to England by way of the United States, gathering impressions for the volume from which the following essay is taken,* From Sea to Sea *(1899). In London, he added to his reputation with* The Light That Failed *(1890) and* Barrack-Room Ballads *(1902). Following a trip to the South Seas, he settled in Brattleboro, Vermont for four years (his wife was American), where he produced* The Jungle Books *(1894-95),* The Seven Seas *(1896) and* Captains Courageous *(1897). His restless spirit carried him back to England, then to South Africa to report the Boer War. By 1922 when he became the rector of St. Andrews University, he was wealthy and famous. Before he died in 1936 he had become the symbol of British imperialism and conservatism. The Nobel Prize for Literature was given to him in 1907 when he was forty-two, the youngest man and the first Englishman to win the award.*

They said in Buffalo that he was in Hartford, Conn.; and again they said "perchance he is gone upon a journey to Portland"; and a big, fat drummer vowed that he knew the great man intimately, and that Mark was spending the summer in Europe—which information so upset me that I embarked upon the wrong train, and was incontinently turned out by the conductor three-quarters of a mile from the station, amid the wilderness of railway tracks. Have you ever, encumbered with great-coat and valise, tried to dodge diversely-minded locomotives when the sun was shining in your eyes? But I forgot that you have not seen Mark Twain, you people of no account!

Saved from the jaws of the cowcatcher, me wandering devious a stranger met.

"Elmira is the place. Elmira in the State of New York—this State, not two hundred miles away"; and he added, perfectly unnecessarily, "Slide, Kelley, slide."

I slid on the West Shore line, I slid till midnight, and they dumped me down at the door of a frowzy hotel in Elmira. Yes, they knew all about "that man Clemens," but reckoned he was not in town; had gone East somewhere. I had better possess my soul in patience till the morrow, and then dig up the "man Clemens' " brother-in-law, who was interested in coal.

The idea of chasing half a dozen relatives in addition to Mark Twain up and down a city of thirty thousand inhabitants kept me awake. Morning revealed Elmira, whose streets were desolated by railway tracks, and whose suburbs were given up to the manufacture of door-sashes and window-frames. It was surrounded by pleasant, fat, little hills, rimmed with timber and topped with cultivation. The Chemung River flowed generally up and down the town, and had just finished flooding a few of the main streets.

The hotel-man and the telephone-man assured me that the much-desired brother-in-law was out of town, and no one seemed to know where "the man Clemens" abode. Later on I discovered that he had not summered in that place for more than nineteen seasons, and so was comparatively a new arrival.

A friendly policeman volunteered the news that he had seen Twain or "someone very like him" driving a buggy the day before. This gave me a delightful sense of nearness. Fancy living in a town where you could see the author of *Tom Sawyer*, or "someone very like him," jolting over the pavements in a buggy!

"He lives out yonder at East Hill," said the policeman; "three miles from here."

Then the chase began—in a hired hack, up an awful hill, where sunflowers blossomed by the roadside, and crops waved, and *Harper's Magazine* cows stood in eligible and commanding attitudes knee-deep in clover, all ready to be transferred to photogravure. The great man must have been persecuted by outsiders aforetime, and fled up the hill for refuge.

Presently the driver stopped at a miserable, little, white wood shanty, and demanded "Mister Clemens."

"I know he's a big-bug and all that," he explained, "but you can never tell what sort of notions those sort of men take into their heads to live in, anyways."

There rose up a young lady who was sketching thistletops and goldenrod, amid a plentiful supply of both, and set the pilgrimage on the right path.

"It's a pretty Gothic house on the left-hand side a little way farther on."

"Gothic h——," said the driver. "Very few of the city hacks take this drive, specially if they know they are coming out here," and he glared at me savagely.

It was a very pretty house, anything but Gothic, clothed with ivy, standing in a very big compound, and fronted by a verandah full of chairs and hammocks. The roof of the verandah was a trellis-work of creepers, and the sun peeping through moved on the shining boards below.

Decidedly this remote place was an ideal one for work, if a man could work among these soft airs and the murmur of the long-eared crops.

Appeared suddenly a lady used to dealing with rampageous outsiders. "Mr. Clemens has just walked downtown. He is at his brother-in-law's house."

Then he was within shouting distance, after all, and the chase had not been in vain. With speed I fled, and the driver, skidding the wheel and swearing audibly, arrived at the bottom of that hill without accidents. It was in the pause that followed between ringing the brother-in-law's bell and getting an answer that it occurred to me for the first time Mark Twain might possibly have other engagements than the entertainment of escaped lunatics from India, be they never so full of admiration. And in another man's house— anyhow, what had I come to do or say? Suppose the drawing-room should be full of people—suppose a baby were sick, how was I to explain that I only wanted to shake hands with him?

Then things happened somewhat in this order. A big, darkened drawing-room; a huge chair; a man with eyes, a mane of grizzled hair, a brown mustache covering a mouth as delicate as a woman's, a strong, square hand shaking mine, and the slowest, calmest, levellest voice in all the world saying:—

"Well, you think you owe me something, and you've come to tell me so. That's what I call squaring a debt handsomely."

"Piff!" from a cob-pipe (I always said that a Missouri meerschaum was the best smoking in the world), and, behold! Mark Twain had curled himself up in the big armchair, and I was smoking reverently, as befits one in the presence of his superior.

The thing that struck me first was that he was an elderly man; yet, after a minute's thought, I perceived that it was otherwise, and in five minutes, the eyes looking at me, I saw that the grey hair was an accident of the most trivial. He was quite young. I was shaking his hand. I was smoking his cigar, and I was hearing him talk—this man I had learned to love and admire fourteen thousand miles away.

Reading his books, I had striven to get an idea of his personality, and all my preconceived notions were wrong and beneath the reality. Blessed is the man who finds no disillusion when he is brought face to face with a revered writer. That was a moment to be remembered; the landing of a twelve-pound salmon was nothing to it. I had hooked Mark Twain, and he was treating me as though under certain circumstances I might be an equal.

About this time I became aware that he was discussing the copyright question. Here, so far as I remember, is what he said. Attend to the words of the oracle through this unworthy medium transmitted. You will never be able to imagine the long, slow surge of the drawl, and the deadly gravity of the countenance, the quaint pucker of the body, one foot thrown over the arm of the chair, the yellow pipe clinched in one corner of the mouth, and the right hand casually caressing the square chin:—

"Copyright? Some men have morals, and some men have— other things. I presume a publisher is a man. He is not born. He is created—by circumstances. Some publishers have morals. Mine have. They pay me for the English productions of my books. When you hear men talking of Bret Harte's works and other works and my books being pirated, ask them to be sure of their facts. I think they'll find the books are paid for. It was ever thus.

"I remember an unprincipled and formidable publisher. Perhaps he's dead now. He used to take my short stories—I can't call it steal or pirate them. It was beyond these things altogether. He took my stories one at a time and made a book of it. If I wrote an essay on dentistry or theology or any little thing of that kind —just an essay that long (he indicated half an inch on his finger), any sort of essay—that publisher would amend and improve my essay.

"He would get another man to write some more to it or cut it about exactly as his needs required. Then he would publish a book called *Dentistry by Mark Twain*, that little essay and some other things not mine added. Theology would make another book, and so on. I do not consider that fair. It's an insult. But he's dead now, I think. I didn't kill him.

"There is a great deal of nonsense talked about international copyright. The proper way to treat a copyright is to make it exactly like real-estate in every way.

"It will settle itself under these conditions. If Congress were to bring in a law that a man's life was not to extend over a hundred and sixty years, somebody would laugh. That law wouldn't concern anybody. The man would be out of the jurisdiction of the court. A term of years in copyright comes to exactly the same thing. No law can make a book live or cause it to die before the appointed time.

"Tottletown, Cal., was a new town, with a population of three thousand—banks, fire-brigade, brick buildings, and all the modern improvements. It lived, it flourished, and it disappeared. To-day no man can put his foot on any remnant of Tottletown, Cal. It's dead. London continues to exist. Bill Smith, author of a book read for the next year or so, is real-estate in Tottletown. William Shakespeare, whose works are extensively read, is real-estate in London. Let Bill Smith, equally with Mr. Shakespeare now deceased, have as complete a control over his copyright as he would over his real-estate. Let him gamble it away, drink it away, or— give it to the church. Let his heirs and assigns treat it in the same manner.

"Every now and again I go up to Washington, sitting on a board to drive that sort of view into Congress. Congress takes its arguments against international copyright delivered ready made, and—Congress isn't very strong. I put the real-estate view of the case before one of the Senators.

"He said: 'Suppose a man has written a book that will live for ever?'

"I said: 'Neither you nor I will ever live to see that man, but we'll assume it. What then?'

"He said: 'I want to protect the world against that man's heirs and assigns, working under your theory.'

"I said: 'You think that all the world has no commercial sense. The book that will live for ever can't be artificially kept up at inflated prices. There will always be very expensive editions of it and cheap ones issuing side by side.'

"Take the case of Sir Walter Scott's novels," Mark Twain continued, turning to me. "When the copyright notes protected them, I bought editions as expensive as I could afford, because I liked them. At the same time the same firm was selling editions that a cat might buy. They had their real estate, and not being fools, recognized that one portion of the plot could be worked as a gold mine, another as a vegetable garden, and another as a marble quarry. Do you see?"

What I saw with the greatest clearness was Mark Twain being forced to fight for the simple proposition that a man has as much right to the work of his brains (think of the heresy of it!) as to the labor of his hands. When the old lion roars, the young whelps growl. I growled assentingly, and the talk ran on from books in general to his own in particular.

Growing bold, and feeling that I had a few hundred thousand folk at my back, I demanded whether Tom Sawyer married Judge Thatcher's daughter and whether we were ever going to hear of Tom Sawyer as a man.

"I haven't decided," quoth Mark Twain, getting up, filling his pipe, and walking up and down the room in his slippers. "I have a notion of writing the sequel to *Tom Sawyer* in two ways. In one I would make him rise to great honor and go to Congress, and in the other I should hang him. Then the friends and enemies of the book could take their choice."

Here I lost my reverence completely, and protested against any theory of the sort, because, to me at least, Tom Sawyer was real.

"Oh, he *is* real," said Mark Twain. "He's all the boy that I have known or recollect; but that would be a good way of ending the book"; then, turning round, "because, when you come to think of it, neither religion, training, nor education avails anything against the force of circumstances that drive a man. Suppose we took the next four and twenty years of Tom Sawyer's life, and gave a little joggle to the circumstances that controlled him. He would, logically and according to the joggle, turn out a rip or an angel."

"Do you believe that, then?"

"I think so. Isn't it what you call Kismet?"

"Yes; but don't give him two joggles and show the result, because he isn't your property any more. He belongs to us."

He laughed—a large, wholesome laugh—and this began a dissertation on the rights of a man to do what he liked with his own creations, which being a matter of purely professional interest, I will mercifully omit.

Returning to the big chair, he, speaking of truth and the like in literature, said that an autobiography was the one work in which a man, against his own will and in spite of his utmost striving to the contrary, revealed himself in his true light to the world.

"A good deal of your life on the Mississippi is autobiographical, isn't it?" I asked.

"As near as it can be—when a man is writing to a book and about himself. But in genuine autobiography, I believe it is impossible for a man to tell the truth about himself or to avoid impressing the reader with the truth about himself.

"I made an experiment once. I got a friend of mine—a man painfully given to speak the truth on all occasions—a man who wouldn't dream of telling a lie—and I made him write his autobiography for his own amusement and mine. He did it. The manuscript would have made an octavo volume, but—good, honest man that he was—in every single detail of his life that I knew about he turned out, on paper, a formidable liar. He could not help himself.

"It is not in human nature to write the truth about itself. None the less the reader gets a general impression from an autobiography whether the man is a fraud or a good man. The reader can't give his reasons any more than a man can explain why a woman struck him as being lovely when he doesn't remember her hair, eyes, teeth, or figure. And the impression that the reader gets is a correct one."

"Do you ever intend to write an autobiography?"

"If I do, it will be as other men have done—with the most earnest desire to make myself out to be the better man in every little business that has been to my discredit; and I shall fail, like the others, to make my readers believe anything except the truth."

This naturally led to a discussion on conscience. Then said Mark Twain, and his words are mighty and to be remembered:—

"Your conscience is a nuisance. A conscience is like a child. If you pet it and play with it and let it have everything that it wants, it becomes spoiled and intrudes on all your amusements and most of your griefs. Treat your conscience as you would treat anything else. When it is rebellious, spank it—be severe with it, argue with it, prevent it from coming to play with you at all hours, and you will secure a good conscience; that is to say, a properly trained one. A spoiled one simply destroys all the pleasure in life. I think I have reduced mine to order. At least, I haven't heard from it for some time. Perhaps I have killed it from over-severity. It's wrong to kill a child, but, in spite of all I have said, a conscience differs from a child in many ways. Perhaps it's best when it's dead."

Here he told me a little—such things as a man may tell a stranger—of his early life and upbringing, and in what manner he had been influenced for good by the example of his parents. He spoke always through his eyes, a light under the heavy eyebrows; anon crossing the room with a step as light as a girl's, to show me some book or other; then resuming his walk up and down the room, puffing at the cob pipe. I would have given much for nerve enough to demand the gift of that pipe—value, five cents when new. I understood why certain savage tribes ardently desired the liver of brave men slain in combat. That pipe would have given me, perhaps, a hint of his keen insight into the souls of men. But he never laid it aside within stealing reach.

Once, indeed, he put his hand on my shoulder. It was an investiture of the Star of India, blue silk, trumpets, and diamond-studded jewel, all complete. If hereafter, in the changes and chances of this mortal life, I fall to cureless ruin, I will tell the superintendent of the workhouse that Mark Twain once put his hand on my shoulder; and he shall give me a room to myself and a double allowance of paupers' tobacco.

"I never read novels myself," said he, "except when the popular persecution forces me to—when people plague me to know what I think of the last book that everyone is reading."

"And how did the latest persecution affect you?"

"Robert?" said he, interrogatively.

I nodded.

"I read it, of course, for the workmanship. That made me think I had neglected novels too long—that there might be a good many books as graceful in style somewhere on the shelves; so I began a course of novel reading. I have dropped it now; it did not amuse me. But as regards Robert, the effect on me was exactly as though a singer of street ballads were to hear excellent music from a church organ. I didn't stop to ask whether the music was legitimate or necessary. I listened, and I liked what I heard. I am speaking of the grace and beauty of the style."

"You see," he went on, "every man has his private opinion about a book. But that is my private opinion. If I had lived in the beginning of things, I should have looked around the township to see what popular opinion thought of the murder of Abel before I openly condemned Cain. I should have had my private opinion, of course, but I shouldn't have expressed it until I had felt the way. You have my private opinion about that book. I don't know what my public ones are exactly. They won't upset the earth."

He recurled himself into the chair and talked of other things.

"I spend nine months of the year at Hartford. I have long ago satisfied myself that there is no hope of doing much work during those nine months. People come in and call. They call at all hours, about everything in the world. One day I thought I would keep a list of interruptions. It began this way:—

"A man came and would see no one but Mr. Clemens. He was an agent for photogravure reproductions of Salon pictures. I very seldom use Salon pictures in my books.

"After that man another man, who refused to see any one but

Mr. Clemens, came to make me write to Washington about something. I saw him. I saw a third man, then a fourth. By this time it was noon. I had grown tired of keeping the list. I wished to rest.

"But the fifth man was the only one of the crowd with a card of his own. He sent up his card. 'Ben Koontz, Hannibal, Mo.' I was raised in Hannibal. Ben was an old schoolmate of mine. Consequently I threw the house wide open and rushed with both hands out at a big, fat, heavy man, who was not the Ben I had ever known—nor anything like him.

" 'But *is* it you, Ben?' I said. 'You've altered in the last thousand years.'

"The fat man said: 'Well, I'm not Koontz exactly, but I met him down in Missouri, and he told me to be sure and call on you, and he gave me his card, and'—here he acted the little scene for my benefit—'if you can wait a minute till I can get out the circulars—I'm not Koontz exactly, but I'm traveling with the fullest line of rods you ever saw.' "

"And what happened?" I asked breathlessly.

"I shut the door. He was not Ben Koontz—exactly—not my old school-fellow, but I had shaken him by both hands in love, and . . . I had been bearded by a lightning-rod man in my own house.

"As I was saying, I do very little work in Hartford. I come here for three months every year, and I work four or five hours a day in a study down the garden of that little house on the hill. Of course, I do not object to two or three interruptions. When a man is in the full swing of his work these little things do not affect him. Eight or ten or twenty interruptions retard composition."

I was burning to ask him all manner of impertinent questions, as to which of his works he himself preferred, and so forth; but, standing in awe of his eyes, I dared not. He spoke on, and I listened, grovelling.

It was a question of mental equipment that was on the carpet, and I am still wondering whether he meant what he said.

"Personally I never care for fiction or story-books. What I like to read about are facts and statistics of any kind. If they are only facts about the raising of radishes, they interest me. Just now, for instance, before you came in"—he pointed to an encyclopedia on the shelves—"I was reading an article about 'Mathematics.' Perfectly pure mathematics.

"My own knowledge of mathematics stops at 'twelve times twelve,' but I enjoyed that article immensely. I didn't understand a word of it; but facts, or what a man believes to be facts, are always delightful. That mathematical fellow believed in his facts. So do I. Get your facts first, and"—the voice dies away to an almost inaudible drone—"then you can distort 'em as much as you please."

Bearing this precious advice in my bosom, I left; the great man assuring me with gentle kindness that I had not interrupted him in the least. Once outside the door, I yearned to go back and ask some questions—it was easy enough to think of them now—but his time was his own, though his books belonged to me.

I should have ample time to look back to that meeting across the graves of the days. But it was sad to think of the things he had not spoken about.

In San Francisco the men of *The Call* told me many legends of Mark's apprenticeship in their paper five and twenty years ago; how he was a reporter delightfully incapable of reporting according to the needs of the day. He preferred, so they said, to coil himself into a heap and meditate until the last minute. Then he would produce copy bearing no sort of relationship to his legitimate work—copy that made the editor swear horribly, and the readers of *The Call* ask for more.

I should like to have heard Mark's version of that, with some stories of his joyous and variegated past. He has been journeyman printer (in those days he wandered from the banks of the Missouri even to Philadelphia), pilot cub and full-blown pilot, soldier of the South (that was for three weeks only), private secretary to a Lieutenant-Governor of Nevada (that displeased him), miner, editor, special correspondent in the Sandwich Islands, and the Lord only knows what else. If so experienced a man could by any means be made drunk, it would be a glorious thing to fill him up with composite liquors, and, in the language of his own country, "let him retrospect." But these eyes will never see that orgy fit for the gods!

Selma Lagerlöf

ORIENTAL SINGING

SELMA LAGERLÖF, *the first woman to win the Nobel Prize for Literature (1909) and the first to gain a seat in the Swedish Academy (1914), was born in 1858 in Varmland, the scene of most of her writings. She gave up a teaching career after her first and greatest novel, Gosta Berling (1891), proved to be immediately successful. Based on old folk legends, it is a pure example of the storyteller's art at its best—warm, simple, personal, and poetic—the same qualities that make the following travel sketch from Harvest (1934) a memorable essay. Her deeply religious spirit and her intuitive understanding of the forces that move men, warm the pages of her novel Jerusalem (1902), her trilogy The Ring of the Lowenskolds (1931), her several collections of short stories, her poetry, and her two autobiographical volumes, while her lively sense of fantasy and fun make The Wonderful Adventures of Nils one of the world's best books for children. In her later years, she traveled widely but always returned to her birthplace, where she died in 1940.*

We are in Egypt, away down at Assuan, and we have ridden out early in the morning to see the island of Philæ and the first cataract.

The road passes through the desert; to the right of us rises a mountain chain, and to the left, a short distance away, we have the Nile. Between the mountain and the river there is nothing but yellow-white desert sand.

The opposite shore of the Nile is bordered by a row of tall black stones. They have been shaped in the most fantastic way by the river, and as long as I look at them I must ponder over what I can best liken them to. They look like a row of broad pillars which have been driven down into the river bed, but which have been heaved hither and thither, every which way, by some inundation. Or maybe they look more like a long row of fishermen, who in their various postures—sitting, lying, standing, bending out over the river to look at their floats, leaning back to pull the fish out of the water—have all of them been turned to stone in the same instant.

Beyond the row of black stones extends once more the yellow sand desert, terminated by a range of mountains. Its rocks are dark, but the sand has not failed to powder with yellow its crevices and slopes as far up as it has been able to find something to hold it.

All this appears to us beautiful; or perhaps it really fascinates us because it is so unusual. We have never before seen a landscape in black and yellow. A setting for fairy tales, it seems to me—for savagery and cruelty. The night before, the Nile, which now is black as a forest river, had lain absolutely red at sundown, like a broad stream of blood. It had looked gorgeous, had provided the touch of red for which nature seems to yearn.

Since we are in Egypt it is almost unnecessary to say that the weather is wonderful now in the morning, fresh and just warm enough, with clear air and a sun which has recently risen over the mountain rim and which still acts quite gentle and safe. Wonderful also are the little donkeys which carry us, and the merry, tireless donkey boys who trot ahead of us. Wonderful above all is the feeling of health, of strength, and of contentment which surges through us every day while we travel on the blessed Nile or stay in its vicinity.

As a matter of fact the river has completely bewitched us. We came to Assuan on a steamboat, but now we contemplate making the return trip to Cairo in the proper way—that is to say, on a river boat. Yesterday we began to negotiate with the owner of a dahabeah about engaging his boat.

It will be a long boat trip to Cairo, and if the wind is contrary it can stretch out into a month, indeed, perhaps even longer. But that is exactly what we wish. To glide down the river in the fascinating little craft with the fantastic sail and the tidy little cabin, to sit on the brightly polished deck and watch palm groves, and Negro villages, waterworks, and, now and then, a temple ruin pass by—that is what we should like to keep on doing without interruption not only for a month but to the end of life.

We are completely mad. It is not at all apprehension over the fact that we two women are to set off with an Arab skipper and his crew, without any other European on board, which prevented us from completing the agreement yesterday; neither is it the thought that in this way we shall perhaps not have time to visit Jerusalem, which after all has been the real objective of our trip; nor that we shall be without mail from home for weeks. All these things we consider insignificant in comparison with the chance to see Africa's sparkling sky of stars reflect itself in the Nile night after night, and to see the river, day after day, spread out like a wide breadth of light blue satin, to inhale this marvelous air, which makes existence a blissful intoxication. No, what had hindered us was simply the impossibility of getting a regular contract drawn up yesterday with the skipper. Today was to be dedicated to old Philæ, the morrow again was to be devoted to the drawing up of a contract, to the purchase of a certain amount of food supplies and other necessities such as blankets and comfortable deck chairs.

No, we feel no anxiety whatever in regard to the good-natured, splendid-looking Arab who is to conduct us. We are not at all afraid of the Orientals. We have made the acquaintance of quite a number in Cairo and Luxor. We have found them quite human, not at all heroic, to be sure, but sympathetic, frank, and naïve. We believe we have quite a rare gift of getting on good terms with them, of entering into their feelings and reactions—in a word, of winning their devotion.

A change in the scenery has taken place. The road has turned in among the mountains, and we have before us quite a wide desert plain, surrounded on all sides by ridges. At the foot of the mountain wall quite close to us stands a mastaba, or tomb of a saint, a small square building covered with a low cupola.

What luck for us! The tomb does not stand lonely and deserted as it does most of the days in the year. It is surrounded by a fairly large crowd of people already, and more are on their way. There must be some sort of a festival going on there.

Why is it so beautiful to see the desert people come riding

down the sand-covered mountain slopes on horses, camels, and donkeys—whole village groups, men and women, children and old folks? Is it the unexpected in seeing the desert come to life? Is it the incredible in the existence here of so many people? It is not a colorful crowd. The men wear black cloaks and white turbans, the women are black from top to toe. Not even the saddle beasts are in any way gaudily decorated.

But that is the way it is under the sky of Egypt. Everything becomes beautiful, but not at all dreamy or melting away in any kind of shadow. Let the eye rejoice at seeing everything outlined definitely and clearly. It is not men and beasts one sees, but a succession of statues in bronze and granite, which come trooping down from the interior of the mountains, bright and shining, molded by a master's hand.

We give our guide a sign that we would like to stop here a few minutes to see a little more of the desert people, and the next moment we are out of the saddles. Then we walk up toward the mastaba.

On the ground outside sit a circle of men, easily forty in number, on their crossed legs, singing at the top of their lungs. We have seen similar singing groups before at Cairo, and we assume that here as well as there they sing from the Koran. But here the singing has a few characteristics which are new to us.

It was, of course, the same howl, forced out through the nose, the same astounding crescendos in high treble, the same total lack of rhythm and melody which had appalled us the first time we had heard singing from the Koran, but now there is added something wild, I should almost say animalistic. It is the roaring of lions and hyenas, the trumpeting of elephants, the bellowing of aurochs, that these singers imitate. In the meantime they devote themselves to their singing with all their might and main. Their eyes protrude from their heads, their cheeks glow, they lean far backward and emit these inhuman sounds with their faces turned toward the sky.

We stand there absolutely quiet and listen. No one pays the slightest attention to us. Suddenly we nudge each other with the elbows. We have both recognized at the same time the fine-looking captain of the dahabeah who in a few days is to take us

down to Cairo. He squats there like the others, completely absorbed in the singing, and to our tortured ears it seems as if he
howls and shrieks worse than anyone else.

Quite unexpectedly we begin to feel a great terror. Everything
about us is extremely tranquil. Groups of unveiled women stand
all around, visibly enjoying the men's singing. Out of the mountain, new little caravans keep coming; others approach across the
desert plain. Some of the new arrivals unload their camels. What
is there that is terrifying in all this?

I hardly know how to explain it. The horror lay in the singing.
It must have lain in the fact that these people could enjoy as
beauty what to us was ear-splitting noise.

The horror must have lain in the fact that here opened a wide
gulf which separated them from us. The gulf which we had not
seen before.

We had seen that they dressed differently from us, that they ate
in a different manner, had another faith, another color of the skin,
but all that had seemed to us immaterial. They were nevertheless
human beings like ourselves.

And as human beings we still regarded them; we did not feel
superior, but we felt the difference. Here was something we would
never understand. If these people were to hear a Mass at St. Peter's,
or a symphony by Beethoven, or an opera by Mozart, they would
probably feel the same consternation as that which now had
seized us. They would be incapable of comprehending that the
Occidentals could enjoy these abominable floods of tunes. They
would feel separated from us by a yawning, impassable chasm.

And as it was in one respect, so perhaps it was in all others. We
felt consternation before what was alien in these people, and we
hurried back to our donkeys to continue our ride.

The next day we concluded no contract with the captain of the
dahabeah, we gave up the long sojourn on the Nile, the starry
nights, the delightful life of idlers on the river boat. Our souls
ached, but our suspicions had been aroused. To anyone who had
sung like that captain, one could not entrust oneself for a whole
month on a small Nile boat.

As soon as this was decided, a hotel employee came up to me
and whispered in confidence that the dahabeah which we had in-

tended to hire had shortly before made a veritable death journey. It had had cholera on board.

And this he told us now for the first time!

"I no could tell about it before now," he said, "now when the ladies don't want to go. If I tell before, I prevent captain make much money. He never forget it."

Beyond a doubt no one else in all Assuan would have dared warn us. But the thing that had saved us—was it only chance, or who had been that time the keeper of fools?

Anatole France

W O M E N

JACQUES ANATOLE THIBAULT, *born in Paris in 1844, took his pen-name, Anatole France, from his father, a bookseller who made occasional ventures into literature. He started his career as a writer after quitting his librarian's job over a quarrel with a superior. Ignoring the naturalistic trends current in French fiction, he wrote in a fanciful and imaginative vein. Within the framework of legend and history, he ironically surveyed the human being and the world in which he lived. But his sense of social justice remained undiminished, and when the Dreyfus case arose, he actively supported Emile Zola in his defense of Dreyfus. Thereafter his works became increasingly ironical, and his skillful writing in this vein, demonstrated by the following essay on the Frenchmen's favorite subject, reached its peak in* Penguin Island *(1909). Three years before he died, he received the Nobel Prize in 1921 for his essays, criticism, novels, plays and poetry, all characterized, according to the citation, by "an exalted style, generous humanity and beauty; and bearing a stamp of true French spirit."*

Christianity has done much for love by making a sin of it. The Church excludes woman from the priesthood; it fears her, and thereby shows how dangerous she is. It repeats with the Ecclesiast: "The arms of a woman are like the nets of the hunters,—*laqueus venatorum.*" It warns us not to put our hope in her: "Lean not upon a reed shaken in the wind, and put not your trust therein, for all flesh is grass, and the glory thereof passeth away like the flower of the fields." It dreads the wiles of this pest of the human race: "All cunning is small beside the cunning of a woman's heart. *Brevis omnis malitia super malitiam mulieris.*" But by the very terror it betrays of her, it makes her strong and formidable.

To grasp the full significance of these maxims you must have lived with the mystics. You must have passed your childhood in a religious atmosphere. You must have gone into "retreat"; followed the observances of the Church. You must have read, at twelve years old, those little books of edification that reveal the supernatural world to simple souls. You must have known the story of St. Francis de Borgia gazing into the open coffin of Queen Isabella, or the apparition of the Abbess of Vermont to her daughters in Christ. The Abbess had died in the odor of sanctity, and the nuns, who had shared in her works of angelic piety, believing her in Heaven, were wont to invoke her in their prayers. But one day she appeared to them, with wan face and flames licking the border of her robe. "Pray for me," she bade them; "in the days when I was alive, joining my hands in prayer, I thought what pretty hands they were. To-day I am expiating that sinful thought in the torments of Purgatory. Know, my daughters, the adorable goodness of God, and pray for me." These little books of childish theology contain a thousand tales of the kind—tales that give purity too exalted a price not to add an infinite zest to carnal pleasures.

In consideration of their beauty, the Church made Aspasia, Laïs, and Cleopatra into demons, ladies of Hell. What glory for them! Why, a Saint would have appreciated the compliment! The most modest and austere of womankind, who has no faintest wish to destroy any man's peace of mind, would fain have the power to destroy all men's. Her pride is flattered by the precautions the Church takes against her. When poor St. Antony shouts at her: "Begone, foul beast!" his very alarm tickles her vanity deliciously. She is ravished to find herself more dangerous than she had ever suspected.

But never think too highly of yourselves, my sisters; you were not, at your first appearance in the world, perfect and fully armed. Your grandmothers of the days of the mammoth and the giant bear did not wield the same domination over the prehistoric hunters and cavemen which you possess over us. You were useful then, and necessary, but you were not invincible. To tell the truth, in those far-off ages, and for long afterwards, you lacked charm. In those days you were like men, and men were like brutes. To make of you the fearful and wonderful thing you are to-day, to become the indifferent and sovereign cause of countless sacrifices and crimes, you still needed two things: Civilization, which gave you veils, and Religion, which gave you scruples. Since then your powers are perfected; you are now a mystery, and you are a sin. Men dream of you and lose their souls for you. You inspire longing and alarm; love's delirium has come into the world. Yes, it is an infallible instinct inclines you to piety. You are well advised to love Christianity. It has multiplied your puissance tenfold. Do you know St. Jerome? At Rome and in Asia you inspired him with such panic terror that he fled to escape you into a frightful desert. There he fed on roots, and the skin clung to his fleshless bones and was burnt black by the sun, yet he found you there also. His solitude was peopled with your phantoms, yet more alluring even than yourselves.

For it is a truth, only too well proven by the ascetics, that the dreams you excite are more seductive, if that is possible, than the realities you have in your power to offer. Jerome rejected with equal horror your presence and the remembrance of your presence. But in vain he gave himself up to fasts and prayers; you filled his life, from which he had expelled you, with hallucinations. Such was the power of woman over a Saint. I doubt if it is as great over an habitué of the Moulin-Rouge. Take heed your empire be not diminished along with men's belief in God; beware you do not lose a portion of your influence through ceasing to be a sin.

Candidly I do not think rationalism is good for you. In your place, I should not be overfond of the physiologists who are so indiscreet, who are so over ready to explain things to you, who say you are sick when we think you are inspired, and who attribute to the predominance of reflex actions your sublime potentialities for love and suffering. That is not the way they speak of you in the *Golden Legend*; "white dove," "lily of purity," "rose of love," are the names they give you there. Surely this is more agreeable than to be dubbed hysterical, cataleptic, subject to hallucinations,—as you are every day since science has ruled the roost.

Moreover, if I were one of you, I should cordially detest all those emancipators of the sex who are for making you into men's equals. They are urging you to take a false step. Fine promotion, to be sure, for you, to be as good as an attorney or a druggist! Take care, I say; already you have stripped off some particles of your mystery and fascination. All is not lost. Men still fight, and ruin and kill themselves for you; but the young fellows in tramcars leave you to stand on the platform while they sit snug inside. Your cult is declining along with other things once held sacrosanct.

George Bernard Shaw

KILLING FOR SPORT

GEORGE BERNARD SHAW *was born in 1856 to a family of Dublin "downstarts." As a young man he went to London, found some odd writing jobs, and became a music critic under the pseudonym of Cornetto di Basso. He joined the Fabian Society in 1884 and for many years was active in writing political tracts and protests against accepted practices, similar in tone to the following selection. After a fling at the novel—in nine years the pen that was to earn his fortune made no more than twelve pounds—he turned to the drama with greater success. By 1904, his plays began to reach the stage and by 1910, he was internationally successful with his witty, brilliant attacks upon conventional English ideas and institutions. Among his plays are* Caesar and Cleopatra (1901), Man and Superman (1903), The Doctor's Dilemma (1911), Heartbreak House (1917), *and* Saint Joan

(1923). *He delighted in his role as difficult eccentric, opposing vivi-section and innoculations and espousing vegetarianism (which, he once said, would entitle his funeral to be followed by "herds of oxen, sheep, swine, flocks of poultry, and a small traveling aquarium of live fish, all wearing white scarves"). He died in his home at Ayot St. Lawrence, England in 1950. His plays (and the musical and motion picture versions of them) continue to be played and produced throughout the civilized world.*

Sport is a difficult subject to deal with honestly. It is easy for the humanitarian to moralize against it; and any fool on its side can gush about its glorious breezy pleasures and the virtues it nourishes. But neither the moralizings nor the gushings are supported by facts: indeed they are mostly violently contradicted by them. Sportsmen are not crueler than other people. Humanitarians are not more humane than other people. The pleasures of sport are fatigues and hardships: nobody gets out of bed before sunrise on a drizzling wintry morning and rides off into darkness, cold, and rain, either for luxury or thirst for the blood of a fox cub. The humanitarian and the sportsman are often the self-same person drawing altogether unaccountable lines between pheasants and pigeons, between hares and foxes, between tame stags from the cart and wild ones from the heather, between lobsters or *paté de foie gras* and beefsteaks: above all, between man and the lower animals; for people who are sickened by the figures of a *battue* do not turn a hair over the infantile death-rate in Lisson Grove or the slums of Dundee.

Clearly the world of sport is a crystal palace in which we had better not throw stones unless we are prepared to have our own faces cut by the falling glass. My own pursuits as a critic and as a castigator of morals by ridicule (otherwise a writer of comedies) are so cruel that in point of giving pain to many worthy people I can hold my own with most dentists, and beat a skilful sportsman hollow. I know many sportsmen; and none of them are ferocious. I know several humanitarians; and they are all ferocious. No book of sport breathes such a wrathful spirit as this book of humanity. No sportsman wants to kill the fox or the pheasant as I want to kill him when I see him doing it. Callousness is not cruel. Stupidity is not cruel. Love of exercise and of feats of skill is not cruel. They may and do produce more destruction and suffering than all the neuroses of all the Neros. But they are characteristic of quite amiable and cheerful people, mostly lovers of pet animals. On the other hand, humane sensitiveness is impatient, angry, ruthless, and murderous. Marat was a supersensitive humanitarian, by profession a doctor who had practiced successfully in genteel circles in England. What Marat felt towards marquesses most humanitarians feel more or less towards sportsmen. Therefore let no sportsman who reads these pages accuse me of hypocrisy, or of claiming to be a more amiable person than he. And let him excuse me, if he will be so good, for beginning with an attempt to describe how I feel about sport.

To begin with, sport soon bores me when it does not involve killing; and when it does, it affects me much as the murder of a human being would affect me, rather more than less; for just as the murder of a child is more shocking than the murder of an adult (because, I suppose, the child is so helpless and the breach of social faith therefore so unconscionable), the murder of an animal is an abuse of man's advantage over animals: the proof being that when the animal is powerful and dangerous, and the man unarmed, the repulsion vanishes and is replaced by congratulation. But quite humane and cultivated people seem unable to understand why I should bother about the feelings of animals. I have seen the most horrible pictures published in good faith as attractive in illustrated magazines. One of them, which I wish I could forget, was a photograph taken on a polar expedition, showing a murdered bear with its living cub trying to make it attend to its maternal duties. I have seen a photograph of a criminal being cut into a thousand pieces by a Chinese executioner, which was by comparison amusing. I have also seen thrown on a screen for the entertainment of a large audience a photograph of an Arctic explorer taking away a sledge dog to shoot it for food, the dog jumping about joyously without the least suspicion of its human friend's intentions. If the doomed dog had been a man or a woman, I believe I should have had less sense of treachery. I do not say that this is reasonable: I simply state it as a fact. It was quite evident that the lecturer had no suspicion of the effect the picture was producing on me; and as far as I could see, his audience was just as callous; for if they had all felt as I felt there would have been at least a very perceptible shudder, if not an articulate protest. Now this was not a case of sport. It was necessary to shoot the dog: I should have shot it myself under the same circumstances. But I should have regarded the necessity as a horrible one; and I should have presented it to the audience as a painful episode, like cannibalism in a crew of castaways, and not as a joke. For I must add that a good many people present regarded it as a bit of fun. I absolve the lecturer from this extremity of insensibility. The shooting of a dog was a trifle to what he had endured; and I did not blame him for thinking it by comparison a trivial matter. But to us, who had endured nothing, it might have seemed a little hard on the dog, and calling for some apology from the man.

I am driven to the conclusion that my sense of kinship with animals is greater than most people feel. It amuses me to **talk to** animals in a sort of jargon I have invented for them; and it **seems** to me that it amuses them to be talked to, and that they respond to the tone of the conversation, though its intellectual content may to some extent escape them. I am quite sure, having made the experiment several times on dogs left in my care as part of the furniture of hired houses, that an animal who has been treated as a brute, and is consequently undeveloped socially (as human beings remain socially undeveloped under the same circumstances) will, on being talked to as a fellow-creature, become friendly and companionable in a very short time. This process has been described by some reproachful dog owners as spoiling the dog, and sincerely deplored by them, because I am glad to say it is easier to do than to undo except by brutalities of which few people are capable. But I find it impossible to associate with animals on any other terms. Further, it gives me extraordinary gratification to find a wild bird treating me with confidence, as robins sometimes do. It pleases me to conciliate an animal who is hostile to me. What is more, an animal who will not be conciliated offends me. There is at the Zoo a morose maned lion who will tear you to pieces if he gets half a chance. There is also a very handsome maneless lion with whom you may play more safely than with most St. Bernard dogs, as he seems to need nothing but plenty of attention and admiration to put him into the best of humors. I do not feel towards these two lions as a carpenter does towards two pieces of wood, one hard and knotty, and the other easy to work; nor as I do towards two motor bicycles, one troublesome and dangerous, and the other in perfect order. I feel towards the two lions as I should towards two men similarly diverse. I like one and dislike the other. If they got loose and were shot, I should be distressed in the one case whilst in the other I should say "Serve the brute right!" This is clearly fellow-feeling. And it seems to me that the plea of the humanitarian is a plea for widening the range of fellow-feeling.

The limits of fellow-feeling are puzzling. People who have it in a high degree for animals often seem utterly devoid of it for human beings of a different class. They will literally kill their dogs with kindness whilst behaving to their servants with such utter inconsideration that they have to change their domestic staff once a month or oftener. Or they hate horses and like snakes. One could fill pages with such inconsistencies. The lesson of these apparent contradictions is that fellow-feeling is a matter of dislikes as well as of likes. No man wants to destroy the engine which catches him in its cog-wheels and tears a limb from him. But many a man has tried to kill another man for a very trifling slight. The machine, not being our fellow, cannot be loved or hated. The man, being our fellow, can.

Let us try to get down to the bottom of this matter. There is no use in saying that our fellow-creatures must not be killed. That is simply untrue; and the converse proposal that they must be killed is simply true. We see the Buddhist having his path swept before him lest he should tread on an insect and kill it; but we do not see what that Buddhist does when he catches a flea that has kept him awake for an hour; and we know that he has to except certain poisonous snakes from his forbearance. If mice get into your house and you do not kill them, they will end by killing you. If rabbits breed on your farm and you do not exterminate them, you will end by having no farm. If you keep deer in your park and do not thin them, your neighbors or the authorities will finally have to save you the trouble. If you hold the life of a mosquito sacred, malaria and yellow fever will not return the compliment. I have had an interview with an adder, in the course of which it struck repeatedly and furiously at my stick; and I let it go unharmed; but if I were the mother of a family of young children, and I found a cobra in the garden, I would vote for *"La mort sans phrase,"* as many humane and honorable persons voted in the case, not of a serpent, but of an anointed king.

I see no logical nor spiritual escape from the theory that evolution (not, please observe, Natural Selection) involves a deliberate intentional destruction by the higher forms of life of the lower. It is a dangerous and difficult business; for in the course of natural selection the lower forms may have become necessary to the existence of the higher; and the gamekeeper shooting everything that could hurt his pheasants or their chicks may be behaving as foolishly as an Arab lunatic shooting horses and camels. But where Man comes, the megatherium must go as surely as where the poultry farmer comes the fox must go unless the hunt will pay for the fox's depredations. To plead for the tiger, the wolf, and the poisonous snake, is as useless as to plead for the spirochete or the tetanus bacillus: we must frankly class these as early and disastrous experiments in creation, and accept it as part of the mission of the later and more successful experiments to recognize them as superseded, and to destroy them purposely. We should, no doubt, be very careful how we jump from the indisputable general law that the higher forms of life must exterminate or limit the lower, to the justification of any particular instance of the slaughter of non-human animals by men, or the slaughter of a low type of man by a high type of man. Still, when all due reservations are made, the fact remains that a war of extermination is being waged daily and necessarily by man against his rivals for possession of the earth, and though an urban humanitarian and vegetarian who never has occasion to kill anything but a microbe may shudder at the callousness with which a farmer kills rats and rabbits and sparrows and moles and caterpillars and ladybirds and many more charming creatures, yet if he were in the farmer's place he would have to do exactly the same, or perish.

In that case why not make a pleasure of necessity, and a virtue of pleasure, as the sportsmen do? I think we must own that there is no objection from the point of view of the animals. On the contrary, it is quite easy to show that there is a positive advantage to them in the organization of killing as sport. Fox hunting has saved the existing foxes from extermination; and if it were not for the civilization that makes fox hunting possible, the fox would still be hunted and killed by packs of wolves. I am so conscious of this that I have in another place suggested that children should be hunted or shot during certain months of the year, as they would then be fed and preserved by the sportsmen of the counties as generously and carefully as pheasants now are; and the survivors would make a much better nation than our present slum products. And I go further. I maintain that the abolition of public executions was a very bad thing for the murderers. Before that time, we did exactly as our sportsmen now do. We made a pleasure of the necessity for exterminating murderers, and a virtue of the pleasure. Hanging was a popular sport, like racing. Huge crowds assembled to see it and paid large prices for seats. There would have been betting on the result if it had been at all uncertain. The criminal had what all criminals love: a large audience. He had a procession to Tyburn: he had a drink: he was allowed to make a speech if he could; and if he could not, the speech was made for him and published and sold in great numbers. Above all, such fair play as an execution admits of was guaranteed to him by the presence of the public, whereas now he perishes in a horrible secrecy which lends itself to all the abuses of secrecy. Whether the creature slain be man or what we very invidiously call brute, there is no case to be made against sport on its behalf. Even cruelty can justify itself, as far as the victim is concerned, on the ground that it makes sport attractive to cruel people, and that sport is good for the quarry.

The true objection to sport is the one taken by that wise and justly famous Puritan who objected to bear baiting not because it gave pain to the bear but because it gave pleasure to the spectators. He rightly saw that it was not important that we should be men of pleasure, and that it was enormously important that we should be men of honor. What the bear would have said if it had had any say in the matter can only be conjectured. Its captors might have argued that if they could not have made money by keeping it alive whilst taking it to England to be baited, they would have killed it at sight in the Pyrenees; so that it owed several months of life, with free board and lodging, to the institution of bear baiting. The bear might have replied that if it had not been for the bear pit in England they would never have come to hunt for it in the Pyrenees, where it could have ended its days in a free and natural manner. Let us admit for the sake of a quiet life that the point is disputable. What is not disputable by any person who has ever seen sport of this character is that the man who enjoys it is degraded by it. We do not bait bears now (I do not quite know why); but we course rabbits. I lived for a time on the south slope of the Hog's Back; and every Sunday morning rabbits were coursed within earshot of me. And I noticed that it was quite impossible to distinguish the cries of the excited terriers from the cries of the sportsmen, although ordinarily the voice of a man is no more like the voice of a dog than like the voice of a nightingale. Sport reduced them all, men and terriers alike, to a common denominator of bestiality. The sound did not make me more humane: on the contrary, I felt that if I were an irresponsible despot with a park of artillery at my disposal, I should (especially after seeing the sportsmen on their way to and from their sport) have said: "These people have become subhuman, and will be better dead. Be kind enough to mow them down for me."

As a matter of fact there is always a revulsion against these dehumanizing sports in which the killing can be seen, and the actual visible chase shared, by human beings: in short, the sports in which men revert to the excitements of beasts of prey. Several have been abolished by law: among them bear baiting and cock fighting: both of them sports in which the spectators shared at close quarters the excitement of the animals engaged. In the sports firmly established among us there is much less of this abomination. In fox hunting and shooting, predatory excitement is not a necessary part of the sport, and is indeed abhorred by many who practice it. Inveterate foxhunters have been distressed and put off their hunting for days by happening to see a fox in the last despairing stage of its run from the hounds: a sight which can be avoided, and often is, by the hunters, but which they may happen upon some day when they are not hunting. Such people hunt because they delight in meets and in gallops across country as social and healthy incidents of country life. They are proud of their horsemanship and their craftiness in taking a line. They like horses and dogs and exercise and wind and weather, and are unconscious of the fact that their expensive and well equipped hunting stables and kennels are horse prisons and dog prisons. It is useless to pretend that these ladies and gentlemen are fiends in human form: they clearly are not. By avoiding being in at the death they get all the good out of hunting without incurring the worst of the evil, and so come out with a balance in their favor.

Shooting is subtler: it is a matter of skill with one's weapons. The expert at it is called, not a good chicken butcher, but a good shot. When I want, as I often do, to pick him off, I do so not because I feel that he is cruel or degraded but because he is a nuisance to me with the very disagreeable noise of his explosions, and because there is an unbearable stupidity in converting an interesting, amusing, prettily colored live wonder like a pheasant into a slovenly unhandsome corpse. But at least he does not yap like a terrier, and shake with a detestable excitement, and scream out frantic bets to bookmakers. His expression is that of a man performing a skilled operation with an instrument of precision: an eminently human expression, quite incompatible with the flush of blood to the eyes and the uncovering of the dogtooth that makes a man like a beast of prey. And this is why it is impossible to feel that skilled shooting or foxhunting are as abominable as rabbit coursing, hare-hunting with beagles, or otter-hunting.

And yet shooting depends for its toleration on custom as much as on the coolness with which it has to be performed. It may be illogical to forgive a man for shooting a pheasant and to loathe him for shooting a seagull; but as a matter of plain fact one feels that a man who shoots seagulls is a cad, and soon makes him feel it if he attempts to do it on board a public ship, whereas the snipe shooter excites no such repulsion. And "fair game" must be skilfully shot if the maximum of toleration is to be enjoyed. Even then it is not easy for some of us to forget that many a bird must have been miserably maimed before the shooter perfected his skill. The late King Edward the Seventh, immediately after his recovery from a serious operation which stirred the whole nation to anxious sympathy with him, shot a stag, which got away to die of just such internal inflammation as its royal murderer had happily escaped. Many people read the account without the least emotion. Others thought it natural that the King should be ashamed, as a marksman, of his failure to kill, but rejected as sentimental nonsense the notion that he should feel any remorse on the stag's behalf. Had he deliberately shot a cow instead, everyone would have been astounded and horrified. Custom will reconcile people to any atrocity; and fashion will drive them to acquire any custom. The English princess who sits on the throne of Spain goes to bullfights because it is the Spanish fashion. At first she averted her face, and probably gave offense by doing so. Now, no doubt, she is a *connoisseuse* of the sport. Yet neither she nor the late King Edward can be classed as cruel monsters. On the contrary, they are conspicuous examples of the power of cruel institutions to compel the support and finally win the tolerance and even the enjoyment of persons of full normal benevolence.

But this is not why I call shooting subtle. It fascinates even humane persons not only because it is a game of skill in the use of the most ingenious instrument in general use, but because killing by craft from a distance is a power that makes a man divine rather than human.

> *"Oft have I struck*
> *Those that I never saw, and struck them dead"*

said the statesman to Jack Cade (who promptly hanged him); and something of the sense of power in that boast stimulates every boy with a catapult and every man with a gun. That is why there is an interest in weapons fathoms deeper than the interest in cricket bats and golf clubs. It is not a question of skill or risk. The men who go to Africa with cameras and obtain photographs and even cinematographs of the most dangerous animals at close quarters, show much more skill and nerve than the gentlemen who disgust us with pictures of themselves sitting on the body of the huge creatures they have just killed with explosive bullets. Shooting "big game," like serving as a soldier in the field, is glorified conventionally as a proof of character and courage, though everyone knows that men can be found by the hundred thousand to face such ordeals, including several who would be afraid to walk down Bond Street in an unfashionable hat. The real point of the business is neither character nor courage, but ability to kill. And the greater cowards and the feebler weaklings we are, the more important this power is to us. It is a matter of life and death to us to be able to kill our enemies without coming to handgrips with them; and the consequence is that our chief form of play is to pretend that something is our enemy and kill it. Even to pretend to kill it is some satisfaction: nay, the spectacle of other people pretending to do it is a substitute worth paying for. Nothing more supremely ridiculous as a subject of reasonable contemplation could be imagined than a sham fight in Earls Court between a tribe of North American Indians and a troop of cowboys, both imported by Buffalo Bill as a theatrical speculation. To see these grown-up men behaving like children, galloping about and firing blank cartridges at one another, and pretending to fall down dead, was absurd and incredible enough from any rational point of view; but that thousands of respectable middle-aged and elderly citizens and their wives, all perfectly sober, should pay to be allowed to look on, seems flat madness. Yet the thing not only occurred in London, but occurs now daily in the cinema theaters and yearly at the Military Tournaments. And what honest man dare pretend that he gets no fun out of these spectacles? Certainly not I. They revived enough of my boyish delight in stage fights and in the stories of Captain Mayne Reid to induce me to sit them out, conscious as I was of their silliness.

Please do not revile me for telling you what I felt instead of what I ought to have felt. What prevents the sport question and every other question from getting squarely put before us is our habit of saying that the things we think should disgust us and fill us with abhorrence actually do disgust us and fill us with abhorrence, and that the persons who, against all reason and decency, find some sort of delight in them, are vile wretches quite unlike ourselves, though, as everyone can see, we and they are as like as potatoes. You may not agree with Mr. Rudyard Kipling about war, or with Colonel Roosevelt about sport; but beware how you pretend that war does not interest and excite you more than printing, or that the thought of bringing down a springing tiger with a well-aimed shot does not interest you more than the thought of cleaning your teeth. Men may be as the poles asunder in their speculative views. In their actual nervous and emotional reactions they are "members one of another" to a much greater extent than they choose to confess. The reason I have no patience with Colonel Roosevelt's tedious string of rhinoceros murders in South Africa is not that I am not interested in weapons, in marksmanship, and in killing, but because my interest in life and creation is still greater than my interest in death and destruction, and because I have sufficient fellow-feeling with a rhinoceros to think it a frightful thing that it should be killed for fun.

Consider a moment how one used to feel when an Irish peasant shot his landlord, or when a grand duke was blown to pieces in Russia, or when one read of how Charlotte Corday killed Marat. On the one hand we applauded the courage, the skill, the resolution of the assassin; we exalted in the lesson taught to tyrants and in the overthrow of the strong oppressor by the weak victim; but we were horrified by the breach of the law, by the killing of the accused at the decree of an irresponsible Ribbon Lodge under no proper public control, by the execution of the grand duke without trial and opportunity of defense, by the suspicion that Charlotte Corday was too like Marat in her lust for the blood of oppressors to have the right to kill him. Such cases are extremely complicated, except for those simple victims of political or class prejudice who think Charlotte Corday a saint because she killed a Radical, and the Ribbonmen demons because they were common fellows who dared to kill country gentlemen. But however the cases catch us, there is always that peculiar interest in individual killing, and consequently in the means and weapons by which individuals can kill their enemies, which is at the root of the sport of shooting.

It all comes back to fellow-feeling and appetite for fruitful activity and a high quality of life: there is nothing else to appeal to. No commandment can meet the case. It is no use saying "Thou shalt not kill" in one breath, and, in the next "Thou shalt not suffer a witch to live." Men must be killed and animals must be killed: nay, whole species of animals and types of men must be exterminated before the earth can become a tolerable place of habitation for decent folk. But among the men who will have to be wiped out stands the sportsman: the man without fellow-feeling, the man so primitive and uncritical in his tastes that the destruction of life is an amusement to him, the man whose outlook is as narrow as that of his dog. He is not even cruel: sport is partly a habit to which he has been brought up, and partly stupidity, which can always be measured by wastefulness and by lack of sense of the importance and glory of life. The horrible murk and grime of the Pottery towns is caused by indifference to a stupid waste of sunlight, natural beauty, cleanliness, and pleasant air, combined with a brutish appetite for money. A *battue* is caused by indifference to the beauty and interest of bird life and song, and callousness to glazed eyes and blood-bedabbled corpses, combined with a boyish love of shooting. All the people who waste beauty and life in this way are characterized by deficiency in fellow-feeling: not only have they none of St. Francis' feeling that the birds are of our kin, but they would be extremely indignant if a loader or a gamekeeper asserted any claim to belong to their species. Sport is a sign either of limitation or of timid conventionality.

And this disposes of the notion that sport is the training of a conquering race. Even if such things as conquering races existed, or would be tolerable if they did exist, they would not be races of sportsmen. The red scalp-hunting braves of North America were the sportingest race imaginable; and they were conquered as easily as the bisons they hunted. The French can boast more military glory to the square inch of history than any other nation; but until lately they were the standing butt of English humorists for their deficiencies as sportsmen. In the middle ages, when they fought as sportsmen and gentlemen, they were annihilated by small bodies of starving Englishmen who carefully avoided sportsmanlike methods and made a laborious business (learnt at the village target) of killing them. As to becoming accustomed to risks, there are plenty of ways of doing that without killing anything except occasionally yourself. The motor-cyclist takes more trying risks than the foxhunter; and motor-cycling seems safety itself compared to aviation. A dive from a high springboard will daunt a man as effectually as a stone wall in the hunting field. The notion that if you have no sportsmen you will have no soldiers (as if more than the tiniest fraction of the armies of the world had ever been sportsmen) is as absurd as the notion that burglars and garrotters should be encouraged because they might make hardier and more venturesome soldiers than honest men; but since people foolishly do set up such arguments they may as well be mentioned in passing for what they are worth.

The question then comes to this: which is the superior man? the man whose pastime is slaughter, or the man whose pastime is creative or contemplative? I have no doubt about the matter myself, being on the creative and contemplative side by nature. Slaughter is necessary work, like scavenging; but the man who not only does it unnecessarily for love of it but actually makes as much of it as possible by breeding live things to slaughter, seems to me to be little more respectable than one who befouls the streets for the pleasure of sweeping them. I believe that the line of evolution leads to the prevention of the birth of creatures whose lives are not useful and enjoyable, and that the time will come when a gentleman found amusing himself with a gun will feel as compromised as he does now when found amusing himself with a whip at the expense of a child or an old lame horse covered with sores. Sport, like murder, is a bloody business; and the sportsmen will not always be able to outface that fact as they do at present.

But there is something else. Killing, if it is to give us heroic emotions, must not be done for pleasure. Interesting though the slaying of one man by another may be, it is abhorrent when it is done merely for the fun of doing it (the sportsman's way) or to satisfy the envious spite of the worse man towards the better (Cain's way). When Charlotte Corday stabbed Marat, and when Hamilton of Bothwellhaugh shot the Regent Murray, they were stung by intolerable social wrongs for which the law offered them no redress. When Brutus and his fellow-conspirators killed Cæsar, they had persuaded themselves that they were saving Rome. When Samson slew the lion, he had every reason to feel convinced that if he did not, the lion would slay him. Conceive Charlotte Corday stabbing Marat as an exercise of manual and anatomical skill, or

Hamilton bringing down the Regent as a feat of marksmanship! Their deeds at once become, not less, but more horrifying than if they had done them from a love of killing. Jack the Ripper was a madman of the most appalling sort; but the fascination of murder for him must have been compounded of dread, of horror, and of a frightful perversion of an instinct which in its natural condition is a kindly one. He was a ghastly murderer; but he was a hot-blooded one. The perfection of callousness is not reached until a life is sacrificed, and often cruelly sacrificed, solely as a feat of skill. Peter the Great amusing himself by torturing his son to death was a revolting monster; but he was not so utterly inhuman in that crime as he was when, on being interested by a machine for executing criminals which he saw in a museum on his travels, he proposed to execute one of his retinue to see how the machine worked, and could with difficulty be brought to understand that there was a sentimental objection to the proceeding on the part of his hosts which made the experiment impossible. When he tortured his son he knew that he was committing an abomination. When he wanted to try an experiment at the cost of a servant's life he was unconscious of doing anything that was not a matter of course for any nobleman. And in this he was worse than abominable: he was deficient, imbecile, less than human. Just so is the sportsman, shooting quite skilfully and coolly without the faintest sense of any murderous excitement, and with no personal feeling against the birds, really further from salvation than the man who is humane enough to get some sense of wickedness out of his sport. To have one's fellow-feeling corrupted and perverted into a lust for cruelty and murder is hideous; but to have no fellow-feeling at all is to be something less than even a murderer. The man who sees red is more complete than the man who is blind.

The triviality of sport as compared with the risk and trouble of its pursuit and the gravity of its results makes it much sillier than crime. The idler who can find nothing better to do than to kill is past our patience. If a man takes on himself the heavy responsibility of killing, he should not do it for pastime. Pastimes are very necessary; for though a busy man can always find something to do, there comes a point at which his health, his sanity, his very existence may depend on his doing nothing of the smallest importance; and yet he cannot sit still and twiddle his thumbs: besides, he requires bodily exercise. He needs an idle pastime. Now "Satan finds some mischief still for idle hands to do" if the idler lets his conscience go to sleep. But he need not let it go to sleep. There are plenty of innocent idle pastimes for him. He can read detective stories. He can play tennis. He can drive a motor-car if he can afford one. He can fly. Satan may suggest that it would be a little more interesting to kill something; but surely only an outrageous indifference to the sacredness of life and the horrors of suffering and terror, combined with a monstrously selfish greed for sensation, could drive a man to accept the Satanic suggestion if sport were not organized for him as a social institution. Even as it is, there are now so many other pastimes available that the choice of killing is becoming more and more a disgrace to the chooser. The wantonness of the choice is beyond excuse. To kill as the poacher does, to sell or eat the victim, is at least to act reasonably. To kill from hatred or revenge is at least to behave passionately. To kill in gratification of a lust for death is at least to behave villainously. Reason, passion, and villainy are all human. But to kill, being all the time quite a good sort of fellow, merely to pass away the time when there are a dozen harmless ways of doing it equally available, is to behave like an idiot or a silly imitative sheep.

Surely the broad outlook and deepened consciousness which admits all living things to the commonwealth of fellow feeling, and the appetite for fruitful activity and generous life which come with it, are better than this foolish doing of unamiable deeds by people who are not in the least unamiable.

Thomas Mann

THOMAS MANN *was born amid comfortable middle-class sur-roundings in Lübeck in 1875. He worked in a Munich insurance office briefly and during his attendance at the university there, married the daughter of a professor. His family background inspired his first great novel,* Buddenbrooks, *written at the age of 24. In the next decades, he produced many marvelous stories—particularly* Death in Venice *and* Mario and the Magician—*along with critical essays of wide influence, but his important work continued to be in the field of fiction:* The Magic Mountain (1924) *and the* Joseph *tetralogy (1933-43), both landmarks of modern literature. After a political disagreement with the Nazi government and a short residence in Switzerland, Mann came to America to teach at Princeton University. In 1941, he settled in California, where he wrote* The Holy Sinner *and* Dr. Faustus. *During the fifties, dissatisfied with the climate of conformity in America, he again took up residence in Switzerland. There he died in 1955 while working on* The Confessions of Felix Krull. *Awarded the Nobel Prize for 1929, he stands with James Joyce and Marcel Proust among the great novelists of the century.*

When Anton Chekhov died in Badenweiler in July 1904 of tuberculosis of the lungs, I was a young man who had embarked upon literature with some short stories and a novel which owed a great deal to the art of fiction in nineteenth-century Russia. Yet I seek in vain today to recall the impression made upon me then by the death of the Russian writer only fifteen years my senior. My mind is a blank. For, like the rest of my country-men, I was little familiar with Chekhov's work.

What were the causes of this ignorance? Speaking for myself, it was probably because I was under the spell of the *magnum opus*, fascinated by those monumental epics, which are the fruit of sustained inspiration and are brought to completion by the power of indomitable patience; for I worshiped the great achievers like Balzac, Tolstoy, and Wagner, and it was my dream to emulate them if I could. Whereas Chekhov (like Maupassant, whom by the way I knew much better) confined himself to the modest dimension of the short story; and this did not call for heroic endurance throughout years and decades, but could be tossed off by some happy-go-lucky artist in a day or two or a week or two, at most. I felt a certain disdain for this, hardly realizing then that genius can be bounded in a nutshell and yet embrace the whole fulness of life by virtue of a brevity and terseness deserving the highest admiration. Such works attain to full epic stature and can even surpass in intensity the great towering novels which inevitably flag at times and subside into noble boredom. If I understood that better in later life than in my youth, this was largely owing to my growing intimacy with Chekhov's art; for his short stories rank with all that is greatest and best in European literature.

Speaking more generally, it seems to me that Chekhov was underestimated for so long in western Europe, and in Russia, too, because of his extremely sober, critical, and doubting attitude towards himself—a most disarming quality which, however, far from inspiring respect, set a bad example to the world at large. For the opinion we have of ourselves is not without influence on the picture which our fellow-men make of us: it colors their notions and may falsify them. This short-story teller was for too long convinced of the slightness of his gifts and of his lack of artistic distinction. Until the end he had nothing of the literary grand seigneur about him, still less of the prophet or the sage, unlike Tolstoy who looked down on Chekhov amicably and according to Gorky, saw in him "an excellent, quiet, *modest* creature."

There is something disconcerting in such praise from a man whose colossal conceit did not fall short even of Wagner's. Chekhov would probably have repaid it with a calm, polite, ironical smile. For politeness and dutiful veneration mixed with some irony characterized Chekhov's attitude to the great man of Yasnaya Polyana; and at times the irony developed into open rebellion; not of course in his personal intercourse with that overpowering personality, but in letters to third persons. On his return from his self-sacrificing journey to the exiles' island of Sachalin (a descent into hell if ever there was one), he wrote: "What a sour and sullen fellow I should be now if I had remained between my four walls. *Before* my journey for instance I regarded Tolstoy's *Kreutzersonata* as a great event; now on the other hand it seems to me silly and absurd." Tolstoy's imperial but also questionable prophetic airs got on his nerves. "May the devil take the philosophy of the great ones of this earth!" he wrote. "All the great sages are as despotic as generals, and as uncivil as generals, too, because they are convinced of their impunity." That was chiefly aimed at Tolstoy's abuse of doctors as worthless scoundrels. For Chekhov was a doctor, a doctor by passionate conviction, a man of science, and of faith in science; he believed science to be one of the forces making for progress, the great antagonist of scandalous conditions, since it enlightens the heads and hearts of men.

In short he was a positivist—from modesty; a simple servant of remedial truth, who never for a moment laid claim to any of the liberties taken by the great.

His long-persisting doubts of himself as an artist extended, in my opinion, beyond the self to literature altogether. Literature, to use his own words, was his mistress; whereas science was his lawfully-wedded wife, in whose presence he felt guilty of unfaithfulness because of his love for the other. Hence, the exhausting journey to Sachalin, endangering his already weakened constitution, and his report on the fearful conditions prevailing on the island, a report which caused a sensation and actually resulted in some reforms. Hence, too, his tireless activity as a country doctor which kept pace with his literary work; the administration of the district hospital of Svenigorod near Moscow; the fight against cholera which he conducted in Molichovo, his own small property. Meanwhile his fame as an author was growing, but he viewed this skeptically, with conscience-stricken modesty. "Am I not bamboozling the reader," he asked, "and throwing dust in his eyes? For after all I am unable to answer the really vital questions."

Those words moved me to the core. Indeed they impelled me

to study Chekhov's biography in detail, one of the most touching and engaging that I know. He came from Taganrog on the Sea of Azov in south Russia, a typically provincial town, in which his father (lower-middle-class, bigoted, and the son of a serf) ran a small shop and tyrannized over his wife and children. Old Chekhov was also a painter, or rather a dauber, of sacred images, and a self-taught performer on the violin; furthermore he had a passion for liturgical music and assembled a church choir in which his boys were obliged to sing. Probably these amateur sidelines were responsible for the failure of the shop, which went bankrupt while Anton Pavlovitch was still at school, and his father had to flee from his creditors to Moscow. Yet in this narrow, bigoted, lower-middle-class breast there lurked something embryonically artistic, although it was only to germinate, develop, and unfold in one of his offspring. All the same, one of Anton's elder brothers became a "publicist" and the other a painter; an insignificant publicist, it is true, and a painter who (like the other) eventually drowned what little talent he may have possessed in vodka.

At home in Taganrog the boys had to help their father in the shop, run errands, and get up at three o'clock in the morning on high days and holidays to rehearse with the rest of the choir for the services. On the top of all this, there was attendance at the local grammar-school, a soulless drilling-ground in which teachers as well as taught were directed from above to shun independent thinking like the plague. So that life resembled forced labor; boring, oppressive, and wearisome. But one of the brothers, Anton Pavlovitch, the one who had been secretly marked out, had his own peculiar compensation in the shape of an inborn tendency to merriness, merry-making, clowning, and mimicry. This was nourished by observation and translated into caricature. The boy could imitate anyone: a simple-minded deacon; a pompous official, treading a measure at a ball; a dentist; or the rigid deportment of a police-sergeant in church. He mimicked them all and he did it so comically, so well, and with such truth to life that his audience was amazed: "Do that again," they said. "My word! Has one ever . . . ? We were there too and found nothing to laugh about. Yet this little rogue does it right and twice as natural as life! What nonsense! Ha, ha, ha! Stop it now, that unseemly nonsense! Or, rather, before you stop, that police sergeant on his way to church, let's have *him* once more!"

It was the *primum mobile* of art that made its appearance then, the talent for primitive aping, the will and the gift to amuse by acting the buffoon. It was to use very different means in the future and pour itself into quite other forms; it was to become imbued with spiritual elements, to experience moral ennoblement and to rise from the ridiculous to the sublime, from merely amusing mimicry to imitations that would shake the soul. Yet even in his deepest, bitterest, and most serious moods, Chekhov never lost his comic vision of life, and his work was always to retain a great deal of the gifted mimicry of the police-sergeant and the dancing official. . . .

The father, then, had to close shop and make off to Moscow, while the sixteen-year-old Anton Pavlovitch stayed behind for three years in Taganrog at his school-desk. For if his dearest wish, to study medicine, was to be granted, he must complete the grammar-school course. Subsisting as best he might, on a tiny scholarship supplemented by wretchedly paid private lessons to younger students, he finished the course, and, passing out through the upper forms, he obtained his school-leaving certificate and followed his parents to Moscow to study at the university.

He had escaped from the narrowness of provincial existence. Would life in the great city make him happy, and did he breathe more freely there? Alas, no one could breathe freely in the Russia of those days, in that gloomy and stifling atmosphere. Men went about, sneakingly devout, brutally badgered and bullied by those in authority. It was a life led under surveillance and censorship, a cringing life made hideous by the wrathful bellowing of the state. The somber system of absolute autocracy under Alexander III and his terrible Minister, Pobyodonostsov, brooded over the country; and many a fine mind in Chekhov's vicinity, spirits delicately poised and in need of the ozone of freedom, fell as victims to melancholia. Insanity darkened the mind of Gleb Uspenski, an honest and upright chronicler of Russian peasant life. Garshin, whose mournful fiction Chekhov much admired, committed suicide. The attraction of vodka increased greatly among the intellectuals. They drank because they were without hope.

Anton Pavlovitch did not take to drinking; neither did he become melancholy or insane. For one thing, he had an outlet in his medical studies which he pursued zestfully and which were outside the sphere of Pobyodonoststov's interference; and then, faced with the universal dejection, he adopted the same humorous attitude towards it with which he had countered the boredom of Taganrog. He made jokes; he aped the police-sergeant, the silly deacon, the official at the ball, or their counterparts; but he no longer mimicked them in the flesh, he took them off on paper. There he sat in his parents' house, writing for any of the comic papers which liked to indulge in a little cautious satire. He would fling off all kinds of amusing sketches, quite short and hastily jotted down: anecdotes, dialogues, humorous news items, pen-portraits; and all this with such verve that people exclaimed, just as they had done at home in Taganrog: "I say! Did you ever? He's got something there! Just do that again!" And he did it again, and again and again; bubbling over with wit, inexhaustible in minute observations of everyday life and waggish imitations. For vast numbers of these little pieces had to be delivered if the measly fees they earned were to mount up sufficiently not only to defray the costs of his studies but also to contribute something substantial to the upkeep of his parents and his younger brothers and sisters; for his father earned hardly a penny, and Anton at the age of nineteen was the mainstay of the family. "Antosha Chechonte" was the name he used as contributor to the comic papers.

Then something very strange came to pass, something indicative of the autonomous spirit of literature and exemplifying the totally unexpected results that may arise from any kind of meddling with it, however utilitarian, unimportant, and light-hearted such meddling may be. This spirit acts as a "goad to the conscience"—Antosha Chechonte, the joker, said so himself. In one of his letters he described himself sitting at his unprotected table in his parents' house. Children were yelling round him, a chiming clock kept chiming, there was any amount of coming and going, his father was reading out loud in the next room, and his literary work lay before him, "goading my conscience unmercifully." That was hardly fair, since he was only writing to raise a laugh and amuse the bourgeoisie. But that is where the something strange, significant, and unexpected I mentioned just now entered in. Gradually, without his knowledge or consent, something broke through into his little sketches which was originally no part of their plan; something that came from the conscience of literature and from his own personal conscience, too. That something, although still gay and entertaining, could now also be bitter and sad, accusing and exposing life and society, suffering, criticizing; it was literature, in short. For the thing that broke through was directly connected with the actual writing, with the form and the language. The critical sadness and rebelliousness sprang from the desire for a better reality, for a purer, truer, lovelier, nobler life, for a human society in which the spirit could take delight. But this desire was imagined in the language, in the obligation to exploit it aesthetically, an "unmerciful" obligation, yet an absolutely vital factor in that element which broke through into Antosha's care-free prose. Fifteen years were to pass, and then Gorky, speaking about this same Antosha, passed the following judgment: Chekhov is unsurpassed as a stylist, and the future historian of literature, reflecting on the growth of the Russian language, will conclude that it has been created by Pushkin, Turgenev, and Chekhov."

That pronouncement was made in 1900. At the moment we are considering the years 1884-1885. Anton, now twenty-four years old, had completed his studies and had entered the district hospital of Voskressensk as an internee, where he undertook post-mortem examinations of the corpses of suicides and others who had died under suspicious circumstances. Yet he still went on writing comic literature; it had become a habit with him; and a few other things had crept in (*The Death of an Official, The Fat and the Lean, A Delinquent*) whose composition had given him singular pleasure. The rank and file of his readers may have liked them less because there was a bitter tang to the humor; but here and there one or another raised his brows, sat up and took notice. Amongst those was D. V. Grigoróvitch. Who knows Dimitri Vassilyovitch Grigoróvitch? Not I. To be honest, I had never heard of him before I began to study Chekhov's biography. And yet he was at that time a widely esteemed author, a writer of serious literature.

It was this man who wrote a letter from Petersburg to young Dr. Chekhov in Voskressensk, a very earnest letter which was perhaps the most moving, astonishing, and epoch-making event in Chekhov's whole life. This literary celebrity, already advanced in years, wrote as follows: "My dear Sir, you possess a quite extraordinary talent which, I am convinced, need not shrink back from even the greatest tasks. It would be a tragedy if you continued to dissipate your powers on literary small talk. I feel compelled to implore you not to do that, but to concentrate on genuinely artistic work." Anton Pavlovitch read this in black and white signed by that great name. He wrote in reply:

> I nearly burst into tears. I am dumbfounded and quite incapable of judging whether I have earned this great reward or not. . . . If I possess a talent deserving of respect, then let me confess to one who is pure in heart that until now I have not respected it. . . . There are always sufficient reasons to be unjust to oneself, extremely mistrustful and hypochondriacal. . . . Until this moment I have adopted a completely frivolous, careless and superficial attitude towards my literary activity. . . . In writing I was careful above all things not to waste on the story of the moment those images and figures which were dear to me, and which, God knows why, I have carefully guarded and kept hidden away.

This is what he wrote in his letter of thanks to the aged Grigoróvitch, a letter which was later made public. After he had written it, he went out to perform a post-mortem or to visit a case of typhus in the district hospital; let us say, to visit a case of typhus, in remembrance of the spotted typhus of Lieutenant Klimov, the tale of an illness told from the point of view of the stricken man with consummate mastery in later years by Anton Chekhov, who never signed himself Antosha Chechonte again after the receipt of that letter.

His allotted span of life was short. He was only twenty-nine years of age when the first symptoms of tuberculosis declared themselves; he was a doctor; he knew what that meant, and one cannot help wondering if his foresight as to the brevity of his guest performance here below did not contribute its quota to that strange modesty of his, that skeptical, infinitely winning and unobtrusive humility which continued to characterize his spiritual and artistic bearing as a whole, including even the instinct to turn it to account as a typical feature of his art and as the peculiar magic of his existence. Twenty-five years—that was roughly the time allowed him for his creative life; and truly he made full use of it; for a good six hundred stories bear his name, not a few of which have the compass of the long short story; and there are masterpieces, such as *Ward Number Six*, among them. In this tale a doctor, sickened by the stupidity and wretchedness of the world of normal men, becomes so friendly with an interesting madman that the world judges him to be mad himself and locks him up. This story of eighty-seven pages, written in 1892, makes no direct accusation; but it is so frighteningly symbolic of the debasement of humanity under the decline of autocracy that young Lenin said to his sister: "When I had finished that story yesterday evening, I found that it positively haunted me. I couldn't stay in my room. I got up and went out. I felt as if I myself were locked up in Ward Number Six."

But, if references are to be made and praises bestowed, then I must certainly mention *A Tedious Tale*, for it is my favorite among all Chekhov's stories, an outstandingly fascinating work which for gentleness, sadness, and strangeness has no equal in the literary world. It is an astonishing production; if for no other reason, because this tale, allegedly "tedious" yet actually overwhelming, is put into the mouth of an old man by a young man of thirty with the utmost sympathy and understanding. The hero is a world-renowned scholar with the rank of a general, an Excellency, who often calls himself by that title in his confessions. "My Excellency," he says, adding, as it were, an inaudible "Good Lord!" or "Dear me!" For, high though he stands in the official hierarchy, he stands high enough spiritually for his self-critical and altogether critical mind to regard his fame and the veneration shown him as ludicrous; and to despair in the depths of his soul because his life, so full of honors, has always lacked a spiritual center, a "central idea," and that therefore at bottom it has been a life without sense and without hope. He writes:

> Every feeling and every thought lives an isolated existence in my mind; and the most experienced analyst will not discover in my judgments on science, the theater, literature, etc., etc., what people call a central idea, or the God of living men. And if that is lacking, there is nothing but the void. . . . It is not in the least surprising therefore that the last months of my life have been darkened by thoughts and feelings worthy of a slave and a barbarian and that indifference is now my portion. For if something higher and stronger than all external circumstances does not inform the life of a man, then indeed a common cold is enough to disturb his equilibrium; and all his pessimism or optimism together with his great and little thoughts are merely symptoms and nothing else. I am defeated. Why, then, should I continue to think or to argue? No, I shall simply sit and wait for what is coming in silence.

"And my ending is despair"; Prospero's last words keep on recurring to the mind when reading the confessions of Nikolai Stepanovitch, so old and so famous, who says: "But as it happens, I fail to love the popularity of my name. I am afraid it has deceived me." Anton Chekhov was not old, he was young when he put those words into the mouth of the general; but he had not very long to live; and perhaps that was why he was able to anticipate the mood of old age with such incredible, uncanny prescience. "I fail to love the popularity of my name." For Chekhov, too, did not love his increasing fame; he felt "for some inexplicable reason uneasy about it." Was he not deceiving his readers by dazzling them with his talent, since he was "unable to answer the really vital questions?" "A conscious life without a definite philosophy of life," he wrote to a friend, "is no life at all, but a burden and a nightmare." In *A Tedious Tale*, Katya, the ward of the famous scholar, turns to him in vain. She has suffered shipwreck as an actress; and she, the one human being whom he still cares for, loving her with the secret tenderness of old age, asks him in her helplessness and distress: "What shall I do? Answer me, Nikolai Stepanovitch, I implore you. What shall I do?" And the only answer he can give is this: "I don't know, Katya. Upon my honor, I don't know." Then she leaves him. The question: "What is to be done?" haunts Chekhov's writings at every turn in a deliberately confused way which even borders on the ludicrous because of the odd, helpless, stilted manner in which his characters indulged in fruitless speculations on the subject of this vital question. The truth about life which this author felt it his bounden duty to proclaim devalues the very ideas and opinions which he has his figures argue and fight about. That truth is by nature ironical.

But, if that is so, then must it not also follow that art itself is nihilistic by nature? And yet art is so industrious! Art is the very essence of work, the prototype of all work, work itself, performed for its own sake. And Chekhov was devoted to work as few others have ever been. He worked incessantly and tirelessly, regardless of his delicate constitution and of the wasting nature of his disease, every day and right to the end. More than that, he spent himself heroically in perpetual doubt as to his labor's ultimate value and in spite of the guilty feeling that it lacked any central or "root idea"; that he had no answer to the question: "What can be done?" and evaded it by descriptions of life which were merely entertaining. "We only draw life as it is," he said, "and never go a step further than that." Or again: "As things are, the life of an artist has no sense; and the more gifted he is, the stranger and more incomprehensible is the part he plays; since it is obvious that he works for the amusement of an unclean beast of prey and by doing so helps to maintain the existing order."

The existing order: that meant the impossible state of affairs in the Russia of the 'nineties under which Chekhov lived. But his despondency, his doubts about the value of his work, the feeling of the strangeness and incomprehensibility of his role as an artist, all these are timeless and not dependent on the conditions prevailing in Russia then. "Conditions," that is to say bad conditions, in which a disastrous gulf divides truth from reality, are always with us; and Chekhov has brothers in misfortune today, artists whose fame torments them because they "are amusing a doomed world without offering it even the shadow of a saving truth," or so it is said, and who, just like him, feel themselves at one with the hero of A *Tedious Tale* who could not answer the question "What shall I do?" And these artists, too, are unable to convince themselves of the value of their work: nevertheless they go on working right up to the bitter end.

"Nevertheless"; this strange word must have a meaning and must have a sense which makes some sense of the work they do. Can it be that in art itself, however much it resembles mere entertainment, there resides something ethical, something social imbued with the spirit of service; something which may perhaps finally approach the "saving truth" towards which humanity stretches out its hands? I touched earlier on the autonomy of literature with its unexpected results, and tried to show how this spirit, without any desire or expectation on young Chekhov's part, broke through into his sprightly penny-a-liners and automatically raised their moral level. One biographer says of him: "What is remarkable in Chekhov's development is the fact that, closely connected with his attainment to mastery of form, there went his altered attitude towards his times, an attitude giving proof of an unerring instinct and the gift of subtle discrimination between those forces which will soon belong to the past and those which herald the future."

What interests me in this observation is the recognition of the connection between Chekhov's gradual mastery of form and his increasing sensitiveness to the moral evils of his age; in other words, the interdependence of his aesthetic and ethical conscience. It is this connection which gives to the diligence of art its meaning, its dignity, and its spirit of service; and it explains Chekhov's great regard for work altogether and his condemnation of all idle drones and parasites, his increasingly definite rejection of a life that, as he said, "is based on slavery."

With the working class Chekhov had no contact at all and he never studied Marx. He was not a workers' poet like Gorky. But he found accents for his haunting chagrin in the face of existing conditions which went to the heart of his people, as for instance in *The Peasants*, that great and awful social document. During a religious festival a sacred image, "The Giver of Life," is carried around in a procession from village to village. A vast concourse of villagers and visitors, surrounded by dust and noise, streams out to meet it; they all stretch out their hands towards it, gazing at it ardently and calling out with tears: "Our Protectress! Our Mother!"

> It was as if all of them suddenly understood that there was something else besides empty space between earth and heaven, that the rich and the mighty had not snatched everything away, that there was still some protection against injuries and wrongs, against slavish oppression, against deep, unbearable misery, and against the fearful evil of drink . . . "Our Protectress! Our Mother!" But hardly was the ceremony over and the sacred image borne away, than everything went on in the same old way as before, and coarse, drunken voices were heard again from the inn.

The compassion and the bitterness ("everything went on in the same old way") are typical of Chekhov; and I am inclined to think that his popularity, so strikingly manifested at his death and burial in Moscow, had its roots in descriptions of this nature. This manifestation caused a "loyal" newspaper to remark that Anton Pavlovitch must have belonged to the "stormy petrels of the Revolution."

He did not look like a stormy petrel, nor like a moujik turned genius, nor yet like Nietzsche's pale criminal. The portraits show a slightly built man in the fashion of the day: a starched collar, a pince-nez on a narrow cord, a short pointed beard, regular, rather suffering features and a melancholy regard. His features express intelligent attention, modesty, skepticism, and kindness. They betray no symptoms of a stormy inner life, either; it is almost as if he were too modest to entertain such passions; there is no sign in his life that he ever felt passionately about a woman; and his biographers are of the opinion that he, who could describe love so well, never experienced erotic rapture. Yet he married none the less, three years only before his death, a marriage which came to pass as a result of his happy relationship with the Moscow Arts Theatre and his friendship with Stanislavsky; for the bride-elect was the gifted actress Olga Knipper. His letters to her have been preserved, written in his own hand; and they too are wary of the extreme of emotion and keep to a whimsically ironical tone.

These last years in Crimea, where his health forced him to re-side and where the Arts Theatre visited him *en bloc* to play his pieces to him, were perhaps the happiest of his life, owing to his marriage, his friendship with Gorky, and the honor of Tolstoy's company; for the latter would spend periods of convalescence from time to time in a castle near Yalta. In addition the invalid rejoiced like a child over his election to honorary membership in the literary section of the Petersburgh Academy of Science. But when, two years later, Gorky's membership was rejected by the Government because of his radical views, Chekhov, like Korolenko, resigned as protest. His last story was *The Bride* (1903) and his last play *The Cherry Orchard;* and in these works, calmly facing the coming dissolution and refusing to make much ado even about his illness and death, he left us with a message of hope. His life's work, which made no claim to the monumental dimensions of the epic, nevertheless enfolds the whole of Russia, that vast country where eternal nature exists side by side with the hopelessly unnatural conditions of its pre-revolutionary social fabric. "The insolence and idleness of the strong; the ignorance of the weak vegetating like animals—and everywhere incredible poverty, affliction, degeneration, drunkenness, hypocrisy and lying. . . ." But the nearer the end approached the more affectingly the inner light of faith in the future played around the dark picture; and even more brightly and warmly a poet's loving gaze embraced a coming communion of proud, free, and active human beings, "new, noble, and reasonable patterns of life on whose threshold we are perhaps already standing and whose shape we sometimes foresee."

"Good-bye, my dear, dear Sasha," says Nadya, the "bride," to the dead man who has persuaded her to escape from a false existence; "and before her eyes there arose a new life; wide and free; and this new life, still nebulous and mysterious, called to her and allured her." A dying man wrote these words just before the end. Perhaps it was only the mystery of death which called and allured. Or is it permissible to believe that the passionate longing of a poet may after all alter life?

John Galsworthy

JOHN GALSWORTHY, *the English novelist and playwright, was born in 1867 to a prosperous family of Surrey. After attending Harrow and Oxford, he was admitted to the bar, but he practiced little law. Instead, he traveled about the world (on one voyage he became friendly with the ship's captain, a Pole named Joseph Conrad). At the age of 28, he began to write, publishing his first four books under the pseudonym of John Sinjohn because they fell short of his demanding standards. In 1906, he completed the first volume of his greatest work,* The Forsyte Saga. *He turned to the drama with* The Silver Box, *and spurred by a strong sense of justice, attacked social evils of various kinds in other plays such as* Strife, Justice, The Skin Game, *and* Loyalties. *In 1920-21, he completed the Forsyte trilogy and continued to write about the younger generation of Forsytes in a second trilogy called* A Modern Comedy *(1929). He also wrote several volumes of short stories, sketches, letters, poems, and essays. The following essay from* Candelabra, *published in 1932, the year he won the Nobel Prize, reveals the shrewd satirical approach to modern mores, beliefs, and ideals that gives the Forsyte chronicles their flavor. Galsworthy died in London in 1933.*

Of what do we moderns dream? What are our castles in Spain?

This question crossed my mind in Seville cathedral, that stone fabric of man's greatest dream in the ages to which we have been accustomed to apply the word "dark." Travelers in Spain consulting their guide-books, read: "On the eighth day of July, in the year 1401, the Dean and Chapter of Seville assembled in the Court of the Elms and solemnly resolved: 'Let us build us a church so great that those who come after us may think us mad to have attempted it!' The church took one hundred and fifty years to build."

And in that glorious building, raised by five succeeding generations, one could not help wondering wherein lay the superiority of ourselves, Children of Light, over those old Sons of Darkness.

We too dream, no doubt—not always with a Freudian complex; and our dreams have results, such as the Great Dam at Assouan, the Roosevelt Dam in Arizona, the Woolworth Building, the Forth Bridge, the Power Works at Niagara, the Panama Canal (which took one-tenth of the time the Sons of Darkness lavished on Seville cathedral). But all these things were dreamed and fabricked out for immediate material benefit. The old builders of pyramids, mosques and churches built for no physical advantage in this life. They carved and wrought and slowly lifted stone on stone for remote and, as they thought, spiritual ends. We moderns mine and forge and mason-up our monuments to the immediate profit of our bodies. Incidentally they may give pleasure to the spirit, but we did not exactly build them for that purpose. Have we raised anything really great in stone or brick for a mere idea since Christopher Wren built St. Paul's Cathedral?

Sons of Darkness and Children of Light, both have worshiped a half-truth. The ancients built for tomorrow in another world, forgetting that all of us have a today in this. They spent riches and labor to save the souls of their hierarchy, but they kept their laborers so poor that they had no souls to save. They left astounding testimony to human genius and tenacity, but it never seems to have ruffled their consciousness that they fashioned the beautiful with slavery, misery, and blood.

We moderns pursue what we call Progress. All our stupendous achievements have this progressive notion at their back. Brooklyn Bridge may look beautiful in any light, and Sheffield chimney-stacks may look beautiful in the dark, but they were not put up for that reason, nor even because we thought we were thereby handing our Presidents or Prime Ministers the keys of heaven. Modern engineers may be lovers of beauty and men of imagination, but their prime mistresses are Science, Industry, and Trade. We think that if we make the wheels go round fast enough mankind is bound to rise on the wings of wealth. Look after the body, we say, and the spirit will look after itself. Whether we save a greater proportion of our bodies than the ancients did of souls is the question; but no such trifling doubt shakes our belief in Progress. Our modern castle in Spain is in one word: "Production."

Most men and women have an instinctive love of beauty, and some natural pride in the work of their brains and hands: but machinery divides us from the ancients; quietly, gradually, it has shifted the central point of man's philosophy. Before the industrial era set in, men used to make things by hand; they were in some sort artists, with at least the craftsman's pride in their work. Now they press buttons, turn wheels; don't make completed articles; work with monotony at the section of an article—so many hours of machine-driving a day, the total result of which is never a man's individual achievement. "Intelligent specialism," says a writer on Labor Policy, "is one thing. It consists in one man learning how to do one thing specially well. But the sort of specializing which consists in setting thousands of human beings during their whole working lives to such soul-destroying jobs as fixing the bristles into a hairbrush, pasting labels on jampots, or nearly any one of the varieties of machine-tending, is quite another thing. It is the utter negation of human nature."

The tendency of modern "Production" is to center a man's interest not in his working day, but outside of it—at least, in the lower ranks of industry. The old artificers absorbed culture, such as it was, from their work. In these days culture, such as it is, is grafted on to the workman in his leisure, as antidote to wheel-driving. Hewers, delvers, drawers of water in the past never, perhaps, took interest in their work; and there are still many among us today to whom their work is of absorbing interest. But, on the whole, the change has put pride of quantity above pride of quality. In old days the good thing was often naturally supplied; nowadays it is more often artificially demanded.

No one objects to production sanely and coherently directed to fine purposes. But this Progress of ours, which is supposed to take care of our bodies, and of which machinery is the mistress—does it progress? We used to have the manor-house with half-a-dozen hovels in its support. Now we have twenty miles of handsome residences with a hundred and twenty miles of ugly back streets, reeking with smoke and redolent of dullness, dirt, and discontent. The proportions are still unchanged, and the purple patches of our great towns are too often as rouge on the cheeks and salve on the lips of a corpse. Is this really Progress?

True progress would mean leveling up and gradually extinguishing the disproportion between manor and hovel, residence and back street.

Let us fantastically conceive the civic authorities of London on the eighth day of July, in this year of grace, solemnly resolving: "We will remake of London a city so beautiful and sweet to dwell in, that those who come after us shall think us mad to have attempted it." It might well take five generations to remake of London a stainless city of Portland stone, full of baths and flowers and singing birds—not in cages. We should need a procession of civic authorities who steadily loved castles in Spain. For a civic body only lives about four years; and cannot bind its successor. I wonder if we have even begun to realize the difficulty of true progress in a democratic age. He who furnishes an antidote to the wasteful, shifting tendency of short immediate policies under a system of government by bodies elected for short terms, might be the greatest benefactor of the age. For find that antidote we must, or discover democracy to be fraudulent.

Again, are we not unfortunate in letting civic life be run by those who were born seeing two inches before their noses, and whose education, instead of increasing, has reduced those inches to one? It seems ungrateful to criticize the practical businessman, whose stamina and energy make the more imaginative gasp. One owes him much, but one would like to owe him more. For does his vision as a rule extend beyond keeping pace with the present? And without vision—the people perish! Has not the word "visionary" come to have a slighting significance? And yet, unless we incorporate beauty in our scheme of life today, and teach the love of beauty to our children, the life of tomorrow and the children thereof must needs be as far from beauty as we are now. Isn't it, then, peculiar to set men to direct the education, housing, and amusements of their fellow-citizens, unless they have a love of beauty and some considerable knowledge of art? And have not the present generation of businessmen—with notable exceptions —a sort of indulgent contempt for art and beauty? A few years ago the Headmaster of a great Public School made use of these words: "I'm glad to see so many boys going in for art; it is an excellent hobby to pass the time *when you have nothing better to do!*" He had been teaching Greek for half a century; yet it was Greek to him that art has been the greatest factor in raising mankind from its old savage state. The contemplation of beautiful visions, emotions, thoughts, and dreams, expressed beautifully in words, stone, metal, paint, and music, has slowly, generation by generation, uplifted man and mollified his taste for "long pig"— as the South Sea Islander calls his edible enemy. Even the uplifting part of religion is but the beautiful expression of exalted feeling. The rest of religion (including the ceremony of eating "long pig") is only superstition. Think of the thousand wars fought in the name of superstition; the human sacrifices, the tortures of the Inquisition; the persecutions, intolerances, and narrow cruelties perpetrated even to this day! The teachings of Buddha, of Christ, of St. Francis d'Assisi were the expression of exalted feeling; simple, and touching the hearts of men, as all true beauty does. They have done an ennobling work. But who shall deny that they belong to the cult of beauty?

Trade—they say—has been a mollifying factor, an elevator in the human hotel. Yes, in so far as it opens up communications, and is the coach in which art and beauty ride; but *of itself*—it has no elevating influence.

Beauty, alone, in the largest sense of the word—the yearning for it, the contemplation of it—has civilized mankind. And no human being ever contributed to that process who thought he had "something better to do." And yet, we don't take beauty seriously. Immediate profit rules the roost in this Age of ours, and I leave it to the conscience of the Age to decide whether that is good. For every Age has a conscience; though it never comes to life till the Age is on its death-bed.

The mistake of all Ages, perhaps, has lain in keeping the knowledge and the love of beauty as a preserve for the few, the possession of a caste or clique. No great proportion of us are capable of creating or expressing beauty; but an immensely greater proportion of us are capable of appreciating it than have ever been given the chance of so doing. It should be our castle in Spain to clear our Age of that defect, and put beauty within the reach of all.

Machinery, of course, has come to stay; and though it may be true that engineers, authors, stone-cutters, artists, and many others still love beauty and take pride in their work, the great majority of us—label-pasters, wheel-drivers, stokers, clerks, shop-girls, bristle-fixers—are the slaves of modern machinery. For all such we must rely on grafted culture now; in other words, on education, rousing and fostering in the young that instinct for beauty which is in nearly all of us. For this, we have exceptional facilities nowadays. Besides teaching cooking and the fine art of being clean, we can bring an inkling of the other fine arts, architecture, literature, painting, music, of past and present, to children even in the humblest schools, we can teach children to appreciate the beauty of Nature, and give them some idea of taste. Revolution or evolution—we glibly talk of now one, now the other, but both are vain unless they mean demand for greater dignity of human life. What use in B despoiling A if B is going to use his spoils no better, perhaps worse, than A?

The word beauty is not here used in any precious sense. Its precious definitions are without number, or—value to speak of. No! It is here used to mean everything which promotes the true dignity of human life. For instance, to be "a good sport"—as they say—a man will shun that which lowers his dignity, dims his idea of his own quality; and his conception of his own quality derives obscurely from his sense of beauty. The dignity of human life demands, in fact, not only such desirable embroideries as pleasant sound, fine form, and lovely color but health, strength, cleanliness, balance, joy in living, just conduct and kind conduct. A man who truly loves beauty hates to think that he enjoys it at the expense of starved and stunted human beings or suffering animals. Mere aestheticism can be cruel or pettifogging; but such is not the beauty which gleams on the heights in the sunrise—certainly not our castle in Spain.

Sentiment apart, the ideal of beauty is the best investment modern man can make; for nothing else—not even trade—will keep him from extirpating the human species. Science in the hands of engineers and chemists has developed destructive powers which increase a hundredfold with each decade, while the reproductive powers and inclinations of the human being do not vary. Nothing in the world but the love of beauty in its broad sense stands between Man and the full and reckless exercise of his competitive appetites. The Great War was a little war compared with that which, through the development of scientific destruction, might be waged next time. There is, then, sheer necessity for investment in the ideal of beauty. No other security will give us interest on our money, and our money back. Unbalanced trade, science, industry give, indeed, a high momentary rate of interest, but only till the crash comes again and the world goes even more bankrupt than it is at present. The professor who invented a rocket which would visit the moon, find out all about it, and come back with the story, would have done more real good if he had taught a school full of children to see the beauty of—moonshine.

The next war will be fought from the air, and from under the sea, with explosives, gas, and the germs of disease. It may be over before it is declared. The final war necessary for the complete extirpation of mankind will be fought, perhaps, with atomic energy; and we shall have no occasion to examine the moon, for the earth will be as lifeless.

But it is sentiment which really makes the wheels go round, for not even "big business" rules our instincts and passions, and the question for modern man is: What shall we be sentimental about? Which is the fairer castle in Spain—quantity or quality— blind production or the dignity of human life?

What ideals have we at present? Happiness in a future life. If there be a future life for the individual, shall we find it repaying if we have not striven for quality in this; not had that kind and free and generous philosophy which belongs to the cult of beauty, and alone gives peace of mind? The pursuit of beauty includes, then, whatever may be true in the ideal of happiness in a future life. We have another current ideal: wealth or comfort in this life. But the cult of beauty contains all that is good in that; for it demands physical health and well-being, sane minds in sane bodies, which depend on a sufficiency of material comfort. The rest of the ideal of wealth is mere fat, sagging beyond the point of balance. Modern civilization offers us, in fact, a compound between "happiness in a future life" and "material comfort in this," lip-serving the first, and stomach-serving the second. You get the keys of heaven from your bank, but not unless you have a good balance. Modern civilization, on the whole, is camouflaged commercialism, wherein to do things well for the joy of doing them well is mere eccentricity. We even commercialize salvation—for so much virtue, so much salvation! *Quid pro quo!*

To give the devil its due, ours is the best Age men ever lived in; we are all more comfortable and virtuous than we ever were; we have many new accomplishments, advertisements in green pastures, telephones in bedrooms, more newspapers than we want to read, and extremely punctilious diagnosis of maladies. A doctor examined a young lady the other day, and among his notes were these: "Not afraid of small rooms, ghosts, or thunderstorms —not made drunk by hearing Wagner; brown hair, artistic hands; had a craving for chocolate in 1918." The Age is most thorough and accomplished, but with a kind of deadly practicality. All for today, nothing for tomorrow! The future will never think us mad for attempting what we do attempt; we build no Seville cathedrals. We never get ahead of time. For instance, we have just let slip a chance to re-vitalize the country life of England. At demobilization we might have put hundreds of thousands on the land, which needs them so very badly. And we have put in all not so many as the war took off the land. Life on the land means hard work and fewer cinemas; but it also means hearty stock for the next generation and the power of feeding ourselves on an island which the next war might completely isolate. A nation which never looks ahead is in for rude awakenings.

The pursuit of beauty as a national ideal, the building of that castle in Spain, requires, of course, foresight, long and patient labor, and steadfastness of ideal.

All literary men can tell people what they ought not to be; that is—literature. But to tell them what they ought to do is—politics, and it would be mere impertinence for a literary man to suggest anything practical!

But let him, at least, make a few affirmations. He believes that modern man is a little further from being a mere animal than the men of the Dark Ages, however great the castles in Spain those men left for us to look upon; but he is sure that we are in far greater danger than ever they were of a swift decline. From that decline he is convinced that only the love and cult of beauty will save us.

By the love and cult of beauty he means: *a higher and wider conception of the dignity of human life*; the teaching of what beauty is, to all—not merely to the few; the cultivation of good-will, so that we wish and work and dream that not only ourselves but everybody may be healthy and happy; and, above all, the fostering of the habit of doing things and making things well, for the joy of the work and the pleasure of achievement, rather than for the gain they will bring us. With these as the rules—instead of, as now, the riders—the wheels of an insensate scientific industrialism, whose one idea is to make money and get ahead of other people, careless of direction toward heaven or hell, might conceivably be spoked. Our Age lacks an ideal expressed with sufficient concreteness to be like a vision beckoning. In these unsuperstitious days no other ideal seems worthy of us, or indeed possible to us, save beauty—or call it, if you will, the dignity of human life.

Writers sometimes urge the need for more spiritual beauty in our lives. I distrust the word spiritual. We must be able to smell, and see, hear, feel, and taste our ideal as well; must know by plain evidence that it is lifting human life, and is the heritage of all, not merely of the refined and leisured. The body and soul are one for the purpose of all real evolution, and regrettable is any term suggestive of divorce between them. The dignity of human life is an unmistakable and comprehensive phrase. Offense against it is the modern Satan. We can say "Retro, Satanas," by leaving, each of us, a tiny corner of the universe a little more dignified, lovely, and lovable than we found it.

Latest opinion—unless there is a later—assigns ten thousand years as the time during which what we know as civilization has been at work. But ten thousand years is a considerable period of mollification, and one had rashly hoped that traditions of gentleness and fair-play had more strength among Western peoples than they have been proved to have since 1914; that mob feeling might have been less, instead of, as it seems, more potent. And yet, alongside of stupidity, savagery, greed, and mob violence, run an amazing individual patience, good humor, endurance, and heroism, which save a man from turning his back on himself and the world, with the words: "Cats and monkeys, monkeys and cats; all life is there!" Fear, after all, is at the back of nearly all savagery; and man must infallibly succumb to the infections of fear if there be not present in him that potent antidote—the sense of human dignity, which is but a love of and a belief in beauty. What applies to the individual applies to the civilization of which he forms a part. Our civilization, if it is to endure, must have a star on which to fix its eyes—something distant and magnetic to draw it on, something to strive towards, beyond the troubled and shifting needs and passions and prejudices of the moment. Those who wish to raise the dignity of human life should try to give civilization that star, to equip the world with the only vision which can save it from spite and the crazy competitions which lead thereto. The past few years have been the result of the past few hundred years. The war was no spasmodic visitation, but the culmination of age-long competitions. The past few years have devoured many millions of grown men, more millions of little children—prevented their birth, killed them, or withered them for life. If modern individuals and modern nations pursue again these crazy competitions, without regard for the dignity of human life, we shall live to see ten millions perish for every million who perished in this war. We shall live to curse the day, when, at the end of so great a lesson, we were too practical and businesslike to take it to heart.

Facts must be faced, and ideals should be grounded in reality; for it is no use blinking the general nature of man, or thinking that Rome can be built in a day. But with all our prejudices and passions, and all our "business instinct," we have also the instinct for beauty, and a sense of what is dignified. On that we must build, if we wish to leave to those who come after us the foundations of a castle in Spain such as the world has not yet seen; to leave our successors in mood and heart to continue our work, so that one hundred and fifty years, perhaps, from now human life may really be dignified and beautiful, not just a breathless, grudging, visionless scramble from birth to death, of a night with no star alight.

Roger Martin du Gard

ROGER MARTIN DU GARD, *the French novelist and playwright,
published his first two books in 1908: one was his first novel* Devenir,
*the other his doctoral thesis on archeology. Neither made him famous,
but the painstaking documentation and respect for truth he learned
through the latter helped to make* Jean Barois (1913) *his first successful novel. After service in World War I, he began* Les Thibaults, *a
ten-volume panorama of French life during the period prior to the war.
His reputation was made by, and rests on this* roman-cycle, *for which
he received the Nobel Prize in 1937. He also wrote several plays for
the experimental theater, some long stories, and* Recollections of André
Gide, *a brief but poignant memoir of his friend, from which the following piece has been taken. Martin du Gard died near Paris in 1958,
at the age of 77.*

> Only the very simple or the very
> great may be sure of dying in their
> own way. The others die in imita-
> tion.
>
> JEAN GUÉHENNO

The Clinique de Nice.

He is more than eighty years old; his heart is weak and
may give in at any moment; his liver is swollen, and an abscess
may be forming there; his blood is poisoned with urea. He knows
all that. He knows that his heart may stop beating from one moment to the next, or that he might be carried off, after a few days
of great pain, by a crisis of uremia. But of all this he thinks, if at
all, with a sort of curiosity, as if it were an unprecedented adventure: his last. . . . What is much more, this born insomniac has
not once closed his eyes since he took to his bed. How can he
stand such an ordeal? By what terrors can this old man be haunted
as he lies, forever awake, on what seems to be his deathbed? By

none, is the answer. He laughs when I show my anxiety. "It's just like you to think of such things! I occupy my mind as best I can. I wait, I listen to the clock striking, I daydream, I recite the poems that I still know by heart. . . . That's how I am. I don't deserve any credit for it, my dear Roger. I just have never been afraid of what might happen to me. . . ." * In the endless solitude of his nights, it is not of his own end that he thinks: it is of a passage in the *Aeneid* that he has just reread for the fifth or sixth time, and in which, to his great delight, he thinks that he has just discovered one of Vergil's hidden intentions, which had hitherto escaped him. Or else he thinks of the scenario that he would like to adapt from the *Caves du Vatican;* or of one of the new ideas which he carries within him, and caresses, and develops, and defines, so that he may be able to put it down in his notebooks, should be ever again have the strength to write. . . .

In the morning, when I hasten into his room and am anxious to know if the fever has at last abated, and what have been the incidents of the night, he won't, at first, let me put any questions to him: what he's in a hurry to tell me is far more important, in his eyes! If I insist, and want to question the nurse, or inspect his temperature chart, he grows angry, signs to me to come nearer, makes me sit right beside his bed in order to strain his breathing as little as possible, and then, in a low voice, and with many a pause, he goes over the things he has thought of in the night.

"Have you ever thought about this, Roger? For centuries men had hardly any doubts of their double nature. . . . They knew that their bodies would perish, but as for their immortal souls . . . And then, all of a sudden, they no longer feel sure! All of a sudden humanity no longer believes in the immortality of the spirit! Think how important that is! It's overwhelming, Roger, isn't it? Overwhelming!"

Another day he was full of the stupidity of the higher clergy. During the night he had been looking at an anthology of Car-

---

* As early as the 20th of December, 1924, we read in the *Journal:* ". . . I believe it comes rather from my lack of a certain *sense of reality.* . . . I can no longer manage to be afraid. . . . Yet I have known what fear was; when I was a child I was extremely funky. . . ."

dinal Mindszenty's writings. He was disgusted, indignant, in full rebellion—and very aggressive.

"Of course I was horror-struck by that tragic trial in Budapest. But just look at the poor Cardinal's sermons, and his pastoral letters! The platitudes! The childishness! The poverty of thought! I've never read anything—anything—like it." His feverish face contracted, his eyes grew hard. He was struggling for breath, but he insisted on going on. "No, no! The Churches and the Faith have really done too much harm! I cannot remain indifferent to that: right to the end I shall refuse to accept it! Those Churches must come down off their pedestals! We've got to outwit them! Mankind must be set free from their black magic! You're too easygoing, my dear Roger! Tolerance puts weapons in the Enemy's hands. If we don't fight them, we might as well give in at once: we might as well admit our defeat. . . . I, for one, am not going to give in! While there's a breath left in me I shall cry 'No!' to the Churches!"

This morning, after a bad night, he was rather sorry for himself —which is rare. He made a smiling catalogue of the infirmities, the distresses of his sick old body, now riddled with injections.

"It's at moments like these," I said, "that it would be marvelously consoling to believe in one's immortal soul."

He laughed. "No, no, not at all! In that respect neither old age nor illness, nor the nearness of death has any effect upon me. . . . I don't dream of any after life. On the contrary: the farther I go, the more inacceptable I find the hypothesis of the Beyond. *Instinctively* and *intellectually!*" Then, after a pause, "And I think that in saying that I prove myself much more genuinely *spiritual* than the believers. . . . It's an idea I often think over. I'd like to develop it a little, if I were given the time. . . ."

He said that, with a sort of smiling serenity, on the day after Maurice Maeterlinck had died of a heart attack, just over a mile from here, murmuring, according to the local papers, "Long live Immortality!"

Herman Hesse

THE BROTHERS KARAMAZOV
or The Downfall of Europe
Thoughts on Reading Dostoevsky

HERMAN HESSE *was born in southern Germany in 1877, and after an irregular career as student, book-seller, and mechanic, he became a popular author through his first novel,* Peter Camenzind (1904). *When his opposition to World War I won him enmity and accusations of treason, he left his native country to become a Swiss citizen in 1919, even as* Demian, *one of the earliest and finest novels based upon psychoanalysis, was being hailed by a whole generation emerging from the war as the perfect expression of its troubled and desperate temper. To satisfy his fascination with mystical religion, he made a long trip to India, and wrote* Siddhartha *and later* Journey to the East *as a result. A fictional companion-piece to the following essay,* Steppenwolf (1927), *is a strange and exciting experimental novel which condemns modern civilization as only a thin veneer over bestial instincts. His other novels, his short stories, poems, and belle-lettres, many yet untranslated, were cited in the award of the Nobel Prize for 1947. T. S. Eliot quotes him in his famous* The Waste Land *and Thomas Mann and André Gide acclaimed him as one of the outstanding writers of our time.*

Motto: *Nichts ist aussen, nichts ist innen, denn was aussen ist, ist innen.*

In the writings of Dostœvsky, and most concentratedly in the Karamazovs, there appears with terrifying clarity an expression and a prophecy of what I term "the downfall of Europe." That European youth, particularly German youth, feels Dostœvsky and not Goethe or even Nietzsche their great writer seems to me decisive of our lot. One examines recent literature and finds everywhere approximations of Dostœvsky; these are of-

ten merely imitations and childish in effect. The ideal of the
Karamazovs, primitive, Asiatic, occult, is becoming the European
ideal, and has begun to devour the spirit of Europe. That is what
I term the downfall of Europe. This downward journey is a return
home to the Mother, a turning back toward Asia, to the sources,
to the Faustian mothers; and will obviously lead, like every death
on earth, to a new birth. We only feel these events as "downfall,"
we contemporaries, as the aged feel a sense of sadness when they
leave an old and beloved home. On the other hand, the young
see only the new, the future.

But what is this "Asiatic ideal" that I find in Dostœvsky, and
which I feel is on the verge of capturing Europe by force?

Briefly it is the renunciation of every strongly established ethic
and moral in favor of a comprehensive *laissez-faire:* a new, dangerous, terrible holiness prophesied by old Zossima, lived by Alyosha
and Dmitri; and, most importantly, brought to articulate expression by Ivan. The ideal of righteousness dominates old Zossima;
for him there is always good and evil, but he prefers to give his
love to sinners. This new kind of holiness is far freer and livelier
in Alyosha; he passes through the slime and mud of his surroundings with a nearly amoral naïveté. He often reminds me of Zarathustra's noblest vow: "One day I swore to renounce all disgust!"

But see, Alyosha's brothers compel these thoughts further; the
Karamazovs follow a straight, clear path. It seems, flatly and without contradiction, that in the course of this thick book the situation of the Brothers Karamazov slowly reverses itself: everything
definite becomes equivocal, the saintly Alyosha becomes worldlier,
the worldlier brothers become holier. The most criminal and licen-
tious brother Dmitri moves toward a nearly godly, most sensitive
and fervent presentiment of a new holiness, a new morality, and a
new mankind. That is very strange. The more Karamazov-like the
book drives forward, the more unrestrained and brutal, the more
inwardly holy the Brothers become. The new ideal glimmers
through the bodies of these barbaric men and events. And alongside the drunk, murderous, and violent Dmitri and the cynical, intellectual Ivan, the outward triumphs of the respectable district
attorney and the other champions of the bourgeois become more
and more shabby, hollow, and worthless.

Thus, the "new ideal" which threatens the roots of the European spirit appears to be a completely amoral mentality and sensibility, a faculty to sense the godly, the necessary, the fated, in the wickedest and the ugliest; and to offer this ideal respect and worship. In his great speech the district attorney attempts to present the affair Karamazov in ironic exaggeration and expose it to the scorn of the citizens. This attempt distorts nothing; it is, in effect, mild.

This speech depicts from the conservative bourgeois point of view, the "Russian man," who up to that time had been only a slogan. The disturbing, irresponsible, withal delicately-conscienced, tender, dreamy, cruel, deeply child-like Russian man. Today he is again invoked in this fashion, though he has, I believe, long been on the point of becoming the European man. This precisely is the "downfall of Europe."

We must consider this "Russian man" for a moment. He is far older than Dostœvsky, but Dostœvsky has placed him before the world in his complete and terrifying meaning. The Russian man is Karamazov: he is Feodor Pavlovitch, he is Dmitri, he is Ivan, he is Alyosha. For these four—though they seem so different—necessarily belong together. Together they are Karamazov and the "Russian man"; together they are the imminent man of the European crisis.

In addition: one notices something highly remarkable: namely how Ivan changes in the course of the story from a man of civilization to a Karamazov, from a European to a Russian, from a well defined historical type to the unformed raw material of the future. This emergence of Ivan from his original nimbus of restraint, understanding, coolness, and scientific objectivity has the fable-like logic of a dream; this gradual, anxious, madly exciting decline of apparently the most stable brother into hysteria, into Russianism, into Karamazovism. It is ultimately Ivan the doubter who holds conversations with the Devil. We shall say more about this later.

Therefore: "the Russian man" (whom we have already seen in Germany) is to be designated neither the hysteric, the drunkard, the criminal, nor the poet and saint, but rather the coexistence of all these natures. The Russian man, the Karamazov, is at once murderer and magistrate, brute and the tenderest of souls. He is equally the most consummate egoist and the self-sacrificing hero. He is incomprehensible to us from a European, from a solid, moral, ethical, doctrinal point of view. Outside and Inside, good and evil, God and Satan coexist in this man.

These Karamazovs show a continual yearning toward a highest symbol which has mastered their souls, toward a god who is at the same time a devil. Dostœvsky's Russian man has been circumscribed by this symbol. The god who is at once the devil is the primeval Demiurge. He is that which was before the beginning; he is the one who exists beyond contradictions, who knows neither day nor night, good nor evil. He is the Nothing and the All. He is unknown to us because we can understand only polarities. We are individuals: we are bound to day and night, to heat and cold. We require a God and a Devil. Beyond polarity, in the Nothing and the All, the Demiurge lives uniquely.

Much could be said here, but this suffices. We have discerned the nature of the Russian man. He struggles out of polarities, out of individuality, out of morals; he is on the point of setting himself free: behind the curtain and beyond the *principium individuationis* he is turning back. This man loves everything and nothing; he does everything and nothing. This man is primal substance once more; he is a spiritual embryo. He cannot live in this form; he can only be destroyed, he can only disappear.

Dostœvsky has conjured up this fearful apparition, this man of the downfall. It has often been said that it is lucky his Karamazovs were not finished; otherwise not merely Russian literature but all Russia and all mankind might explode and vanish into air.

Even if no one had suggested these extreme consequences, what has been said cannot be unsaid. The existent, the ordained, the possible could no longer remain obscured. For a long while the Russian man has existed far outside of Russia; he rules in half of Europe, and in these recent years a part of the dreaded explosion has noisily made itself heard. It appears that Europe is tired, that it shall return home, that it shall rest, that it shall be reborn.

Two remarks of a European occur to me, of a European who is certainly an exemplary representative of the old, faded, now declining, doubtless evolving Europe. I mean Kaiser Wilhelm. The

first remark is one which he wrote beneath a rather strange allegorical picture, warning the peoples of Europe to preserve their
"holiest endowments" against the pressing danger from the East.

Kaiser Wilhelm was certainly not a sensitive man; nevertheless
he possessed, as a hearty admirer and defender of an outmoded
ideal, a faculty for sensing dangers which threatened this ideal. He
was not a man of the spirit; he did not like to read good books, and
he was too concerned with politics. A reading of Dostœvsky was
not responsible, as one might think, for that picture with its warning cry to the peoples of Europe. The cry was based on a vague
fear of Eastern hordes brought into prominence by Japan's am-
bitions against Europe.

The Kaiser knew only partially what his remark meant, and
how monstrously right it was. He certainly was not acquainted
with the Karamazovs. He had an aversion to difficult or profound
books. But he had sensed uncannily well. The danger existed exactly as he felt it, and it came nearer daily. It was the Karamazovs
whom he feared. He feared the infection of Europe by the East,
the reeling back of the weary European spirit to its Asiatic
mother.

The second remark of the Kaiser which occurs to me, and
which in its time made a fearful impression on me, is this: "The
nation with the best nerves will win the war." At the time I first
heard this remark, at the very beginning of the war, I took it as
the muffled preliminary shock of an earthquake. It was clear the
Kaiser did not mean it so; rather he meant to say something very
flattering to Germany. He himself had, very possibly, excellent
nerves, and so did the comrades of his hunts and parades. He
also knew the stale old fairy-tale of a depraved and diseased
France and a virtuous and fruitful Germany, and he believed it.
But all the others, the knowing ones, the apprehensive ones, those
with antennæ for tomorrow and the day after—for them that remark was terrifying. They all knew that Germany had by no
means better or worse nerves than the enemy in the West. Thus
this remark from the mouth of the nation's leader sounded like
fearful, fateful *hybris* rushing blindly into destruction.

No, the Germans did not have better nerves than the French,
English, or Americans. At the most they had better nerves than

the Russians. For "to have bad nerves" is the popular expression for hysteria and neurasthenia, for moral insanity, and all these illnesses which one can diagnose variously, but which taken together are almost synonymous with Karamazovism. Germany was infinitely more susceptible, weaker and more open to the Karamazovs, to Dostœvsky, to Asia, than any other European people, with the exception of Austria.

Thus, in his own way, the Kaiser twice had a premonition of, twice prophesied the downfall of Europe.

But now an entirely different question arises: how can one appraise the downfall of the old Europe? Here roads and minds part. The partisans of the past, the devoted admirers of a hallowed, noble form and culture, the knights of an established morality, all can attempt to stop this downfall or weep desperately when it occurs. To them the downfall is the end—to others the beginning. To them Dostœvsky is a criminal—to the others a saint. To them Europe and its spirit is an entity permanently joined together; it is something unique, untouchable, something fixed and essential. To the others it is developing, changing, eternally mutating.

One can positively, as well as negatively, regard the Karamazov element, the chaotic, the wild, the dangerous, the amoral. They who put off, fear, and curse this whole world of Dostœvsky, Karamazov, Russia, Asia, Demiurge fantasies have now a hard time of it, because Karamazov dominates more and more. But they make a mistake; they see only the reality: the visible and the material. They see the "downfall of Europe" coming as a shuddering catastrophe with thunder and drums, or as a revolution filled with massacre and violence, or as the prevalence of crime, corruption, thievery, murder and every depravity.

All this is possible, all this lies in Karamazov. One never knows how a Karamazov will surprise us: perhaps with a murderous blow, perhaps with a touching hymn to God. Among them are Alyoshas and Dmitris, Feodors and Ivans. Indeed, as we have seen, they are not distinguishable by their individual natures, but by their readiness to assume the characteristics of all natures.

But this does not help reassure the anxious that this unpredictable man of the future (he is already here in the present!) does as much good as evil, that he can found a City of God as well as a community of the Devil. What is established or destroyed on earth bothers the Karamazovs little. Their secret lies elsewhere, as well as the value and fruitfulness of their being.

These men are fundamentally set apart from the others, from the more recent, the more regulated, the more predictable, plain and upright men. They live as much within as without; they are in perpetual intercourse with their souls. The Karamazovs are capable of any crime, but they rarely commit one: for the most part they are content with the crime thought or dreamt, with contemplating its possibility. Here lies their secret. We seek the formula for it.

Every human order, every culture and civilization is based on a compromise between the allowed and the forbidden. Mankind, on his way between the animal and the far-off man of the future, has continually to suppress much, hide much, and deny much to be capable of society and of being a decent human being. Man is full of the animal, full of the primeval world, full of gigantic, nearly uncontrollable impulses of a cruel and bestial egotism. All of these dangerous impulses are here, are always here; but culture, compromise, civilization have obscured them, one does not show them; one has learned from childhood on to hide and deny these impulses. But every one of these impulses sometimes comes to light. Each one continues to live, none is killed; none, in the long run, in eternity, is changed or ennobled. Yet each of these impulses is in itself good, is not worse than any other; it is just that each age and each culture has impulses which it fears more than others, which it more rigidly forbids. When these impulses reawaken, as unredeemed and only superficially subdued natural forces, when these animals howl and stir again, with the wail of long suppressed and whipped slaves, and with the primeval heat of their naturalness, then the Karamazovs break out. When a culture, the attempt to domesticate mankind, becomes tired and begins to stagger, then greater numbers of men become remarkable, become hysterical, have unusual lusts; they resemble young people in puberty or women in childbirth. Longings for which one has no name arise in the soul; which one, from the point of view of the old culture and morality, must designate as evil; but which can speak with so strong, so natural, so guiltless a voice that all good and evil become ambiguous and every law wavers.

Such men are the brothers Karamazov. Every law appears to them simply a convention, every lawful man a Philistine; they easily prize every freedom and peculiarity: they all too lovingly listen to the many voices in their own breasts.

But it is not necessary that the chaos in these souls give rise only to crime and disorder. Give this primeval force which has broken out a new direction, a new name, a new valuation; then we have the roots of a new culture, a new order, a new morality. For thus it is with every culture: we cannot kill the animal impulses within us, for then we ourselves die—but we can to some extent guide them, to some extent calm them, to some extent make the "good" useable as one can hitch an unruly nag to a good wagon. From age to age the luster of this "good" becomes old and tarnished; the impulses refuse to be subjugated any longer: they also do not believe in this "good." Then the culture breaks down—most of the time slowly, like the ancient world which took centuries to die.

And before the old, dying culture and morality can be succeeded by a new one, in this uneasy, dangerous, painful state of affairs, man must again look into his soul, again see the animal rising in himself, again acknowledge the presence of primitive forces which are beyond morality. Those selected and condemned to do this, destined and ripe for this, are the Karamazovs. They are hysterical and dangerous; they become criminals as easily as ascetics; they believe in nothing except the mad doubt in all belief.

Every symbol has a hundred meanings, and every meaning may be correct. The Karamazovs also have a hundred meanings; mine is only one of them. In a time of revolutions, at the turning point of a new epoch, mankind has created itself a symbol in this book, has constructed a world as the mind of sleeping man creates in dreams an image of the forces and powers struggling within him.

That a single man was able to write the Karamazovs is a miracle. Now that the wonder has occurred, there is no need to explain it. However, a need exists, a very deep need, to interpret this miracle: to read its writing as fully as possible and in the full light of its magic. This essay of mine is no more than a thought, a note, an idea toward an interpretation.

One should not believe that all the thoughts and ideas which I express about this book were uttered consciously by Dostœvsky. To the contrary: no great prophet and poet has the power fully to interpret his own vision.

In the end I might indicate how this myth-like novel, this dream of humanity, not only depicts the threshold which Europe is passing over, not only perceives the anxious, dangerous moment of suspension between the Nothing and All, but also everywhere feels and senses the rich possibilities of the new.

In this regard the figure of Ivan is especially astounding. We meet him as a modern, accommodating, cultivated man, somewhat cool, somewhat disappointed, somewhat skeptical, somewhat tired. But he becomes increasingly younger, warmer, significant, more Karamazov-like. It is he who composed the "Grand Inquisitor." It is he who is finally driven from contempt and coolness toward his brother (whom he believes the murderer) to a deep sense of his own guilt and to self-accusation. And it is he who undergoes the spiritual experience of an argument with the unconscious. (Everything hinges on this! It is the meaning of the Downfall, the Rebirth!)

There is an unusually strange chapter in the last book of the novel in which Ivan, coming home from Smerdyakov, sees the Devil sitting in his rooms and converses with him for a whole hour. This Devil is nothing less than Ivan's unconscious, the aroused crowd of long sunken thoughts, the apparently forgotten contents of his soul. And Ivan knows this; Ivan knows it with astonishing certitude and clearly expresses it. Nevertheless he speaks with the Devil, he believes in him—for what is within, is without! He becomes angry with him, seizes him, even throws a glass of water at him. He knows that this Devil is inside him. Scarcely ever in all literature has the dialogue of a man with his unconscious been so clearly and intuitively presented. And this dialogue (in spite of Ivan's anger), this communion with the Devil is clearly the path which the Karamazovs are invoked to show us. So here, in Dostœvsky, the unconscious is represented as the Devil. Rightly so, for to the tamed, cultivated, and moral vision, everything within us is suppressed, that which we bear within us Satanic and odious. But somehow a combination of Ivan and Alyosha yields up a higher, more fruitful attitude, which must shape the foundation of the imminent future. Then the unconscious is no longer the Devil, but rather the god-devil, the Demiurge: he who always was and who comes out of everything. To redefine good and evil is not the concern of the Demiurge, rather the business of man and his lesser gods.

A special chapter could be written about another, a fifth Karamazov who plays a sinister, leading part, although he always remains half obscured. This is Smerdyakov, an illegitimate Karamazov. It is he who murdered the old man. It is he who stands convicted of murder before the omnipresence of God. It is he who instructs Ivan, the know-it-all, about the god-like and the mystical. He is the most incapable of life and at the same time the wisest of all the Karamazovs. But I find no room in this essay to do justice to him, the most mysterious one.

Dostœvsky's book is not to be exhausted. I could, for days, hunt out and find tracks which all indicate the same direction. One, a very clear and fascinating one, occurs to me: the hysteria of the two Hohlakovs. We have here the Karamazov element, the infection of the new, sick, and wicked in two characters. The former, the mother Hohlakov is only sick. In her, whose being is rooted in the old and the conventional, hysteria is merely illness, weakness, and folly. But it is not tiredness which plunges the splendid daughter into hysteria, but rather excess and expectation. She, in the despair between childhood and love's ripeness, develops thoughts and visions of deeper evil than her unimportant mother. With the daughter, confusion, wickedness, and shamelessness are of an innocence and power which point wholly to a fruitful future. The mother Hohlakov is the hysterical one, ripe for a sanatorium, nothing more. The daughter is the neurotic, whose sickness is the symptom of exalted but inhibited powers.

Yes, and should these happenings in the souls of fictitious characters imply the downfall of Europe?

Certainly. They imply it as surely as an inspired eye regards the spring grass as life and its immortality, and regards every drifting leaf in November as death and its inevitability. It is possible that the whole "downfall of Europe" is enacted only within, only in the souls of a generation; its true meaning revealed in a reinterpretation of exhausted symbols and in the revaluation of spiritual values. Thus the ancient world, that first gleaming coinage of European culture, did not crash down with Nero, nor with Spartacus, nor with the Germans; but rather with the germ of thought coming out of Asia: that simple, old, homely thought, which had always been there, but at that time had taken the form of the teachings of Jesus.

Of course one can regard the Karamazovs from a literary point of view, as a "work of art." When the unconscious of an age and a continent has been compressed into the nightmare of a single prophetic dreamer, when it has gushed forth in his rattling, horrifying scream, one can, of course, examine this scream from the standpoint of a singing teacher. Dostœvsky was doubtless a highly gifted poet, in spite of the horror to be found in his books, horror from which a more respectable non-poet such as Turgenev is free. Isaiah was also a richly gifted poet, but is that important? In Dostœvsky, and especially in the Karamazovs, one can find some of that heroic tastelessness which is never tolerable to the artist and which first appears when one stands beyond art. Be that as it may. This Russian prophet everywhere declares himself an artist, an artist of world rank, and one thinks it peculiar that the Europe of Dostœvsky's age considered entirely different men its great writers.

However, I come to a by-road. I wish to say: the less such a world-book is a work of art, the truer perhaps is its prophecy. Nevertheless, the "novel," the "fable," the "fiction" of the *Karamazovs* says so much that is not merely arbitrary, not only the experience of a single man, not the work of deliberate art. For example: that which says everything, the chief point of the whole novel—the Karamazovs are innocent!

These Karamazovs, all four, father and sons, are suspected, dangerous, unpredictable men; they have strange impulses, strange consciences, even stranger lacks of conscience. One is a drunkard, another a woman hunter, one a fantastic fugitive from the world, another a writer of secret, blasphemous poems. They portend much danger, these queer brothers; they tweak other people by the beards, they are prodigal with other people's money, they threaten others with death—and yet they are innocent, all of them together have not really committed a crime. The only murderers in this long novel, which treats of almost nothing but murder, robbery and guilt, the only ones guilty of murder are the prosecutor and the jurymen, the representatives of the old, good, approved order, the citizens, the irreproachables. They condemn the guiltless Dmitri; they judge God and the world after their own code. And straightway they are misled, they commit a horrible injustice, they become murderers—murderers out of narrow-mindedness, out of anxiety, stupidity.

This is no fiction; this is nothing "literary." Neither is it the fevered plotting of the detective story writer (though Dostœvsky can be that), nor the satirical brilliance of the subtle author playing the social critic from ambush. We know all about that; the note is too familiar, and we have long ceased to believe in it.

But no, in Dostœvsky the innocence of the criminal and the guilt of the judge is no clever bit of plotting. It is so frightening, it arises and grows so furtively and so deep down that suddenly, and almost with the last book of the novel, one stands before this fact like a wall; as if before the whole sorrow and madness of the world, before all its trouble and misunderstanding.

I said Dostœvsky is not a poet, or is one only incidentally. I name him a prophet. It is difficult to say what this really means: a prophet! It seems to me he is perhaps a sick man, as Dostœvsky indeed was, genuinely hysterical, almost an epileptic. A prophet is such a sick man. He has lost the healthy, beneficent sense of self-preservation—that sum of all bourgeois virtue. There cannot be many men like these; the world would go to pieces. A sick man of this kind, whether he be called Dostœvsky or Karamazov, has that mysterious, diseased and god-like faculty, whose power the Asiatic reveres in every madman. He is mantic, he is a seer. This means a people, an epoch, a country, or a continent has developed in him an organ, an antenna, a rare, uncommonly precious, uncommonly sympathetic organ which others do not have. This antenna, this sense, is not to be crudely thought of as a kind of imbecile telepathy or conjuring trick, although the gift can manifest itself in such confusing forms. Rather the "sick man" of this kind reads the movements of his own soul from the point of view of mankind and the whole world. Every man has visions; every man has fantasies; every man has dreams. And every vision, every dream, every idea and thought of man can, on the way from unconsciousness to consciousness, undergo a thousand different meanings—and every one can be right. The seer and prophet does not interpret his hallucination personally, the nightmare which oppresses him does not warn him of his own sickness, of a personal death, but of the body whose organ and antenna he is. This may be a family, a party, a people—it may also be all mankind. A certain sickness and sensitivity to the sufferings of mankind, which is otherwise called hysteria, found in the soul of Dostœvsky its indicator and barometer. This is now on the point of being noticed. By this time half of Europe—at least half of Eastern Europe—is on the way to chaos, traveling in holy drunken madness along the edge of the abyss, and singing as it goes along, singing drunkenly and hymn-like as Dmitri Karamazov sang. The insulted citizen laughs at these songs; the saint and prophet hear them with tears.

—*Translated by Harvey Gross*

Thomas Stearns Eliot

HAMLET

THOMAS STEARNS ELIOT, *poet, critic, playwright, editor, and descendant of the New England Eliots, was born in St. Louis in 1888 and educated at Harvard (Bertrand Russell has called him "the best student I ever had"). He went to Europe for further study and in 1914, moved to London, where he has since made his home. For five years he supported himself by teaching and by working as a bank clerk. In*

1922, he startled the public by his now famous The Waste Land, *which expressed the disillusion and despair that the war and the materialism of modern civilization aroused in him and many of his generation. Thereafter poetry was never again the same, and neither was Eliot. In the late twenties, he became associated with the Anglo-Catholic Church, and to the dismay of sociological critics, began to express religious orthodoxy in his essays,* For Lancelot Andrewes *(1928), in his poetry* Ash Wednesday *(1930), and in his immensely popular play,* Murder in the Cathedral *(1935). His* Four Quartets, *composed mostly during World War II while Eliot was an air-raid warden, ranks with the great poetic achievements of the century, but it was the Nobel Prize in 1948 and plays like* The Cocktail Party *(1949),* The Confidential Clerk *(1953), and* The Elder Statesman *(1958) that made his name internationally familiar. Long a widower after the death of his first wife, Eliot recently married an employee of the publishing house which he helps direct. The following essay represents his long-standing interest in dramatic criticism and his penchant for brilliant and unconventional judgments.*

Few critics have even admitted that *Hamlet* the play is the primary problem, and Hamlet the character only secondary. And Hamlet the character has had an especial temptation for that most dangerous type of critic: the critic with a mind which is naturally of the creative order, but which through some weakness in creative power exercises itself in criticism instead. These minds often find in Hamlet a vicarious existence for their own artistic realization. Such a mind had Goethe, who made of Hamlet a Werther; and such had Coleridge, who made of Hamlet a Coleridge; and probably neither of these men in writing about Hamlet remembered that his first business was to study a work of art. The kind of criticism that Goethe and Coleridge produced, in writing of Hamlet, is the most misleading kind possible. For they both possessed unquestionable critical insight, and both make their critical aberrations the more plausible by the substitution— of their own Hamlet for Shakespeare's—which their creative gift effects. We should be thankful that Walter Pater did not fix his attention on this play.

Two writers of our own time, Mr. J. M. Robertson and Professor Stoll of the University of Minnesota, have issued small books which can be praised for moving in the other direction. Mr. Stoll performs a service in recalling to our attention the labors of the critics of the seventeenth and eighteenth centuries,[1] observing that:

> they knew less about psychology than more recent Hamlet critics, but they were nearer in spirit to Shakespeare's art; and as they insisted on the importance of the effect of the whole rather than on the importance of the leading character, they were nearer, in their old-fashioned way, to the secret of dramatic art in general.

Qua work of art, the work of art cannot be interpreted; there is nothing to interpret; we can only criticize it according to standards, in comparison to other works of art; and for "interpretation" the chief task is the presentation of relevant historical facts which the reader is not assumed to know. Mr. Robertson points out, very pertinently, how critics have failed in their "interpretation" of *Hamlet* by ignoring what ought to be very obvious; that *Hamlet* is a stratification, that it represents the efforts of a series of men, each making what he could out of the work of his predecessors. The *Hamlet* of Shakespeare will appear to us very differently if, instead of treating the whole action of the play as due to Shakespeare's design, we perceive his *Hamlet* to be superposed upon much cruder material which persists even in the final form.

We know that there was an older play by Thomas Kyd, that extraordinary dramatic (if not poetic) genius who was in all probability the author of two plays so dissimilar as *The Spanish Tragedy* and *Arden of Feversham*; and what this play was like we can guess from three clues: from *The Spanish Tragedy* itself, from the tale of Belleforest upon which Kyd's *Hamlet* must have been based, and from a version acted in Germany in Shakespeare's lifetime which bears strong evidence of having been adapted from the earlier, not from the later, play. From these three sources it is clear that in the earlier play the motive was a revenge-motive simply; that the action or delay is caused, as in *The Span-*

[1] I have never, by the way, seen a cogent refutation of Thomas Rymer's objections to *Othello*.

ish Tragedy, solely by the difficulty of assassinating a monarch surrounded by guards; and that the "madness" of Hamlet was
feigned in order to escape suspicion, and successfully. In the final
play of Shakespeare, on the other hand, there is a motive which is
more important than that of revenge, and which explicitly
"blunts" the latter; the delay in revenge is unexplained on grounds
of necessity or expediency; and the effect of the "madness" is not
to lull but to arouse the king's suspicion. The alteration is not
complete enough, however, to be convincing. Furthermore, there
are verbal parallels so close to *The Spanish Tragedy* as to leave no
doubt that in places Shakespeare was merely *revising* the text of
Kyd. And finally there are unexplained scenes—the Polonius-
Laertes and the Polonius-Reynaldo scenes—for which there is
little excuse; these scenes are not in the verse style of Kyd, and not
beyond doubt in the style of Shakespeare. These Mr. Robertson
believes to be scenes in the original play of Kyd reworked by a
third hand, perhaps Chapman, before Shakespeare touched the
play. And he concludes, with very strong show of reason, that the
original play of Kyd was, like certain other revenge plays, in two
parts of five acts each. The upshot of Mr. Robertson's examination is, we believe, irrefragable: that Shakespeare's *Hamlet*, so far
as it is Shakespeare's, is a play dealing with the effect of a mother's
guilt upon her son, and that Shakespeare was unable to impose
this motive successfully upon the "intractable" material of the old
play.

Of the intractability there can be no doubt. So far from being
Shakespeare's masterpiece, the play is most certainly an artistic
failure. In several ways the play is puzzling, and disquieting as is
none of the others. Of all the plays it is the longest and is possibly
the one on which Shakespeare spent most pains; and yet he has
left in it superfluous and inconsistent scenes which even hasty
revision should have noticed. The versification is variable. Lines
like

> *Look, the morn, in russet mantle clad,*
> *Walks o'er the dew of yon high eastern hill,*

are of the Shakespeare of *Romeo and Juliet*. The lines in Act v,
sc. ii,

> *Sir, in my heart there was a kind of fighting*
> *That would not let me sleep . . .*
> *Up from my cabin,*
> *My sea-gown scarf'd about me, in the dark*
> *Grop'd I to find out them: had my desire;*
> *Finger'd their packet;*

are of his quite mature. Both workmanship and thought are in
an unstable position. We are surely justified in attributing the play,
with that other profoundly interesting play of "intractable" material and astonishing versification, *Measure for Measure,* to a period of crisis, after which follow the tragic successes which culmi-
nate in *Coriolanus. Coriolanus* may be not as "interesting" as
Hamlet, but it is, with *Antony and Cleopatra,* Shakespeare's most
assured artistic success. And probably more people have thought
Hamlet a work of art because they found it interesting, than have
found it interesting because it is a work of art. It is the "Mona
Lisa" of literature.

The grounds of *Hamlet's* failure are not immediately obvious.
Mr. Robertson is undoubtedly correct in concluding that the essential emotion of the play is the feeling of a son towards a guilty
mother:

> [Hamlet's] tone is that of one who has suffered tortures on the
> score of his mother's degradation. . . . The guilt of a mother is an
> almost intolerable motive for drama, but it had to be maintained
> and emphasized to supply a psychological solution, or rather a hint
> of one.

This, however, is by no means the whole story. It is not merely
the "guilt of a mother" that cannot be handled as Shakespeare
handled the suspicion of Othello, the infatuation of Antony, or
the pride of Coriolanus. The subject might conceivably have expanded into a tragedy like these, intelligible, self-complete, in the
sunlight. *Hamlet,* like the sonnets, is full of some stuff that the
writer could not drag to light, contemplate, or manipulate into
art. And when we search for this feeling, we find it, as in the sonnets, very difficult to localize. You cannot point to it in the
speeches; indeed, if you examine the two famous soliloquies you
see the versification of Shakespeare, but a content which might

be claimed by another, perhaps by the author of the *Revenge of Bussy d'Ambois*, Act v, sc. i. We find Shakespeare's Hamlet not in the action, not in any quotations that we might select, so much as in an unmistakable tone which is unmistakably not in the earlier play.

The only way of expressing emotion in the form of art is by finding an "objective correlative"; in other words, a set of objects, a situation, a chain of events which shall be the formula of that *particular* emotion; such that when the external facts, which must terminate in sensory experience, are given, the emotion is immediately evoked. If you examine any of Shakespeare's more successful tragedies, you will find this exact equivalence; you will find that the state of mind of Lady Macbeth walking in her sleep has been communicated to you by a skillful accumulation of imagined sensory impressions; the words of Macbeth on hearing of his wife's death strike us as if, given the sequence of events, these words were automatically released by the last event in the series. The artistic "inevitability" lies in this complete adequacy of the external to the emotion; and this is precisely what is deficient in *Hamlet*. Hamlet (the man) is dominated by an emotion which is inexpressible, because it is in *excess* of the facts as they appear. And the supposed identity of Hamlet with his author is genuine to this point: that Hamlet's bafflement at the absence of objective equivalent to his feelings is a prolongation of the bafflement of his creator in the face of his artistic problem. Hamlet is up against the difficulty that his disgust is occasioned by his mother, but that his mother is not an adequate equivalent for it; his disgust envelops and exceeds her. It is thus a feeling which he cannot understand; he cannot objectify it, and it therefore remains to poison life and obstruct action. None of the possible actions can satisfy it; and nothing that Shakespeare can do with the plot can express Hamlet for him. And it must be noticed that the very nature of the *données* of the problem precludes objective equivalence. To have heightened the criminality of Gertrude would have been to provide the formula for a totally different emotion in Hamlet; it is just *because* her character is so negative and insignificant that she arouses in Hamlet the feeling which she is incapable of representing.

The "madness" of Hamlet lay to Shakespeare's hand; in the earlier play a simple ruse, and to the end, we may presume, understood as a ruse by the audience. For Shakespeare it is less than madness and more than feigned. The levity of Hamlet, his repetition of phrase, his puns, are not part of a deliberate plan of dissimulation, but a form of emotional relief. In the character Hamlet it is the buffoonery of an emotion which can find no outlet in action; in the dramatist it is the buffoonery of an emotion which he cannot express in art. The intense feeling, ecstatic or terrible, without an object or exceeding its object, is something which every person of sensibility has known; it is doubtless a subject of study for pathologists. It often occurs in adolescence: the ordinary person puts these feelings to sleep, or trims down his feelings to fit the business world; the artist keeps them alive by his ability to intensify the world to his emotions. The Hamlet of Laforgue is an adolescent; the Hamlet of Shakespeare is not, he has not that explanation and excuse. We must simply admit that here Shakespeare tackled a problem which proved too much for him. Why he attempted it at all is an insoluble puzzle; under compulsion of what experience he attempted to express the inexpressibly horrible, we cannot even know. We need a great many facts in his biography; and we should like to know whether, and when, and after or at the same time as what personal experience, he read Montaigne, II. xii, *Apologie de Raimond Sebond*. We should have, finally, to know something which is by hypothesis unknowable, for we assume it to be an experience which, in the manner indicated, exceeded the facts. We should have to understand things which Shakespeare did not understand himself.

William Faulkner

Though WILLIAM FAULKNER *is not an essayist, his address accepting the 1949 Nobel Prize for Literature has already become one of the classics of American prose. The novelist, whose vision of man's fate is expressed in these few words, was born in New Albany, Mississippi in 1897. Most of his life has been spent in the town of Oxford, the Jefferson of his fiction. Faulkner attended the local high school, joined the Canadian Air Force during World War I, then after a year at the state university, he started to write poetry. During a brief period as a member of the artists' colony in New Orleans, he began to write novels and within a few years was producing such fictional masterpieces as* The Sound and the Fury (1929), Light in August (1932), Absolom, Absolom (1936) *which brought him international renown. Faulkner had shunned literary and intellectual associations, but since receiving the Nobel award, he has visited Japan as a cultural representative for the State Department and has lectured at several universities. His sequel to* Sanctuary, Requiem for a Nun, *was turned into a successful stage production by Albert Camus.*

I feel that this award was not made to me as a man but to my work—a life's work in the agony and sweat of the human spirit, not for glory and least of all for profit, but to create out of the materials of the human spirit something which did not exist before. So this award is only mine in trust. It will not be difficult to find a dedication for the money part of it commensurate with the purpose and significance of its origin. But I would like to do the same with the acclaim too, by using this moment as a pinnacle from which I might be listened to by the young men and women already dedicated to the same anguish and travail, among whom is already that one who will some day stand here where I am standing.

Our tragedy today is a general and universal physical fear so long sustained by now that we can even bear it. There are no longer problems of the spirit. There is only the question: When will I be blown up? Because of this, the young man or woman writing today has forgotten the problems of the human heart in conflict with itself which alone can make good writing because only that is worth writing about, worth the agony and the sweat.

He must learn them again. He must teach himself that the basest of all things is to be afraid; and, teaching himself that, forget it forever, leaving no room in his workshop for anything but the old verities and truths of the heart, the old universal truths lacking which any story is ephemeral and doomed—love and honor and pity and pride and compassion and sacrifice. Until he does so he labors under a curse. He writes not of love but of lust, of defeats in which nobody loses anything of value, of victories without hope and worst of all without pity or compassion. His griefs grieve on no universal bones, leaving no scars. He writes not of the heart but of the glands.

Until he relearns these things he will write as though he stood among and watched the end of man. I decline to accept the end of man. It is easy enough to say that man is immortal simply because he will endure; that when the last ding-dong of doom has clanged and faded from the last worthless rock hanging tideless in the last red and dying evening, that even then there will still be one more sound: that of his puny inexhaustible voice, still talking. I refuse to accept this. I believe that man will not merely endure: he will prevail. He is immortal, not because he alone among creatures has an inexhaustible voice, but because he has a soul, a spirit capable of compassion and sacrifice and endurance. The poet's, the writer's, duty is to write about these things. It is his privilege to help man endure by lifting his heart, by reminding him of the courage and honor and hope and pride and compassion and pity and sacrifice which have been the glory of his past. The poet's voice need not merely be the record of man, it can be one of the props, the pillars to help him endure and prevail.

December 10, 1950

François Mauriac

AN AUTHOR AND HIS WORK

FRANÇOIS MAURIAC *is regarded by many readers as the out-standing Catholic novelist of our time. He was born in 1885 in Bor-deaux, the background for most of his fiction. He remained there at the University until his twentieth year and then attended the École de Chartres in Paris, which he left when he began to publish poetry and criticism in avant-garde magazines. After completing two volumes of verse, he founded a magazine to publish Catholic writing. During World War I, he served in the hospital corps in Salonika until he was sent home suffering from malaria. After* The Kiss of the Leper (1922), *his reputation grew rapidly with the appearance of* Genetrix (1924), The Desert of Love (1929), The Viper's Tangle (1933), The Weak-ling (1951) *and* The Enemy (1955). *In 1933 he was elected to the French Academy and in 1952, awarded the Nobel Prize for Literature. As the following essay, his Nobel Prize acceptance speech, indicates, the principal themes of his fiction are based on the constant struggle between human love and divine love, between sin and divine grace.*

When I first began to describe the little world of yester-year that lives again in my books, that small corner of a French province, scarcely known even to Frenchmen, where the vacations of my school days were spent, I had no idea that I would attract the attention of foreign readers. We are all quite convinced of our utter singularity. We forget that the books which we ourselves found enchanting, those of George Eliot or of Dickens, of Tolstoy or Dostœvsky, or of Selma Lagerlöf, describe countries very different from our own, people of another race and another religion; and yet we loved them, because we recognized ourselves in them. All humanity is in this or that peasant back home, and all the landscapes in the world coalesce in the horizons familiar to our childish eyes. The novelist's gift is precisely his power to make plain the universal quality concealed in that sheltered world where we were born, and where we first learned to love and suffer.

That mine has appeared so somber to many readers in France and elsewhere, has, I must admit, never ceased to surprise me. Mortal men, by the very fact that they are mortal, dread even the name of death. And so, too, those who have never loved nor been loved, or those who have been forsaken and betrayed, or who have in vain pursued someone beyond their reach, without so much as glancing back at the one who in turn pursued them and whom they did not love—even such people are astonished and dismayed by works of fiction which describe the loneliness of human beings even in the arms of love. "Tell us the things that please us," they say, as the Jews said to the prophet Isaiah, "deceive us with pleasant falsehoods."

Yes, the reader asks to be deceived by pleasant falsehoods. And yet the works that have lived and still live in the memory of man are those that accepted the human drama as a whole, and did not falter before that incurable solitariness in whose bosom each one of us must live and face his destiny until death, that final solitude, since in the end we die alone.

Such is the world as a novelist without hope depicts it. Such is the dismal world into which the great Strindberg transports you. And it would have been my world also, if from the first strivings of conscious life, I had not possessed a great hope. A hope that pierces like a flash of fire the gloom I have described. Black is my color, and people judge me by this, and, for some reason or other, not by the light that penetrates it and burns there secretly. In France every time a wife attempts to poison her husband or strangle her lover, people say to me, "There's a subject for you. . . ." I am supposed to have a kind of museum of horrors. I specialize in monsters. And yet, on one essential point my characters differ from almost all of those that populate our present-day fiction: they are aware that they have a soul. In this post-Nietzschean Europe where the echo of Zarathustra's cry: "God is dead," reverberates still, and where the fearful results of it have not yet fully run their course, perhaps all my characters do not believe in the living God; but they are all aware of that part of their being which knows evil and which is capable of not committing it. They know what evil is. They all feel somehow that they are responsible for their actions, and that their actions in turn affect the destiny of others.

For my heroes, however worthless they may be, to live is to participate in an infinite movement, an indefinite surpassing of self. Human beings who do not doubt that life has a direction and a goal are not prone to despair. The despair of modern man is born of his belief in the absurdity of the world—his despair and also similarly his addiction to myths of substitution. It is, in the last analysis, the sense of the absurd that makes man inhuman. The day Nietzsche proclaimed the death of God, he heralded at the same time the terrible days we have lived through and the days still to come in which the human person, emptied of his soul and thus denied a personal destiny, is made into a beast of burden. More abused than beasts of burden, in fact, by the Nazis and by those who still employ their methods today; for a horse, a mule, or an ox at least have cash value, but the human animal, procured without cost thanks to a well devised system of purges, is worth only as much as he can produce—until he collapses.

A writer who focuses his work on human beings made in the image of the Father, redeemed by the Son, and illumined by the Holy Spirit, could never, possibly, as I see it, be considered a master of despair, no matter how somber a picture he paints.

True, the coloring still remains somber. That is because he sees human nature as wounded, if not corrupted. It stands to reason that the human story as told by a Christian novelist is no idyll, since he is forbidden to shut his eyes to the mystery of evil.

But to be obsessed by evil is also to be obsessed by purity, by childlike goodness. I am sorry that some of my critics, reading too hastily, fail to notice the place that children occupy in my stories. A child's dream is the keystone of all my books; children love and exchange their first kisses, and for the first time experience loneliness—all the things I cherish in the music of Mozart. People see the vipers plainly in my novels, but fail to see the dove that nests in many a chapter, because in my works childhood is the lost paradise where the first acquaintance with the mystery of evil is made.

The mystery of evil. . . . There are no two ways about it: ei-

ther we must deny its existence, or else accept it in all its manifestations within and without, in our personal history and passions
as well as in the history of external events, written in human blood
by the will to power of empires. I have always been convinced that
individual and collective crimes are closely linked; and in my
capacity of journalist I have only tried to make clear that the day
to day horrors of our political history are no more than the visible consequences of the invisible history unfolding in the secrecy
of the human heart.

We who live beneath a sky still streaked with the smoke of
crematoriums, have paid a high price to find out that evil is really
evil. Before our very eyes we have seen the crematoriums devour
millions of innocent people, including children. And the story goes
on. The concentration camp system is taking deep root in the age-
old lands where Christ has been loved, adored, and worshiped
for centuries. With terror we watched that portion of the globe
where men still enjoy the rights of man, where the human mind
is still free, contract before our eyes like the piece of shagreen
leather in Balzac's tale.

Do not imagine for a moment that I am blind to the challenge
which the existence of evil in the world poses for my faith. In the
Christian outlook evil still remains the most agonizing of mysteries.
The man who in the midst of the crimes of history perseveres in
his faith has still to reckon with the perduring scandal: the seeming uselessness of the Redemption. The reasons given by the the-
ologians for the existence of evil have always left me unpersuaded,
reasonable as they are, in fact just because they are so reasonable.
The answer that eludes us is not of the order of reason, but of
charity. An answer contained wholly and entirely in St. John's
words: "God is love." Nothing is impossible to that Living Love,
not even to draw all things to itself, and that too, is written.

Forgive me for broaching a problem that in every age has stirred
up so many commentaries, disputes, heresies, persecutions, and
martyrdoms. But, after all, it is a novelist talking to you, the one
you have preferred to all others; so it must be that you attach some
value to what has served as his inspiration. Very well, he can assure you that the things he has written in the light of faith and
hope does not contradict the experience of faith and hope and

does not contradict the experience of his readers who share neither his faith nor his hope. To cite another case, we find that Graham Greene's Christian view of life does not disturb agnostics among his admirers. Chesterton remarked that whenever something extraordinary occurs in Christianity it is ultimately because something extraordinary in reality corresponds to it. If we were to pursue this point further, we would perchance discover the reason for the mysterious appeal that works of Christian inspiration, such as those of my friend, Graham Greene, have for the vast dechristianized public which devours his books and delights in his films.

Yes, a vast dechristianized public! As André Malraux has expressed it: "Revolution today plays the role once played by eternal life." But what if the revolution is the myth? And life eternal the unique reality?

Whatever the answer, we all agree on one point: this dechristianized humanity is a humanity crucified. What power on earth can ever destroy the complicity between the suffering of mankind and the Cross? Even Strindberg, who plumbed the lowest depths from which the psalmist cried out, yes, Strindberg himself expressed the desire, I am told, to have engraved on his tomb a single phrase, a phrase which alone suffices to force the gates of eternity: *Crux ave, spes unica!* (Hail, oh Cross, our only hope.) He, also, who suffered so much sought repose in the shelter of that hope, and in the shadow of that love. And it is in his name that your laureate begs to be forgiven for these all too personal remarks, which perhaps struck too serious a note. Yet could he better repay you for the honors you have heaped upon him than by opening to you not only his heart but his soul? And having delivered to you the secret of his torment through his characters he owed it to you to let you know the secret of his peace.

—Translated by the Rev. Edward Flannery

Albert Camus

When ALBERT CAMUS *received the Nobel Prize for Literature in 1957, he was one of the youngest writers ever to receive the award. Born in 1913 in Algeria, he lived in poverty during his early years. Fortunately, his intelligence caught the attention of his teachers and he was awarded a scholarship to the local lycée. While attending the University of Algiers, he helped to organize a company of actors, took up the study of philosophy, and began to write. In recent years, Camus had a profound effect upon modern thought. Though he preferred not to be included within the group known as Existentialists, his concept of the Absurd, his sense of the desperate need of man to re-evaluate his thinking, to face the "benign indifference of the universe," place him in the broad stream of existentialist thought. He presented his ideas in fiction (The Stranger, 1942; The Plague, 1947; The Fall, 1956); in drama (Caligula, 1945; The State of Siege, 1948) and in philosophical treatises (The Myth of Sisyphus, 1941), all distinguished by a lucidity and simplicity of style which brought him an international audience. In 1960, at the age of 46, Albert Camus was killed in an automobile accident. The following essay is from* The Rebel *(1951).*

Art is the activity that exalts and denies simultaneously. "No artist tolerates reality," says Nietzsche. That is true, but no artist can get along without reality. Artistic creation is a demand for unity and a rejection of the world. But it rejects the world on account of what it lacks and in the name of what it sometimes is. Rebellion can be observed here in its pure state and in its original complexities. Thus art should give us a final perspective on the content of rebellion.

The hostility to art shown by all revolutionary reformers must, however, be pointed out. Plato is moderately reasonable. He only

calls in question the deceptive function of language and exiles
only poets from his republic. Apart from that, he considers beauty
more important than the world. But the revolutionary movement
of modern times coincides with an artistic process that is not yet
completed. The Reformation chooses morality and exiles beauty.
Rousseau denounces in art a corruption of nature by society.
Saint-Just inveighs against the theater, and in the elaborate program he composes for the "Feast of Reason" he states that he
would like Reason to be impersonated by someone "virtuous
rather than beautiful." The French Revolution gave birth to no
artists, but only to a great journalist, Desmoulins, and to a clan-
destine writer, Sade. It guillotines the only poet of the times.*
The only great prose-writer† took refuge in London and pleaded
the cause of Christianity and legitimacy. A little later the followers
of Saint-Simon demanded a "socially useful form of art." "Art
for progress" was a commonplace of the whole period, and one
that Hugo revived, without succeeding in making it sound convincing. Vallés alone brings to his malediction of art a tone of im-
precation that gives it authenticity.

This tone is also employed by the Russian nihilists. Pisarev
proclaims the deposition of æsthetic values, in favor of pragmatic
values. "I would rather be a Russian shoemaker than a Russian
Raphæl." A pair of shoes, in his eyes, is more useful than
Shakespeare. The nihilist Nekrassov, a great and moving poet,
nevertheless affirms that he prefers a piece of cheese to all of
Pushkin. Finally, we are familiar with the excommunication of
art pronounced by Tolstoy. Revolutionary Russia finally even
turned its back on the marble statues of Venus and Apollo, still
gilded by the Italian sun, that Peter the Great had had brought
to his summer garden in St. Petersburg. Suffering, sometimes,
turns away from too painful expressions of happiness.

German ideology is no less severe in its accusations. According
to the revolutionary interpreters of Hegel's *Phenomenology*, there
will be no art in reconciled society. Beauty will be lived and no
longer only imagined. Reality, become entirely rational, will satisfy, completely by itself, every appetite. The criticism of formal

* André Chénier. (ED.)
† François René Chateaubriand. (ED.)

conscience and of escapist values naturally extends itself to embrace art. Art does not belong to all times; it is determined, on the contrary, by its period, and expresses, says Marx, the privileged values of the ruling classes. Thus there is only one revolutionary form of art, which is, precisely, art dedicated to the service of the revolution. Moreover, by creating beauty outside the course of history, art impedes the only rational activity: the transformation of history itself into absolute beauty. The Russian shoemaker, once he is aware of his revolutionary role, is the real creator of definitive beauty. As for Raphæl, he created only a transitory beauty, which will be quite incomprehensible to the new man.

Marx asks himself, it is true, how the beauty created by the Greeks can still be beautiful for us. His answer is that this beauty is the expression of the naïve childhood of this world and that we have, in the midst of our adult struggles, a nostalgia for this childhood. But how can the masterpieces of the Italian Renaissance, how can Rembrandt, how can Chinese art still be beautiful in our eyes? What does it matter! The trial of art has been opened definitively and is continuing today with the embarrassed complicity of artists and intellectuals dedicated to calumniating both their art and their intelligence. We notice, in fact, that in the contest between Shakespeare and the shoemaker, it is not the shoemaker who maligns Shakespeare or beauty but, on the contrary, the man who continues to read Shakespeare and who does not choose to make shoes—which he could never make, if it comes to that. The artists of our time resemble the repentant noblemen of nineteenth-century Russia; their bad conscience is their excuse. But the last emotion that an artist can experience, confronted with his art, is repentance. It is going far beyond simple and necessary humility to pretend to dismiss beauty, too, until the end of time, and meanwhile, to deprive all the world, including the shoemaker, of this additional bread of which one has taken advantage oneself.

This form of ascetic insanity, nevertheless, has its reasons, which at least are of interest to us. They express on the æsthetic level the struggle of revolution and rebellion. In every rebellion is to be found the metaphysical demand for unity, the impossibility of capturing it, and the construction of a substitute universe. Rebellion, from this point of view, is a fabricator of universes. This also defines art. The demands of rebellion are really, in part, æsthetic demands. All rebel thought is expressed either in rhetoric or in a closed universe. The rhetoric of ramparts, in Lucretius, the convents and isolated castles of Sade, the island or the lonely rock of the romantics, the solitary heights of Nietzsche, the primeval seas of Lautréamont, the parapets of Rimbaud, the terrifying castles of the surrealists, which spring up in a storm of flowers, the prison, the nation behind barbed wire, the concentration camps, the empire of free slaves, all illustrate, after their own fashion, the same need for coherence and unity. In these sealed worlds, man can reign and have knowledge at last.

This tendency is common to all the arts. The artist reconstructs the world to his plan. The symphonies of nature know no rests. The world is never quiet; even its silence eternally resounds with the same notes, in vibrations that escape our ears. As for those that we perceive, they carry sounds to us, occasionally a chord, never a melody. Music exists, however, in which symphonies are completed, where melody gives its form to sounds that by themselves have none, and where, finally, a particular arrangement of notes extracts from natural disorder a unity that is satisfying to the mind and the heart.

"I believe more and more," writes Van Gogh, "that God must not be judged on this earth. It is one of His sketches that has turned out badly." Every artist tries to reconstruct this sketch and to give it the style it lacks. The greatest and most ambitious of all the arts, sculpture, is bent on capturing, in three dimensions, the fugitive figure of man, and on restoring the unity of great style to the general disorder of gestures. Sculpture does not reject resemblance, of which, indeed, it has need. But resemblance is not its first aim. What it is looking for, in its periods of greatness, is the gesture, the expression, or the empty stare which will sum up all the gestures and all the stares in the world. Its purpose is not to imitate, but to stylize and to imprison in one significant expression the fleeting ecstasy of the body or the infinite variety of human attitudes. Then, and only then, does it erect, on the pediments of teeming cities, the model, the type, the motionless perfection that will cool, for one moment, the fevered brow of man. The frustrated lover of love can finally gaze at the Greek caryatides and grasp what it is that triumphs, in the body and face of the woman, over every degradation.

The principle of painting is also to make a choice. "Even genius," writes Delacroix, ruminating on his art, "is only the gift of generalizing and choosing." The painter isolates his subject, which is the first way of unifying it. Landscapes flee, vanish from the memory, or destroy one another. That is why the landscape painter or the painter of still life isolates in space and time things that normally change with the light, get lost in an infinite perspective, or disappear under the impact of other values. The first thing that a landscape painter does is to square off his canvas. He eliminates as much as he includes. Similarly, subject-painting isolates, in both time and space, an action that normally would become lost in another action. Thus the painter arrives at a point of stabilization. The really great creative artists are those who, like Piero della Francesca, give the impression that the stabilization has only just taken place, that the projection machine has suddenly stopped dead. All their subjects give the impression that, by some miracle of art, they continue to live, while ceasing to be mortal. Long after his death, Rembrandt's philosopher still meditates, between light and shade, on the same problem.

"How vain a thing is painting that beguiles us by the resemblance to objects that do not please us at all." Delacroix, who quotes Pascal's celebrated remark, is correct in writing "strange" instead of "vain." These objects do not please us at all because we do not see them; they are obscured and negated by a perpetual process of change. Who looked at the hands of the executioner during the Flagellation, and the olive trees on the way to the Cross? But here we see them represented, transfigured by the incessant movement of the Passion; and the agony of Christ, imprisoned in images of violence and beauty, cries out again each day in the cold rooms of museums. A painter's style lies in this blending of nature and history, in this stability imposed on incessant change. Art realizes, without apparent effort, the reconciliation of the unique with the universal of which Hegel dreamed. Perhaps that is why periods, such as ours, which are bent on unity to the point of madness, turn to primitive arts, in which stylization is the most intense and unity the most provocative. The most extreme stylization is always found at the beginning and end of artistic movements; it demonstrates the intensity of negation and transposition which has given modern painting its disorderly impetus toward interpreting unity and existence. Van Gogh's admirable complaint is the arrogant and desperate cry of all artists. "I can very well, in life and in painting, too, do without God. But I cannot, suffering as I do, do without something that is greater than I am, that is my life—the power to create."

But the artist's rebellion against reality, which is automatically suspect to the totalitarian revolution, contains the same affirmation as the spontaneous rebellion of the oppressed. The revolutionary spirit, born of total negation, instinctively felt that, as well as refusal, there was also consent to be found in art; that there was a risk of contemplation counterbalancing action, beauty, and injustice, and that in certain cases beauty itself was a form of injustice from which there was no appeal. Equally well, no form of art can survive on total denial alone. Just as all thought, and primarily that of non-signification, signifies something, so there is no art that has no signification. Man can allow himself to denounce the total injustice of the world and then demand a total justice that he alone will create. But he cannot affirm the total hideousness of the world. To create beauty, he must simultaneously reject reality and exalt certain of its aspects. Art disputes reality, but does not hide from it. Nietzsche could deny any form of transcendence, whether moral or divine, by saying that transcendence drove one to slander this world and this life. But perhaps there is a living transcendence, of which beauty carries the promise, which can make this mortal and limited world preferable to and more appealing than any other. Art thus leads us back to the origins of rebellion, to the extent that it tries to give its form to an elusive value which the future perpetually promises, but of which the artist has a presentiment and wishes to snatch from the grasp of history. We shall understand this better in considering the art form whose precise aim is to become part of the process of evolution in order to give it the style that it lacks; in other words, the novel.

It is possible to separate the literature of consent, which coincides, by and large, with ancient history and the classical period, from the literature of rebellion, which begins in modern times. We note the scarcity of fiction in the former. When it exists, with very few exceptions, it is not concerned with a story but with fantasy (*Theagenes and Charicleia* or *Astræa*). These are fairy tales, not novels. In the latter period, on the contrary, the novel form is really developed—a form that has not ceased to thrive and extend its field of activity up to the present day, simultaneously with the critical and revolutionary movement. The novel is born at the same time as the spirit of rebellion and expresses, on the æsthetic plane, the same ambition.

"A make-believe story, written in prose," says Littré about the novel. Is it only that? In any case, a Catholic critic, Stanislas Fumet, has written: "Art, whatever its aims, is always in sinful competition with God." Actually, it is more correct to talk about competition with God, in connection with the novel, than of competition with man's civil status. Thibaudet expresses a similar idea when he says of Balzac: "The *Comédie humaine* is the *Imitation* of God the Father." The aim of great literature seems to be to create a closed universe or a perfect type. The West, in its great creative works, does not limit itself to retracing the steps of its daily life. It consistently presents magnificent images which inflame its imagination and sets off, hotfoot, in pursuit of them.

After all, writing or even reading a novel is an unusual activity. To construct a story by a new arrangement of actual facts has nothing inevitable or even necessary about it. Even if the ordinary explanation of the mutual pleasure of reader and writer were true, it would still be necessary to ask why it was incumbent on a large part of humanity to take pleasure and an interest in make-believe stories. Revolutionary criticism condemns the novel in its pure form as being simply a means of escape for an idle imagination. In everyday speech we find the term *romance* used to describe an exaggerated description or lying account of some event. Not so very long ago it was a commonplace that young girls, despite all appearance to the contrary, were "romantic," by which was meant that these idealized creatures took no account of everyday realities. In general, it has always been considered that the romantic was quite separate from life and that it enhanced it while, at the same time, betraying it. The simplest and most common way of envisaging romantic expression is to see it as an escapist exercise. Common sense joins hands with revolutionary criticism.

But from what are we escaping by means of the novel? From a reality we consider too overwhelming? Happy people read novels, too, and it is an established fact that extreme suffering takes away the taste for reading. From another angle, the romantic universe of the novel certainly has less substance than the other universe where people of flesh and blood harass us without respite. However, by what magic does Adolphe, for instance, seem so much more familiar to us than Benjamin Constant, and Count Mosca than our professional moralists? Balzac once terminated a long conversation about politics and the fate of the world by saying: "And now let us get back to serious matters," meaning that he wanted to talk about his novels. The incontestable importance of the world of the novel, our insistence, in fact, on taking seriously the innumerable myths with which we have been provided for the last two centuries by the genius of writers, is not fully explained by the desire to escape. Romantic activities undoubtedly imply a rejection of reality. But this rejection is not a mere escapist flight, and might be interpreted as the retreat of the soul which, according to Hegel, creates for itself, in its disappointment, a fictitious world in which ethics reigns alone. The edifying novel, however, is far from being great literature; and the best of all romantic novels, *Paul et Virginie*, a really heartbreaking book, makes no concessions to consolation.

The contradiction is this: man rejects the world as it is, without accepting the necessity of escaping it. In fact, men cling to the world and by far the majority do not want to abandon it. Far from always wanting to forget it, they suffer, on the contrary, from not being able to possess it completely enough, estranged citizens of the world, exiled from their own country. Except for vivid moments of fulfillment, all reality for them is incomplete. Their actions escape them in the form of other actions, return in unexpected guises to judge them, and disappear like the water Tantalus longed to drink, into some still undiscovered orifice. To know the whereabouts of the orifice, to control the course of the river, to understand life, at last, as destiny—these are their true aspirations.

But this vision which, in the realm of consciousness at least, will reconcile them with themselves, can only appear, if it ever does appear, at the fugitive moment that is death, in which everything is consummated. In order to exist just once in the world, it is necessary never again to exist.

At this point is born the fatal envy which so many men feel of the lives of others. Seen from a distance, these existences seem to possess a coherence and a unity which they cannot have in reality, but which seem evident to the spectator. He sees only the salient points of these lives without taking into account the details of corrosion. Thus we make these lives into works of art. In an elementary fashion we turn them into novels. In this sense, everyone tries to make his life a work of art. We want love to last and we know that it does not last; even if, by some miracle, it were to last a whole lifetime, it would still be incomplete. Perhaps, in this insatiable need for perpetuation, we should better understand human suffering if we knew that it was eternal. It appears that great minds are sometimes less horrified by suffering than by the fact that it does not endure. In default of inexhaustible happiness, eternal suffering would at least give us a destiny. But we do not even have that consolation, and our worst agonies come to an end one day. One morning, after many dark nights of despair, an irrepressible longing to live will announce to us the fact that all is finished and that suffering has no more meaning than happiness.

The desire for possession is only another form of the desire to endure; it is this that comprises the impotent delirium of love. No human being, even the most passionately loved and passionately loving, is ever in our possession. On the pitiless earth where lovers are often separated in death and are always born divided, the total possession of another human being and absolute communion throughout an entire lifetime are impossible dreams. The desire for possession is insatiable, to such a point that it can survive even love itself. To love, therefore, is to sterilize the person one loves. The shamefaced suffering of the abandoned lover is not so much due to being no longer loved as to knowing that the other partner can and must love again. In the final analysis, every man devoured by the overpowering desire to endure and possess wishes that those whom he has loved were either sterile or dead. This is real rebellion. Those who have not insisted, at least once, on the absolute virginity of human beings and of the world, who have not trembled with longing and impotence at the fact that it is impossible, and have then not been destroyed by trying to love halfheartedly, perpetually forced back upon their longing for the absolute, cannot understand the realities of rebellion and its ravening desire for destruction. But the lives of others always escape us, and we escape them too; they have no firm outline. Life from this point of view is without style. It is only an impulse that endlessly pursues its form without ever finding it. Man, tortured by this, tries in vain to find the form that will impose certain limits between which he can be king. If only one single living thing had definite form, he would be reconciled!

There is not one human being who, above a certain elementary level of consciousness, does not exhaust himself in trying to find formulas or attitudes that will give his existence the unity it lacks. Appearance and action, the dandy and the revolutionary, all demand unity in order to exist, and in order to exist on this earth. As in those moving and unhappy relationships which sometimes survive for a very long time because one of the partners is waiting to find the right word, action, gesture, or situation which will bring his adventure to an end on exactly the right note, so everyone proposes and creates for himself the final word. It is not sufficient to live, there must be a destiny that does not have to wait for death. It is therefore justifiable to say that man has an idea of a better world than this. But better does not mean different, it means unified. This passion which lifts the mind above the commonplaces of a dispersed world, from which it nevertheless cannot free itself, is the passion for unity. It does not result in mediocre efforts to escape, however, but in the most obstinate demands. Religion or crime, every human endeavor in fact, finally obeys this unreasonable desire and claims to give life a form it does not have. The same impulse, which can lead to the adoration of the heavens or the destruction of man, also leads to creative literature, which derives its serious content from this source.

What, in fact, is a novel but a universe in which action is endowed with form, where final words are pronounced, where people possess one another completely, and where life assumes the aspect of destiny?* The world of the novel is only a rectification of the world we live in, in pursuance of man's deepest wishes. For the world is undoubtedly the same one we know. The suffering, the illusion, the love are the same. The heroes speak our language, have our weaknesses and our strength. Their universe is neither more beautiful nor more enlightening than ours. But they, at least, pursue their destinies to the bitter end and there are no more fascinating heroes than those who indulge their passions to the fullest, Kirilov and Stavrogin, Mme Graslin, Julien Sorel, or the Prince de Clèves. It is here that we can no longer keep pace with them, for they complete things that we can never consummate.

Mme de La Fayette derived the *Princesse de Clèves* from the most harrowing experiences. Undoubtedly she is Mme de Clèves and yet she is not. Where lies the difference? The difference is that Mme de La Fayette did not go into a convent and that no one around her died of despair. No doubt she knew moments, at least, of agony in her extraordinary passion. But there was no culminating-point; she survived her love and prolonged it by ceasing to live it, and finally no one, not even herself, would have known its pattern if she had not given it the perfect delineation of faultless prose.

Nor is there any story more romantic and beautiful than that of Sophie Tonska and Casimir in Gobineau's *Pléïades*. Sophie, a sensitive and beautiful woman, who makes one understand Stendahl's confession that "only women of great character can make me happy," forces Casimir to confess his love for her. Accustomed to being loved, she becomes impatient with Casimir, who sees her every day and yet never departs from an attitude of irritating detachment. Casimir confesses his love, but in the tone of one stating a legal case. He has studied it, knows it as well as he knows himself, and is convinced that this love, without which he cannot live, has no future. He has therefore decided to tell her of his love and at the same time to acknowledge that it is vain and to make over his fortune to her—she is rich, and this gesture

---

* Even if the novel describes only nostalgia, despair, frustration, it still creates a form of salvation. To talk of despair is to conquer it. Despairing literature is a contradiction in terms.

is of no importance—on condition that she give him a very modest pension which will allow him to install himself in the suburb of a town chosen at random (it will be Vilna) and there await death in poverty. Casimir recognizes, moreover, that the idea of receiving from Sophie the necessary money on which to live represents a concession to human weakness, the only one he will permit himself, with, at long intervals, the dispatch of a blank sheet of paper in an envelope on which he will write Sophie's name. After being first indignant, then perturbed, and then melancholy, Sophie accepts; and everything happens as Casimir foresaw. He dies, in Vilna, of a broken heart. Romanticism thus has its logic. A story is never really moving and successful without the imperturbable continuity which is never part of real life, but which is to be found on the borderland between reality and reverie. If Gobineau himself had gone to Vilna he would have got bored and come back, or would have settled down comfortably. But Casimir never experienced any desire to change nor did he ever wake cured of his love. He went to the bitter end, like Heathcliff, who wanted to go beyond death in order to reach the very depths of hell.

Here we have an imaginary world, therefore, which is created by the rectification of the actual world—a world where suffering can, if it wishes, continue until death, where passions are never distracted, where people are prey to obsessions and are always present to one another. Man is finally able to give himself the alleviating form and limits which he pursues in vain in his own life. The novel creates destiny to suit any eventuality. In this way it competes with creation and, provisionally, conquers death. A detailed analysis of the most famous novels would show, in different perspectives each time, that the essence of the novel lies in this perpetual alteration, always directed toward the same ends, that the artist makes in his own experience. Far from being moral or even purely formal, this alteration aims, primarily, at unity and thereby expresses a metaphysical need. The novel, on this level, is primarily an exercise of the intelligence in the service of nostalgic or rebellious sensibilities. It would be possible to study this quest for unity in the French analytical novel and in Melville, Balzac, Dostoevsky, or Tolstoy. But a brief comparison between two attempts that stand at different poles of the world of the novel—

the works of Proust and American fiction of the last few years—
will suffice for our purpose.

The American novel* claims to find its unity in reducing man
either to elementals or to his external reactions and to his behavior. It does not choose feelings or passions to give a detailed
description of, such as we find in classic French novels. It rejects
analysis and the search for a fundamental psychological motive
that could explain and recapitulate the behavior of a character.
This is why the unity of this novel form is only the unity of the
flash of recognition. Its technique consists in describing men by
their outside appearances, in their most casual actions, of reproducing, without comment, everything they say down to their
repetitions,† and finally by acting as if men were entirely defined by their daily automatisms. On this mechanical level men, in
fact, seem exactly alike, which explains this peculiar universe in
which all the characters appear interchangeable, even down to
their physical peculiarities. This technique is called realistic only
owing to a misapprehension. In addition to the fact that realism
in art is, as we shall see, an incomprehensible idea, it is perfectly
obvious that this fictitious world is not attempting a reproduction,
pure and simple, of reality, but the most arbitrary form of stylization. It is born of a mutilation, and of a voluntary mutilation, performed on reality. The unity thus obtained is a degraded unity, a
leveling off of human beings and of the world. It would seem
that for these writers it is the inner life that deprives human actions of unity and that tears people away from one another. This
is a partially legitimate suspicion. But rebellion, which is one of
the sources of the art of fiction, can find satisfaction only in con-
structing unity on the basis of affirming this interior reality and
not of denying it. To deny it totally is to refer oneself to an imaginary man. Novels of violence are also love stories, of which they
have the formal conceits—in their own way, they edify.‡ The life
of the body, reduced to its essentials, paradoxically produces an

* I am referring, of course, to the "tough" novel of the thirties and forties and
not to the admirable American efflorescence of the nineteenth century.
† Even in Faulkner, a great writer of this generation, the interior monologue
only reproduces the outer husk of thought.
‡ Bernardin de Saint-Pierre and the Marquis de Sade, with different indications
of it, are the creators of the propagandist novel.

abstract and gratuitous universe, continuously denied, in its turn, by reality. This type of novel, purged of interior life, in which men seem to be observed behind a pane of glass, logically ends, with its emphasis on the pathological, by giving itself as its unique subject the supposedly average man. In this way it is possible to explain the extraordinary number of "innocents" who appear in this universe. The simpleton is the ideal subject for such an enterprise since he can only be defined—and completely defined—by his behavior. He is the symbol of the despairing world in which wretched automatons live in a machine-ridden universe, which American novelists have presented as a heart-rending but sterile protest.

As for Proust, his contribution has been to create, from an obstinate contemplation of reality, a closed world that belonged only to him and that indicated his victory over the transitoriness of things and over death. But he uses absolutely the opposite means. He upholds, above everything, by a deliberate choice, a careful selection of unique experience, which the writer chooses from the most secret recesses of his past. Immense empty spaces are thus discarded from life because they have left no trace in the memory. If the American novel is the novel of men without memory, the world of Proust is nothing but memory. It is concerned only with the most difficult and most exacting of memories, the memory that rejects the dispersion of the actual world and derives, from the trace of a lingering perfume, the secret of a new and ancient universe. Proust chooses the interior life and, of the interior life, that which is more interior than life itself in preference to what is forgotten in the world of reality—in other words, the purely mechanical and blind aspects of the world. But by his rejection of reality he does not deny reality. He does not commit the error, which would counterbalance the error of American fiction, of suppressing the mechanical. He unites, on the contrary, into a superior form of unity, the memory of the past and the immediate sensation, the twisted foot and the happy days of times past.

It is difficult to return to the places of one's early happiness. The young girls in the flower of their youth still laugh and chatter on the seashore, but he who watches them gradually loses his right to love them, just as those he has loved lose the power to be loved.

This melancholy is the melancholy of Proust. It was powerful enough in him to cause a violent rejection of all existence. But his passion for faces and for the light attached him at the same time to life. He never admitted that the happy days of his youth were lost forever. He undertook the task of re-creating them and of demonstrating, in the face of death, that the past could be regained at the end of time in the form of an imperishable present, both truer and richer than it was at the beginning. The psychological analysis of *Remembrance of Things Past* is nothing but a potent means to an end. The real greatness of Proust lies in having written *Time Regained*, which resembles the world of dispersion and which gives it a meaning on the very level of integration. His difficult victory, on the eve of his death, is to have been able to extract from the incessant flight of forms, by means of memory and intelligence alone, the tentative trembling symbols of human unity. The most definite challenge that a work of this kind can give to creation is to present itself as an entirety, as a closed and unified world. This defines an unrepentant work of art.

It has been said that the world of Proust was a world without a god. If that is true, it is not because God is never spoken of, but because the ambition of this world is to be absolute perfection and to give to eternity the aspect of man. *Time Regained*, at least in its aspirations, is eternity without God. Proust's work, in this regard, appears to be one of the most ambitious and most significant of man's enterprises against his mortal condition. He has demonstrated that the art of the novel can reconstruct creation itself, in the form that it is imposed on us and in the form in which we reject it. In one of its aspects, at least, this art consists in choosing the creature in preference to his creator. But still more profoundly, it is allied to the beauty of the world or of its inhabitants against the powers of death and oblivion. It is in this way that his rebellion is creative.

Boris Pasternak

TRANSLATING SHAKESPEARE

BORIS PASTERNAK'S *refusal to accept the Nobel Prize in
1958 was a cause célèbre without parallel in literary history. Although
he is best known in Russia as a poet and as the translator of Shakespeare, he became internationally famous as the author of the frank,
powerful novel,* Doctor Zhivago. *The son of a painter friendly with
Tolstoy, Pasternak grew up in a cultured environment. After studying music and philosophy at Moscow and Marburg, he began his writing career with two volumes of highly individualistic and lyrical verses.
His later poetry, such as* Lieutenant Schmidt, *produced in response
to Soviet poet Mayakovsky's call to serve the cause, are politically and
socially slanted. Besides* Doctor Zhivago *and a number of poems
printed in American periodicals, there are available in English translations a collection of short stories,* Aerial Ways, *and two autobiographical volumes,* Safe Conduct *and* I Remember.

Over the years I have translated several of Shakespeare's
plays: *Hamlet, Romeo and Juliet, Antony and Cleopatra, Othello, King Henry IV* (Parts I and II), *King Lear* and
Macbeth.

The demand for simple and readable translations is great and
seemingly inexhaustible. Every translator flatters himself with the
hope that he, more than others, will succeed in meeting it. I have
not escaped the common fate.

Nor are my opinions on the aims and problems of translating
literary works exceptional. I believe, as do many others, that close-
ness to the original is not ensured only by literal exactness or by
similarity of form: the likeness, as in a portrait, cannot be achieved
without a lively and natural method of expression. As much as
the author, the translator must confine himself to a vocabulary

which is natural to him and avoid the literary artifice involved in stylization. Like the original text, the translation must create an impression of life and not of verbiage.

SHAKESPEARE'S POETIC STYLE

Shakespeare's dramas are deeply realistic in their conception. In his prose passages and in those dialogues in verse which are combined with movement or action his style is conversational. For the rest, the flow of his blank verse is highly metaphorical, sometimes needlessly so and in such cases at the cost of some artificiality.

His imagery is not always equal to itself. At times it is poetry at its highest, at others it falls plainly into rhetoric and is loaded with dozens of inadequate substitutes for the one right word which he had on the tip of his tongue and which escaped him in his hurry. Nevertheless, at its worst as at its best, his metaphorical speech conforms to the essentials of true allegory.

Metaphorical language is the result of the disproportion between man's short life and the immense and long-term tasks he sets himself. Because of this, he needs to look at things as sharply as an eagle and to convey his vision in flashes which can be immediately apprehended. This is just what poetry is. Outsize personalities use metaphor as a shorthand of the spirit.

The stormy quickness of the brushstrokes of a Rembrandt, a Michelangelo, or a Titian was not the fruit of their deliberate choice. Possessed by the need to paint the universe, they could not paint in any other way.

Shakespeare's style combines opposite extremes. His prose is finished and polished. It is the work of a genius in the art of comic detail, a master of conciseness, and a brilliant mimic of everything strange and curious in the world.

In complete contrast to this is his blank verse. Voltaire and Tolstoy were shocked by its inward and outward chaos.

Shakespeare's characters, who often go through several stages of completion, occasionally speak first in poetry and later in prose. In such cases the scenes in verse produce the impression of being sketches and those in prose of being finished and conclusive.

Verse was Shakespeare's most rapid and immediate method of

expression. It was his quickest way of putting down his thoughts. So true is this that many of his verse passages read almost like the rough drafts of his prose.

His poetry draws its strength from its very quality of sketchiness, powerful, uncontrollable, disorderly, and abundant.

SHAKESPEARE'S USE OF RHYTHM

Shakespeare's rhythm is the basic principle of his poetry. Its momentum determines the speed and sequence of questions and answers in his dialogues and the length of his periods and monologues.

It is a rhythm which reflects the enviably laconic quality of English, a quality which makes it possible to compress a whole statement, made up of two or more contrasted propositions, into a single line of iambic verse. It is the rhythm of free speech, the language of a man who sets up no idols and is therefore honest and concise.

HAMLET

Shakespeare's use of rhythm is clearest in *Hamlet*, where it serves a triple purpose. It is used as a method of characterization, it makes audible and sustains the prevailing mood, and it elevates the tone and softens the brutality of certain scenes.

The characters are sharply differentiated by the rhythm of their speech. Polonius, the King, Guildenstern and Rosencrantz speak in one way; Lærtes, Ophelia, Horatio, and the rest in another. The credulity of the Queen is shown not only in her words but also by her singsong manner of drawing out her vowels.

So vivid is the rhythmic characterization of Hamlet himself that it creates the illusion of a leitmotif, as though a musical phrase were reiterated at his every appearance on the stage, although in fact no such leitmotif exists. The very pulse of his being seems to be made audible. Everything is contained in it: his inconsistent gestures, his long, resolute stride and the proud half-turn of his head, as well as the way in which the thoughts he utters in his monologues leap and take flight, the mocking arrogance of his ripostes to the courtiers who mill round him, and his manner of staring into the distance of the unknown whence his father's ghost once summoned him and where it may at any moment speak again.

Neither the music of Hamlet's speech nor that of the play as a whole lends itself to quotation: it is impossible to give an impression of it by any one example. Yet, disembodied though it is, so ominously and so closely is it woven into the texture of the tragedy that, given the subject, one is tempted to describe it as Scandinavian and as suited to the climate of apparitions. It consists in a measured alternation of solemnity and disquiet and, by thickening the atmosphere to its utmost density, it brings out the dominant mood. What is this mood?

According to the well-established view of critics, *Hamlet* is a tragedy of the will. This is true. But in what sense is it to be understood? Absence of will power did not exist as a theme in Shakespeare's time: it aroused no interest. Nor does Shakespeare's portrait of Hamlet, drawn so clearly and in so much detail, suggest a neurotic. Hamlet is a prince of the blood who never, for a moment, ceases to be conscious of his rights as heir to the throne; he is the spoilt darling of an ancient court, and self-assured in the awareness of his natural gifts. The sum of qualities with which he is endowed by Shakespeare leaves no room for flabbiness: it precludes it. Rather, the opposite is true: the audience, impressed by his brilliant prospects, is left to judge of the greatness of his sacrifice in giving them up for a higher aim.

From the moment of the ghost's appearance, Hamlet gives up his will in order to "do the will of him that sent him." *Hamlet* is not a drama of weakness, but of duty and self-denial. It is immaterial that, when appearance and reality are shown to be at variance—to be indeed separated by an abyss—the message is conveyed by supernatural means and that the ghost commands Hamlet to exact vengeance. What is important is that chance has allotted Hamlet the role of judge of his own time and servant of the future. *Hamlet* is the drama of a high destiny, of a life devoted and preordained to a heroic task.

This is the overall tone of the play, so concentrated by the rhythm as to be almost palpable. But the rhythmic principle is applied in still another way. It has a softening effect on certain harsh scenes which would be intolerable without it.

Thus for instance, in the scene in which he sends Ophelia to a nunnery, Hamlet speaks to the girl who loves him, and whom he tramples underfoot, with the ruthlessness of a self-centered Byronic rebel. His irony is out of keeping with his own love for her, which he painfully suppresses in himself. But let us see how this heartless scene is introduced. Immediately before it comes the famous speech, "To be or not to be," and the fresh music of the monologue still echoes in the opening verses which Hamlet and Ophelia exchange. The bitter and disorderly beauty of the monologue in which Hamlet's perplexities crowd and overtake each other and remain unsolved recalls the sudden chords, abruptly cut off, tried out on the organ before the opening of a requiem.

No wonder that the monologue heralds the beginning of the cruel dénouement. It precedes it as the funeral service precedes the burial. The way is opened by it for whatever is inevitable, and whatever follows is washed, redeemed, and lent majesty in advance not only by the spoken thoughts but by the ardor and purity of the tears which ring in it.

ROMEO AND JULIET

If such is the importance of rhythm in *Hamlet*, we might expect it to be greater still in *Romeo and Juliet*. Where, if not in a drama of first love, should harmony and measure have free play? But Shakespeare puts them to an unexpected use. He shows us that lyricism is not what we imagined it to be. He composes no arias, no duets. His intuition leads him by a different path.

Music plays a negative role in *Romeo and Juliet*. It is on the side of the forces which are hostile to the lovers, the forces of worldly hypocrisy and of the hustle of daily life.

Until he meets Juliet, Romeo is full of his imaginary passion for Rosaline, who never appears on the stage. His romantic pose is in the current fashion of his time. It drives him out on solitary walks at night and he makes up for lost sleep by day, shaded by closed shutters from the sun. All the time that this is going on, in the first scenes of the play, he speaks unnaturally in rhymed verse, melodiously declaiming his high-falutin nonsense in the affected drawing-room manner of his day. But from the moment when he sees Juliet at the ball and stops dead in front of her, not a trace is left of his tuneful mode of expression.

Compared to other feelings, love is an elemental cosmic force wearing a disguise of meekness. In itself it is as simple and unconditional as consciousness and as death, as oxygen or uranium. It is not a state of mind, it is the foundation of the universe. Being thus basic and primordial, it is the equal of artistic creation. Its dignity is no less, and its expression has no need of art to polish it. The most that the artist can dream of is to overhear its voice, to catch its ever new, ever unprecedented language. Love has no need of euphony. Truth, not sound, dwells in its heart.

Like all Shakespeare's plays, *Romeo and Juliet* is written for the most part in blank verse, and it is in blank verse that the hero and heroine address each other. But the measure is never stressed, it is never obvious. There is no declamation. The form never asserts itself at the expense of the infinitely discreet content. This is poetry at its best, and like all such poetry it has the freshness and simplicity of prose. Romeo and Juliet speak in half tones, their conversation is guarded, interrupted, secret. It has the very sound of high emotion and mortal danger overheard at night.

The only noisy and emphatically rhythmic scenes are those in crowded rooms and streets. Out in the street, where the blood of Montagues and Capulets is shed, ring the daggers of the quarreling clans. Cooks quarrel and clatter knives in the kitchen as they cook the endless dinners. And to this din of butchery and cooking, as to the brassy beat of a noisy band, the quiet tragedy of feeling develops, spoken for the most part in the soundless whispers of conspirators.

OTHELLO

The division of the plays into acts and scenes was not made by Shakespeare but later, by his editors. Nevertheless it was not forced on them: they lend themselves to it easily by virtue of their inward structure.

The original texts, printed without a break, nevertheless stood out by a rigor of construction and development which is rare in our time.

This applies particularly to the thematic development usually contained in the middle of the drama, that is to say in the third and some parts of the second and fourth acts. This section is, as it were, the box which holds the mainspring of the mechanism.

At the beginning and conclusion of his plays Shakespeare freely improvises the details and, with as light a heart, disposes of the loose ends. The swiftly changing scenes are full of life, they are drawn from nature with the utmost freedom and with a staggering wealth of imagination.

But he denies himself this freedom in the middle section, where the threads have been tied up and must begin to be unraveled; here Shakespeare shows himself to be the child and slave of his age. His third acts are riveted to the mechanics of the plot in a measure unknown to the dramatic art of later centuries, though it was from him that it learned its honesty and daring. They are ruled by too blind a faith in the power of logic and in the real existence of ethical abstractions. The lively portraits drawn at the beginning, with their convincing light and shade, are replaced by personified virtues and vices. The sequence of actions and events ceases to be natural and has the suspect tidiness of rational deductions, as of syllogisms in an argument.

When Shakespeare was a child, moralities constructed in accordance with the formal rules of medieval scholasticism were still shown on the English provincial stage. He may well have seen them, and his old-fashioned industry in working out his plot may have been a remnant of the past which had fascinated him in his childhood.

Four-fifths of his writings are made up of his beginnings and endings. This is the part that made the audience laugh and cry; it is on this that his fame is based, and it accounts for all the talk about his truthfulness to life in opposition to the deadly soullessness of neoclassicism.

But a thing may be rightly observed, yet wrongly explained. One often hears extravagant praise of the "mousetrap" in *Hamlet* or of the iron necessity in the development of this or that passion or in the consequences of this or that crime in Shakespeare. Such admiration starts from false premises. It is not the mousetrap that deserves to be admired, but Shakespeare's genius which shows itself even where his writing is artificial. What should cause wonder is that the third acts, which make up one-fifth of his work and which are often devitalized and contrived, do not circumvent his greatness. He survives, not because of, but in spite of them.

For all the passion and the genius concentrated in *Othello*, and for all its popularity on the stage, what has been said above applies in a considerable measure to this play.

Here we have the dazzling quays of Venice, Brabantio's house, the arsenal; the extraordinary night session of the Senate, and Othello's account of the gradual beginnings of his and Desdemona's feeling for each other. Then the storm at sea off the coast of Cyprus and the drunken brawl at night on the ramparts. And, before the end, the famous scene of Desdemona preparing for the night, in which the still more famous "Willow" song is sung, tragically natural before the dreadful illumination of the finale.

But what happens in between? With a few turns of the key, Iago winds up like an alarm clock the suspicions of his victim, and the course of jealousy, obvious and labored, unwinds, creaking and shuddering like a rusty mechanism. It will be said that such is the nature of jealousy or that such is the tribute paid to the convention of the stage with its insistence on excessive clarity. It may be so. But the damage would be less if the tribute were paid by an artist of less genius and less consistency. In our time another aspect of the play has a topical interest.

Can it be an accident that the hero is black, while all that he holds dear in life is white? What is the significance of this choice of colors? Does it mean only that all peoples have an equal right to human dignity? Shakespeare's thought went much further.

The concept of the equality of peoples did not exist in his time. What did exist and was fully alive was a different and wider notion of their equal opportunities. Shakespeare was not interested in what a man had been at birth, but in the point he had reached, in what he had changed into, what he had become. In Shakespeare's view, Othello, who was black, was a human being and a

Christian who lived in historic times, and this interested him the more because living side by side with Othello was Iago, who was white, and who was an unconverted prehistoric animal.

ANTONY AND CLEOPATRA

There are tragedies in Shakespeare, such as *Macbeth* and *Lear*, which create their own worlds, unique of their kind. There are comedies which belong to the realm of pure fantasy and are the cradle of romanticism. There are chronicles of English history, songs in praise of England sung by the greatest of her sons; some of the events described in them had their counterpart in the circumstances of his time and so his attitude to them could not be sober and dispassionate.

Thus, in spite of the realism in which his work is steeped, it would be vain to look to any of these plays for objectivity. We do, however, find it in his dramas of Roman life.

Julius Caesar was not written only for the sake of poetry and love of art, and still less was *Antony and Cleopatra*. Both are the fruit of his study of plain everyday life. This study is pursued with passion by every representational artist. It was this pursuit which led to the naturalistic novel of the nineteenth century and which accounts for the even more convincing charm of Flaubert, Chekhov, and Leo Tolstoy.

But why should Shakespeare seek the inspiration of his realism in such remote antiquity as Rome? The answer—and there is nothing in it to surprise us—is that just because the subject was remote it allowed Shakespeare to call things by their name. He could say whatever seemed good to him about politics, ethics, or any other thing he chose. He was dealing with an alien and distant world, a world which had long since ceased to exist and was closed, accounted for, and passive. What desire could it arouse? He wished to portray it.

Antony and Cleopatra is the story of a rake and a temptress. In describing them as they burn up their lives Shakespeare uses the tones of mystery fitting to a genuine bacchanalia in the classical sense.

Historians have written that neither Antony nor Cleopatra (nor his companions in his feasts, nor the courtiers who were in her confidence) expected any good to come of the debauchery which they had promoted to the status of a ritual. Foreseeing the end, they spoke of themselves, long before it came, as immortal suicides and promised to die together.

This indeed is the conclusion of the tragedy. At the decisive moment death is the draftsman who lends the story the connecting outline which it had so far lacked. Against the background of campaigns, fires, treason, and defeats, we take leave on two separate occasions of the two principal characters. In the fourth act the hero stabs himself, and the heroine commits suicide in the fifth.

THE AUDIENCE

Shakespeare's chronicles of English history abound in hints at the topical events of his day. There were no newspapers: to hear the news (as G. B. Harrison notes in his *England in Shakespeare's Day*) people gathered in taverns and theaters. Drama spoke in hints. Nor is it surprising that the common people understood them since they concerned facts which were close to everyone.

The political open secret of the time was the difficulties of the war with Spain, started with enthusiasm but which had soon become a bore. For fifteen years it had been waged by land and sea, off the coast of Portugal and in the Netherlands and in Ireland.

Falstaff's parodies of martial speeches amused the simple, peaceful public, which plainly understood what was meant, and which laughed still more heartily at his recruiting scene (where the recruits bribe their way out) because it knew the truth of it by experience.

A great deal more astonishing is another example of the intelligence of the contemporary audience.

The works of Shakespeare, as of all Elizabethans, are full of appeals to history and ancient literature and of mythological examples and names. To understand them nowadays, even reference book in hand, one needs to be a classical scholar; yet we are told that the average Londoner of those days caught these flickering allusions in mid-air and digested them without the least trouble. How are we to believe this?

The explanation is that the school curriculum was very different from ours. A knowledge of Latin, which is now taken for a sign of higher education, was then the lowest step to learning, just as Church Slavonic used to be in Russia. In the primary, so-called grammar schools—and Shakespeare went to one of them—Latin was the spoken language and, according to the historian Trevelyan, the schoolboys were not allowed to use English even in their games. Those London apprentices and shop assistants who could read and write were as much at home with Fortune, Heracles, and Niobe as a modern schoolboy with internal combustion and the elements of electricity.

Shakespeare was born in time to find a well-established, century-old way of life still in being. His age was a festive period in England's history. By the end of the next reign the balance of things had already been upset.

AUTHENTICITY OF SHAKESPEARE'S AUTHORSHIP

Shakespeare's work is a whole and he is everywhere true to himself. He is recognizable by his vocabulary. Certain of his characters appear under different names in play after play and he sings the same song over and over to different tunes. His habit of repeating and paraphrasing himself is particularly noticeable in *Hamlet*.

In a scene with Horatio, Hamlet tells him that he is a man and cannot be played upon like a pipe.

A few pages further on he asks Guildenstern, in the same allegorical sense, whether he would like to play the pipe.

In the first player's monologue about the cruelty of Fortune in allowing Priam to be killed, the gods are urged to punish her by breaking her wheel, the symbol of her power, and flinging the pieces down from heaven to Tartarus. A few pages further on, Rosencrantz, speaking to the King, compares a monarch's power to a wheel fixed on a mount which, if its foundations are shaken, destroys everything on its way as it hurtles down.

Juliet takes the dagger from dead Romeo's side and stabs herself with the words "This is thy sheath." A few lines further on her father uses the same words about the dagger resting in Juliet's breast instead of in the sheath on Romeo's belt. And so on, almost at every step. What does this mean?

Translating Shakespeare is a task which takes time and effort. Once it is undertaken, it is best to divide it into sections long enough for the work not to get stale and to complete one section each day. In thus daily progressing through the text, the translator finds himself reliving the circumstances of the author. Day by day he reproduces his actions and he is drawn into some of his secrets, not in theory but practically, by experience.

Stumbling on such repetitions as I have mentioned and realizing how close together they are, he cannot help asking himself in surprise: "Who and in what conditions would remember so little of what he had put down only a few days earlier?"

Then, with a tangible certainty which is not given to the biographer or the scholar, the translator becomes aware of the personality of Shakespeare and of his genius. In twenty years Shakespeare wrote thirty-six plays, not to speak of his poems and sonnets. Forced to write two plays a year on an average, he had no time to revise and, constantly forgetting what he had written the day before, he repeated himself in his hurry.

At this point the absurdity of the Baconian theory becomes more striking than ever. What need was there to replace the simple and in no way improbable account of Shakespeare's life by a tangle of mysterious substitutions and their alleged discoveries?

Is it conceivable that Rutland, Bacon, or Southampton should have disguised himself so unsuccessfully; that, using a cypher or a faked identity, he should have hidden from Elizabeth and her time only to reveal himself so carelessly to later generations? What cunning, what ulterior purpose can be imagined in the mind of this highly reckless man who undoubtedly existed, who was not ashamed of slips of the pen, and who, yawning with fatigue in the face of history, remembered less of his own work than any high school pupil knows of it today? His strength shows itself in his weaknesses.

There is another puzzling thing. Why is it that ungifted people are so passionately interested in those who are great? They have their own conception of the artist, a conception which is idle, agreeable, and false. They start by assuming that Shakespeare was a genius in the sense in which they understand genius; they apply their yardstick to him and he fails to measure up to it.

His life, they find, was too obscure and workaday for his fame. He had no library of his own and his signature at the bottom of his will is a scrawl. It strikes them as suspicious that a man who knew the soil, the crops, the animals, and all the hours of the day and night as simple people know them should also have been at home with law, history, diplomacy, and the ways and habits of courtiers. And so they are astonished, amazed, forgetting that so great an artist must inevitably sum up everything human in himself.

KING HENRY IV

The period of Shakespeare's life about which there can be least doubt is his youth.

I am thinking of the time when he had just come to London as an unknown young provincial from Stratford. Probably he stayed for a while in the suburbs, further from the center of the town than a cabby would take his fare. Probably, out there, there was a sort of Yamskie village. With travelers to and from London stopping on their way, the place must have had something of the bustling life of a modern railway station; and there were probably lakes, woods, market gardens, stagecoach inns, booths, and amusement parks in the neighborhood. There may have been theaters. Smart people from London came to have a good time.

It was a world which had something about it of the Tverskie-Yamskie of the middle of the last century when, on the outskirts of Moscow, beyond the river—surrounded by the nine muses and by lofty theories, troikas, publicans, gipsy choirs, and educated merchants who patronized the arts—lived and struggled the most distinguished Russian heirs of the young man from Stratford, Apollon Grigoryev and Ostrovsky.

The young man had no definite occupation but an unusually brilliant star. His belief in it had brought him to the capital. He did not yet know his future role, but his sense of life told him that he would play it unbelievably well.

Whatever he took up had been done before him: people had composed verses and plays, acted, obliged the visiting gentry, and tried as hard as they could to make their way in the world. But whatever this young man took up, he felt such an astonishing up-surge of strength that it was clearly best for him to break with all established habits and do everything in his own way.

Before him, only what was artificial and remote from life had been regarded as art. This artificiality was obligatory, and it was a convenient cloak for spiritual impotence and for inability to draw. But Shakespeare had so good an eye and so sure a hand that it was clearly to his advantage to upset the existing convention.

He realized how much he would gain if, instead of staying at the usual distance from life, he walked up to it—not on stilts but on his own legs—and, measuring himself against it, forced it to look down first before his stubbornly unblinking stare.

There was a company of actors, writers, and their patrons who went from pub to pub, baited strangers, and consistently risked their necks by laughing at everything in the world. The most reck-less of them, who yet remained unharmed (he got away with everything), the least moderate and the most sober (drink never went to his head), the one who raised the loudest laugh and who was yet the most reserved, was this gloomy youth who was already striding into the future in his seven-league boots.

Perhaps there really was a fat old Falstaff who went about with these young people. Or perhaps Shakespeare invented him later as an embodiment of that time.

It was not only as a gay memory that it became dear to him: this was the time which saw the birth of Shakespeare's realism. It was not in the solitude of his study that he conceived it but in the early hours in an unmade room in an inn, a room as charged with life as a gun with powder. Shakespeare's realism is not the pro-fundity of a reformed rake nor the hackneyed "wisdom" of later experience. That which is most earnest, grave, tragic, and essential in his art arose out of his consciousness of success and strength in those wild early days of desperate fooling, inventiveness, and hourly mortal danger.

KING LEAR

The productions of *King Lear* are always too noisy. There is the willful, obstinate old man, there are the gatherings in the echoing palace hall, shouts, orders, and afterwards curses and sobs of despair merging with the rolls of thunder and the noises of the wind. But in fact, the only stormy thing in the play is the tempest at night, while the people, huddled in the tent and terrified, speak in whispers.

Lear is as quiet as *Romeo*, and for the same reason. In *Romeo* it is the love of lovers which is persecuted and in hiding; in *Lear* it is filial love and, more widely, the love of one's neighbor, the love of truth.

Only the criminals in *King Lear* wield the notions of duty and honor; they alone are sensible and eloquent, and logic and reason assist them in their frauds, cruelties, and murders. All the decent people are either silent to the point of being indistinguishable from each other or make obscure and contradictory statements which lead to misunderstandings. The positive heroes are the fools, the madmen, the dying, and the vanquished.

Such is the content of this play written in the language of the Old Testament prophets and situated in a legendary epoch of pre-Christian barbarism.

COMEDY AND TRAGEDY IN SHAKESPEARE

There is no pure comedy or tragedy in Shakespeare. His style is between the two and made up of both; it is thus closer to the true face of life than either, for in life, too, horrors and delights are mixed. This has been accounted to him as a merit by all English critics, from Samuel Johnson to T. S. Eliot.

To Shakespeare, the difference between tragedy and comedy was not merely the difference between the lofty and the commonplace, the ideal and the real. He used them rather as the major and minor keys in music. In arranging his material he employed poetry and prose and the transitions from one to the other as variations in music.

These transitions are the chief characteristic of his dramatic art; they are at the very heart of his stagecraft and they convey that hidden rhythm of thought and mood which I referred to in my note on *Hamlet*.

All his dramas are made up of swiftly alternating scenes of tragedy and tomfoolery. One aspect of this method is particularly marked.

On the edge of Ophelia's grave the audience is made to laugh at the philosophizing of the grave-diggers. At the moment when Juliet's corpse is carried out, the boy from the servants' hall giggles at the musicians who have been invited to a wedding, and the musicians bargain with the nurse who is trying to get rid of them. Cleopatra's suicide is preceded by the appearance of the half-wit Egyptian snake-charmer with his absurd reflections on the uselessness of reptiles—almost as in Maeterlinck or in Leonid Andreyev!

Shakespeare was the father and the prophet of realism. His influence on Pushkin, Victor Hugo, and other poets is well known. He was studied by the German romantics. One of the Schlegels translated him into German and the other drew on him for his theory of romantic irony. Goethe, as the symbolist author of *Faust*, was his descendant. Finally, to keep only to the essentials, as a dramatist he is the predecessor of Chekhov and of Ibsen.

It is in this same spirit, which he transmitted to his heirs, that he makes vulgar mediocrity snort and rush in on the funereal solemnity of his finales.

Its irruption makes the mystery of death, already inaccessibly remote from us, withdraw still further. The respectful distance we keep between ourselves and the threshold of what is lofty and frightening grows a little longer still. No situation as seen by the artist or the thinker is final; every position is the last but one. It is as if Shakespeare were afraid lest the audience should believe too firmly in the seemingly unconditional finality of his dénouements. By breaking up the rhythm at the end he re-establishes infinity. In keeping with the character of modern art and in contrast to the fatalism of the ancient world, he dissolves the mortal, temporal quality of the individual sign in its immortal, universal significance.

MACBETH

Macbeth might well have been called *Crime and Punishment.*
All the time I was translating it I was haunted by its likeness to
Dostoevsky's novel.

Planning the murder of Banquo, Macbeth tells his hired murderers:

> *Your spirits shine through you. Within this hour at most*
> *I will advise you where to plant yourselves,*
> *Acquaint you with the perfect spy o' the time,*
> *The moment on't; for 't must be done tonight,*
> *And something from the palace . . .*

A little further on, in the third scene of the third act, the murderers, lying in ambush for Banquo, watch the guests arriving
through the park.

SECOND MURDERER:
> *Then 'tis he: the rest*
> *That are within the note of expectation*
> *Already are i' the court.*

FIRST MURDERER:
> *His horses go about.*

THIRD MURDERER:
> *Almost a mile: but he does usually—*
> *So all men do—from hence to the palace gate*
> *Make it their walk . . .*

Murder is a desperate, dangerous business. Everything must be
thought out, every possibility must be foreseen. Both Shakespeare
and Dostoevsky endow their heroes with their own foresight and
imagination, their own capacities for timeliness, detail, and precision. Both the novel and the play have the sharp, heightened
realism of detection and of detective fiction: the cautious wariness
of the policeman who looks over his shoulder as often as the criminal himself.

Neither Macbeth nor Raskolnikov is a born criminal or a villain
by nature. They are turned into criminals by faulty rationaliza-
tions, by deductions from false premises.

In one case the impetus is given by the prophecy of the witches who set the vanity of Macbeth ablaze. In the other, it comes from the extreme nihilistic proposition that, if there is no God, everything is allowed, and therefore a murder is in no way different from any other human act.

Of the two, Macbeth feels particularly safe from retribution. What could threaten him? A forest walking across a plain? A man not born of woman?—Such things don't exist, they are blatant absurdities. In other words, he may shed blood fearlessly. And what, in any case, has he to fear from justice once he has seized kingly power and become the only source of law? It all seems so clear and logical! What could be more simple and obvious? And so the crimes follow in quick succession—many crimes over a long time—until the forest suddenly moves and sets out on its way and an avenger comes who is not born of woman.

Incidentally, about Lady Macbeth—coolness and will power are not her predominant qualities. I think that what is strongest in her is something more generally feminine. She is one of those active, insistent wives, a woman who is her husband's helper, his support, for whom her husband's interests are her own and who takes his plans on faith once and for all. She neither discusses them nor judges nor selects among them. To reason, to doubt, to make plans—that's her husband's business, it's his lookout. She is his executive, more resolute and consistent than he is himself. Miscalculating her strength, she assumes the excessive burden and is destroyed, not by conscience but by spiritual exhaustion, sadness, and fatigue.

—*Translated by Manya Harari*

PHILOSOPHY AND HISTORY

Theodor Mommsen

THEODOR MOMMSEN, *the German historian and archeologist, was the second writer to win the Nobel Prize for Literature (the first was Rene Sully-Prudhomme). Born in 1817 in Schleswig, he took his Ph.D. at the University of Kiel and then specialized in Roman law and antiquities. When the Danish government in 1843 gave him a grant to study Roman inscriptions in Italy, he made plans to collect all such existing inscriptions and had actually finished the study in one town before he returned to Germany to take a professorship of Roman law at the University of Leipzig. He was soon removed from this post because of his political opinions and his activities in the German Revolution of 1848; he then went to Switzerland, where he taught and embarked upon his great* History of Rome *(1854-56). Mommsen's attitude toward history was unusual for his period: drawing upon his own political experience and adopting a modern tone, he gave the figures with whom he dealt a new life. The following selection from his great work,* The Portrait of Julius Cæsar, *is an outstanding example of his method. Mommsen became professor at Berlin University where he remained until his death in Charlottenberg in 1903, the year after receiving the prize. He also served as Liberal member of the Prussian parliament, where he opposed the domestic policies of Bismarck and once called his tariff policy "Politik von Schwindel." During his lifetime, he produced many articles and other scholarly works of enduring value.*

The first ruler over the whole domain of Romano-Hellenic civilization, Gaius Julius Cæsar, was in his fifty-sixth year (born 12 July 102 B.C.) when the battle at Thapsus, the last link in a long chain of momentous victories, placed the decision as to the future of the world in his hands. Few men have had their elasticity so thoroughly put to the proof as Cæsar—the

sole creative genius produced by Rome, and the last produced by
the ancient world, which accordingly moved on in the path that he
marked out for it until its sun went down. Sprung from one of
the oldest noble families of Latium—which traced back its lineage
to the heroes of the Iliad and the kings of Rome, and in fact to
the Venus-Aphrodite common to both nations—he spent the
years of his boyhood and early manhood as the genteel youth of
that epoch were wont to spend them. He had tasted the sweetness
as well as the bitterness of the cup of fashionable life, had recited
and declaimed, had practiced literature and made verses in his idle
hours, had prosecuted love-intrigues of every sort, and got himself
initiated into all the mysteries of shaving, curls, and ruffles per-
taining to the toilette-wisdom of the day, as well as into the
still more mysterious art of always borrowing and never paying.
But the flexible steel of that nature was proof against even these
dissipated and flighty courses; Cæsar retained both his bodily
vigor and his elasticity of mind and of heart unimpaired. In fenc-
ing and in riding he was a match for any of his soldiers, and his
swimming saved his life at Alexandria; the incredible rapidity of
his journeys, which usually for the sake of gaining time were performed by night—a thorough contrast to the procession-like slow-
ness with which Pompeius moved from one place to another—
was the astonishment of his comtemporaries and not the least
among the causes of his success. The mind was like the body. His
remarkable power of intuition revealed itself in the precision and
practicability of all his arrangements, even where he gave orders
without having seen with his own eyes. His memory was match-
less, and it was easy for him to carry on several occupations simultaneously with equal self-possession. Although a gentleman, a man
of genius, and a monarch, he still had a heart. So long as he lived,
he cherished the purest veneration for his worthy mother Aurelia
(his father having died early); to his wives and above all to his
daughter Julia he devoted an honorable affection, which was not
without reflex influence even on political affairs. With the ablest
and most excellent men of his time of high and of humbler rank,
he maintained noble relations of mutual fidelity, with each after
his kind. As he himself never abandoned any of his partisans after
the pusillanimous and unfeeling manner of Pompeius, but ad-

hered to his friends—and that not merely from calculation—through good and bad times without wavering, several of these, such as Aulus Hirtius and Gaius Martius, gave, even after his death, noble testimonies of their attachment to him.

If in a nature so harmoniously organized any one aspect of it may be singled out as characteristic, it is this—that he stood aloof from all ideology and everything fanciful. As a matter of course, Cæsar was a man of passion, for without passion there is no genius; but his passion was never stronger than he could control. He had had his season of youth, and song, love, and wine had taken lively possession of his spirit; but with him they did not penetrate to the inmost core of his nature. Literature occupied him long and earnestly; but, while Alexander could not sleep for thinking of the Homeric Achilles, Cæsar in his sleepless hours mused on the inflections of the Latin nouns and verbs. He made verses, as everybody then did, but they were weak; on the other hand he was interested in subjects of astronomy and natural science. While wine was and continued to be with Alexander the destroyer of care, the temperate Roman, after the revels of his youth were over, avoided it entirely. Around him, as around all those whom the full luster of woman's love has dazzled in youth, fainter gleams of it continued imperishably to linger; even in later years he had love-adventures and successes with women, and he retained a certain foppishness in his outward appearance, or, to speak more correctly, the pleasing consciousness of his own manly beauty. He carefully covered the baldness, which he keenly felt, with the laurel chaplet that he wore in public in his later years, and he would doubtless have surrendered some of his victories, if he could thereby have brought back his youthful locks. But, however much even when monarch he enjoyed the society of women, he only amused himself with them, and allowed them no manner of influence over him; even his much-censured relation to queen Cleopatra was only contrived to mask a weak point in his political position.

Cæsar was thoroughly a realist and a man of sense; and whatever he undertook and achieved was pervaded and guided by the cool sobriety which constitutes the most marked peculiarity of his genius. To this he owed the power of living energetically in the present, undisturbed either by recollection or by expectation; to this he owed the capacity of acting at any moment with collected vigor, and of applying his whole genius even to the smallest and most incidental enterprise; to this he owed the many-sided power with which he grasped and mastered whatever understanding can comprehend and will can compel; to this he owed the self-possessed ease with which he arranged his periods as well as projected his campaigns; to this he owed the "marvelous serenity" which remained steadily with him through good and evil days; to this he owed the complete independence, which admitted of no control by favorite or by mistress, or even by friend. It resulted, moreover, from this clearness of judgment that Cæsar never formed to himself illusions regarding the power of fate and the ability of man; in his case the friendly veil was lifted, which conceals from man the inadequacy of his working. Prudently as he laid plans and considered all possibilities, the feeling was never absent from his breast that in all things fortune, that is to say accident, must bestow success; and with this may be connected the circumstance that he so often played a desperate game with destiny, and in particular again and again hazarded his person with daring indifference. As indeed occasionally men of predominant sagacity betake themselves to a pure game of hazard, so there was in Cæsar's rationalism a point at which it came in some measure into contact with mysticism.

Gifts such as these could not fail to produce a statesman. From early youth, accordingly, Cæsar was a statesman in the deepest sense of the term, and his aim was the highest which man is allowed to propose to himself—the political, military, intellectual, and moral regeneration of his own deeply decayed nation, and of the still more deeply decayed Hellenic nation intimately akin to his own. The hard school of thirty years' experience changed his views as to the means by which this aim was to be reached; his aim itself remained the same in the times of his hopeless humiliation and of his unlimited plenitude of power, in the times when as demagogue and conspirator he stole towards it by paths of darkness, and in those when, as joint possessor of the supreme power and then as monarch, he worked at his task in the full light of day before the eyes of the world. All the measures of a permanent kind that proceeded from him at the most various times assume their appropriate places in the great building-plan. We cannot therefore properly speak of isolated achievements of Cæsar; he did nothing isolated. With justice men commend Cæsar the orator for his masculine eloquence, which, scorning all the arts of the advocate, like a clear flame at once enlightened and warmed. With justice men admire in Cæsar the author the inimitable simplicity of the composition, the unique purity and beauty of the language. With justice the greatest masters of war of all times have praised Cæsar the general, who, in a singular degree disregarding routine and tradition, knew always how to find out the mode of warfare by which in the given case the enemy was conquered, and which was thus in the given case the right one; who with the certainty of divination found the proper means for every end; who after defeat stood ready for battle like William of Orange, and ended the campaign invariably with victory; who managed that element of warfare, the treatment of which serves to distinguish military genius from the mere ordinary ability of an officer—the rapid movement of masses —with unsurpassed perfection, and found the guarantee of victory not in the massiveness of his forces but in the celerity of their movements, not in long preparation but in rapid and daring action even with inadequate means. But all these were with Cæsar mere secondary matters; he was no doubt a great orator, author, and general, but he became each of these merely because he was a consummate statesman. The soldier more especially played in him altogether an accessory part, and it is one of the principal peculiarities that he began his political activity not as an officer, but as a demagogue. According to his original plan he had purposed to reach his object, like Pericles and Gaius Gracchus, without force of arms, and throughout eighteen years he had as leader of the popular party moved exclusively amid political plans and intrigues—until, reluctantly convinced of the necessity for a military support, he, when already forty years of age, put himself at the head of an army. It was natural that he should even afterwards remain still more statesman than general—just like Cromwell, who also transformed himself from a leader of opposition into a military chief and democratic king, and who in general, little as the prince of Puritans seems to resemble the dissolute Roman, is yet in his development as well as in the objects which he aimed at and the results which he achieved of all statesmen perhaps the most akin to Cæsar. Even in his mode of warfare this improvised generalship may still be recognized; the enterprises of Napoleon against Egypt and against England do not more clearly exhibit the artillery-lieutenant who had risen by service to command than the similar enterprises of Cæsar exhibit the demagogue metamorphosed into a general. A regularly trained officer would hardly have been prepared, through political considerations of a not altogether stringent nature, to set aside the best-founded military scruples in the way in which Cæsar did on several occasions, most strikingly in the case of his landing in Epirus. Several of his acts are therefore censurable from a military point of view; but what the general loses, the statesman gains. The task of the statesman is universal in its nature like Cæsar's genius; if he undertook things the most varied and most remote one from another, they had all without exception a bearing on the one great object to which with infinite fidelity and consistency he devoted himself; and of the manifold aspects and directions of his great activity he never preferred one to another. Although a master of the art of war, he yet from statesmanly considerations did his utmost to avert civil strife and, when it nevertheless began, to earn laurels stained as little as possible by blood. Although the founder of a military monarchy, he yet, with an energy unexampled in history, allowed no hierarchy of marshals or government of praetorians to come into existence. If he had a preference for any one form of services rendered to the state, it was for the sciences and arts of peace rather than for those of war.

The most remarkable peculiarity of his action as a statesman was its perfect harmony. In reality all the conditions for this most difficult of all human functions were united in Cæsar. A thorough realist, he never allowed the images of the past or venerable tradition to disturb him; for him nothing was of value in politics but the living present and the law of reason, just as in his character of grammarian he set aside historical and antiquarian *loquendi* and on the other hand the rule of symmetry. A born ruler, he governed the minds of men as the wind drives the clouds, and compelled the most heterogeneous natures to place themselves at his service —the plain citizen and the rough subaltern, the genteel matrons of Rome and the fair princesses of Egypt and Mauretania, the brilliant cavalry-officer and the calculating banker. His talent for organization was marvelous; no statesman has ever compelled alliances, no general has ever collected an army out of unyielding and refractory elements with such decision, and kept them together with such firmness, as Cæsar displayed in constraining and upholding his coalitions and his legends; never did regent judge his instruments and assign each to the place appropriate for him with so acute an eye.

He was monarch; but he never played the king. Even when absolute lord of Rome, he retained the deportment of the party-leader; perfectly pliant and smooth, easy and charming in conversation, complaisant towards everyone, it seemed as if he wished to be nothing but the first among his peers. Cæsar entirely avoided the blunder into which so many men otherwise on an equality with him have fallen, of carrying into politics the military tone of command; however much occasion his disagreeable relations with the senate gave for it, he never resorted to outrages such as was that of the eighteenth Brumaire. Cæsar was monarch; but he was never seized with the giddiness of the tyrant. He is perhaps the only one among the mighty ones of the earth, who in great matters and little never acted according to inclination or caprice, but always without exception according to his duty as a ruler, and who, when he looked back on his life, found doubtless erroneous calculations to deplore, but no false step of passion to regret. There is nothing in the history of Cæsar's life, which even on a small scale can be compared with those poetico-sensual ebullitions— such as the murder of Kleitos or the burning of Persepolis—which the history of his great predecessor in the east records. He is, in fine, perhaps the only one of those mighty ones, who has preserved to the end of his career the statesman's tact of discriminating between the possible and the impossible, and has not broken down in the task which for greatly gifted natures is the most difficult of all—the task of recognizing, when on the pinnacle of success, its natural limits. What was possible he performed, and never left the possible good undone for the sake of the impossible better, never disdained at least to mitigate by palliatives evils that were incurable. But where he recognized that fate had spoken, he always obeyed. Alexander on the Hypanis, Napoleon at Moscow, turned back because they were compelled to do so, and were indignant at destiny for bestowing even on its favorites merely limited successes; Cæsar turned back voluntarily on the Thames and on the Rhine; and thought of carrying into effect even at the Danube and the Euphrates not unbounded plans of world-conquest, but merely well-considered frontier-regulations.

Such was this unique man, whom it seems so easy and yet is so infinitely difficult to describe. His whole nature is transparent clearness; and tradition preserves more copious and more vivid information about him than about any of his peers in the ancient world. Of such a personage our conceptions may well vary in point of shallowness or depth, but they cannot be, strictly speaking, different; to every not utterly perverted inquirer the grand figure has exhibited the same essential features, and yet no one has succeeded in reproducing it to the life. The secret lies in its perfection. In his character as a man as well as in his place in history, Cæsar occupies a position where the great contrasts of existence meet and balance each other. Of mighty creative power and yet at the same time of the most penetrating judgment; no longer a youth and not yet an old man; of the highest energy of will and the highest capacity of execution; filled with republican ideals and at the same time born to be a king; a Roman in the deepest essence of his nature, and yet called to reconcile and combine in himself as well as in the outer world the Romanic and the Hellenic types of culture—Cæsar was the entire and perfect man. Accordingly we miss in him more than in any other historical personage what are called characteristic features, which are in reality nothing else than deviations from the natural course of human development. What in Cæsar passes for such at the first superficial glance is, when more closely observed, seen to be the peculiarity not of the individual, but of the epoch of culture or of the nation; his youthful adventures, for instance, were common to him with all his more gifted contemporaries of like position, his unpoetical but strongly logical temperament was the tempera-

ment of Romans in general. It formed part also of Cæsar's full
humanity, that he was in the highest degree influenced by the
conditions of time and place; for there is no abstract humanity—
the living man cannot but occupy a place in a given nationality
and in a definite line of culture. Cæsar was a perfect man just because he more than any other placed himself amidst the currents
of his time, and because he more than any other possessed the essential peculiarity of the Roman nation—practical aptitude as a
citizen—in perfection: for his Hellenism in fact was only the Hellenism which had been long intimately blended with the Italian
nationality. But in this very circumstance lies the difficulty, we
may perhaps say the impossibility, of depicting Cæsar to the life.
As the artist can paint everything save only consummate beauty, so
the historian, when once in a thousand years he encounters the
perfect, can only be silent regarding it. For normality admits
doubtless of being expressed, but it gives us only the negative notion of the absence of defect; the secret of nature, whereby in her
most finished manifestations normality and individuality are combined, is beyond expression. Nothing is left for us but to deem
those fortunate who beheld this perfection, and to gain some faint
conception of it from the reflected luster which rest imperishably
on the works that were the creation of this great nature. These
also, it is true, bear the stamp of the time. The Roman hero
himself stood by the side of his youthful Greek predecessor not
merely as an equal, but as a superior; but the world had meanwhile become old and its youthful luster had faded. The action of
Cæsar was no longer, like that of Alexander, a joyous marching
onward towards a goal indefinitely remote; he built on, and out
of, ruins, and was content to establish himself as tolerably and
as securely as possible within the ample but yet definite bounds
once assigned to him. With reason therefore the delicate poetic
tact of the nations has not troubled itself about the unpoetical
Roman, and on the other hand has invested the son of Philip with
all the golden luster of poetry, with all the rainbow hues of legend. But with equal reason the political life of the nations has
during thousands of years again and again reverted to the lines
which Cæsar drew; and that fact, that the peoples to whom the

world belongs still at the present day designate the highest of their monarchs by his name, conveys a warning deeply significant and, unhappily, fraught with shame.

Rudolf Eucken

BACK TO RELIGION

RUDOLF EUCKEN, *the German philosopher, left his native Friesland to study ancient history and classical philology before discovering that his chief interest lay in the field of religious philosophy. In 1874, he was appointed to the chair of philosophy at the University of Jena, a post he held until 1920. Early in his career, he wrote about the philosophic system of Aristotle, but later turned his attention to the ethical and religious problems confronting the ordinary man. The vigorous and idealistic challenge of his books succeeded in reaching a wide popular public, and in 1908, he was awarded the Nobel Prize for Literature. Believing that man is the meeting ground of nature and spirit, he urged the conquest of his non-spiritual nature by incessant striving after the spiritual life. Eucken died in Jena in 1926, at the age of eighty. Among his books available to English-reading audiences are* The Life of the Spirit *and* The Problems of Human Life *(1909),* Collected Essays *(1911) and* Can We Still Be Christians? *(1914). The following essay, typical of his thought, is as pertinent today as when he wrote it during his brief stay in America.*

He is but a superficial observer of the times who can think that the movement of life today is altogether against religion, and that only the denial of religion has the spirit of the age with it.

For, certain as it is that blatant denial still holds the public ear and is more and more permeating the masses, yet in the work of the intellect, and likewise in the depths of men's souls, the case is different. Here, with ever greater vigor, is springing up the feeling that religion is indispensable, the yearning for religion. What is understood by religion is often anything but clear, and often very different from the traditional forms of religion; but the demand is unmistakable for more depth of life and for the establishment of profounder inner connections than our visible existence affords. In the spiritual life of the present day, molecular transformations are taking place, inconspicuous at first but constantly increasing, which will eventually burst upon our view, and which will necessarily provoke essential changes in the entire condition of life. To-day this movement is still an undercurrent, and on the surface the tide flows in the opposite direction. But more and more the undercurrent is rising to the surface, and unless every indication fails, it will soon come into control.

The most fundamental reason for this tendency may be indicated by a single sentence. It is caused by the increasing dissatisfaction with modern civilization, or at least with those aspects of civilization which now occupy the surface of life. All the splendor of external successes of civilization cannot hide the fact that it does not satisfy the whole man with his inner needs, and that the amelioration of the world around us which it has accomplished does not compensate for the inner emptiness of its excessive concentration of effort on the visible world, its secularization of life.

We moderns have set ourselves at work with all our might, have acquired technical perfection, have combined isolated achievements into great systems. By the increased efficiency of our labor we have increasingly subdued the world, and at the same time have imposed upon human society a far more rational form. But, while we have given every care and effort to the means and conditions of life, we have exposed ourselves to the risk of losing life itself, and while performing astounding external feats, inwardly we have become smaller and smaller. Our work has separated itself from our souls, and it now reacts overmasteringly upon them, threatening to absorb them utterly. Our own creations have become our masters and oppressors. Moreover, as the division of labor increases, work constantly becomes more specialized and engages an ever smaller part of each individual soul; the whole man comes less and less to activity, and we lose any superior unity of our nature. Thus more and more we become mere parts of the civilization-machine.

The dangers thus arising were not felt to be so serious a menace, as long as religion and a culture controlled by ideals kept before men's minds another conception of life. But now that these are weakened and repressed, this trend toward the visible world meets less and less resistance. Yet it is true that as a result of the same process the accompanying loss is at least clearly seen and keenly felt. The victory itself is thus calling forth a counter-movement, and the outer triumph, by letting us plainly discern the limits of human power, is being transformed into an inner defeat. An independence once gained for the spiritual life can be temporarily obscured, but not permanently destroyed. At one and the same moment the craving that life should have more soul and depth is expressing itself with elemental power, and, on the other hand, it is becoming clear that, if the All is without soul and no new spiritual world stands open before us, we humans, too, can have no souls. The result is that we are again driven into the path of religion, since without religion life cannot find the longed-for depth.

This craving for soul is accompanied by a craving for continuance and eternity.

Modernity has abandoned religion's mode of conceiving life and the world *sub specie aeternitatis*, has left eternity colorless and empty in its uncurbed desire to plunge full into the current of the time, to uplift conditions here, and from this world to derive all its forces. In all this a special importance has attached to the idea of development. Instead of thinking their position to be fixed and unshakable by the appointment of a higher power, be it God or fate, men have come to think of our life as still in flux, and its condition as susceptible of measureless improvement; above all the immaturity and all the losses of the present has arisen the confident hope of a better and ever better future. Such a conviction has led men to devote endeavor entirely to the living present and carefully to adjust effort to the existing stage of evolution. That contributes great freshness and mobility to life; all rigidity is dispelled, all magnitudes become fluid, infinite increase multiplies the abundant forms.

Without in any wise attacking or disparaging all this, one's own experience of life yet makes it more and more clear that this trend has its dangers and limitations. To yield to the tendency of the times seemed at first to bring clear gain, for a group of persistent convictions still maintained themselves and supplied a counterbalancing repose. More and more, however, the movement drew into itself these survivals; more and more exclusively it mastered all life. It constantly became more swift, more hurried, more agitated; the changes followed faster and faster, one moment crowded on another, and the present was reduced to a passing instant. But in this process it has become apparent that this passionate forward striving leaves no room for true life. And, further, all courage must needs perish, so soon as we are forced to the conviction that everything which we today revere as true, good, beautiful, is subject to change and may tomorrow be cast aside as obsolete. He who unreflectingly lives merely for the moment may in all seriousness look upon that moment as the acme of the whole; but he who looks a little farther cannot doubt that it will be no better with us than with those who went before us, and that the saying still holds which according to Indian doctrines the spirits of the dead cry to the living: "We were what you are; you shall be what we are." In fine, if life is all strung on the thin thread of successive moments, each crowding back its predecessor, so that when the moment vanishes all action at once sinks again into the abyss of nothingness, then, in spite of all the exciting activity of the moment, life becomes a mere shadow.

If only we were quite sure that all our pains and care and haste were bringing about progress for the whole of human life! But that, again, we are not. True, we are constantly advancing in exact science, as we are in the technical mastery of our environment; we are compelling the elements into our service; we are freeing our existence from pain and enriching it with pleasure. But are we by all that winning a closer connection with the depths of reality? Are we growing in spiritual power as in ethical sentiment? Are we becoming greater and nobler men? As life gains in pleasure, do our inner contentment and true happiness increase in due proportion? In truth, we are growing only in our relations to the world outside, not in the essence of our being and hence the question is not to be evaded, whether the unspeakable toil of modern civilization is worth while. We work and work, and know not to what end; for in giving up eternity we have also lost every inner bond of the ages and all power of comprehensive view. Without a guiding star we drift on the waves of time.

As soon as this becomes a fact of clear consciousness and individual experience, either all courage to live must collapse or we must again discover within our domain, and resuscitate, something durable, something eternal, to give us support against the flight of the moments and to permit us to work for durable aims. Otherwise, our life has no sense and no value. That a longing for such an eternity, for a superiority to mere movement, pervades our time, is revealed by many signs. But such a craving leads, if not directly to religion, yet near to religion, as the chief representative of eternal truth.

Again, men crave more love and more solidarity in the human race than modern civilization affords, and that, too, is driving men to religion. Christianity not only had made love the kernel of religion, but also, starting from a Kingdom of God, it had established an inner human solidarity and created an organization on a spiritual foundation. For the modern age, however, so far as it went its own way, other aims came to the front. The chief thing came to be the individual, his emancipation from all hindrances, the development of all his powers, their unlimited enhancement. In all departments of life the independent development of the individual is a chief trait of the modern world; each of the great civilized nations in its own way has contributed to it, according as each has found its high level in art and literature, in religion, or in political and social life. Now for a time this individualism did not come into collision with the old ideals, for the individual found the totality of a spiritual world present within him, so that each one in his proper station could make it his chief task to stamp his own peculiar form on this inner world and to render it his peculiar service. But the situation altered as soon as that world of the spirit faded and disappeared. With it vanished everything that inwardly united individuals and bound their souls together. One individual became inwardly indifferent to another, and the way was opened for a man to make his highest aim his own personal advancement and utmost selfish gain, in total un-concern for anyone else.

The same principles which govern individual conduct are ex-tended to social groups and entire nations; self-interest is the sin-gle rule of action, the moral solidarity of mankind is relaxed and dissolved. The danger is imminent that the end may be a war of all against all. Undoubtedly the resulting rivalry and strife has ef-fected much that is great; it has given life a thorough shaking up, and banished all idle repose. And on this new foundation cohe-sive forces are by no means lacking. Such a force in particular is Work, which with its growth to great combinations perfects or-ganization, assigns to each single element a definite part, and binds them all firmly together. But such gearing together of perform-ances by no means amounts to harmony of sentiment; if it did, the antinomies of the social question and our economic conflicts would be impossible. In truth, combination in work does not pre-vent wide divergence of conviction and opinion, or even mutual hatred and strife. Sects and parties are increasing; common esti-mates and ideals keep slipping away from us; we understand one another less and less, and are falling deeper and deeper into a confused Babel of tongues. Even voluntary association, that form of human unity peculiar to modern times, the free union of many individuals, unites more in accomplishment than in disposi-tion, brings men together outwardly rather than inwardly. Thus, among the monstrous confusions of the present time the demand for stable connections grows insistent, connections which shall take concern both for the common zeal and for the individual. If, however, this demand plants itself wholly on the basis of the visible world and denies everything invisible, it must inevitably assume the form of a harsh oppression and compulsion, for it can produce its effect not through conviction but solely through force. In the social-democratic movement of the present such a danger already shows itself in full distinctness. But while the modern man struggles with all his soul against such a compulsion, a solu-tion of the entanglement is to be sought in no other direction than that of a recovery of inner human bonds and of recourse to an inner world, common to all, of convictions, faith, ideals. We need to upbuild humanity from within, and this cannot be done without a profound deepening of life, and this in turn is not possible without religion.

The fact that today with the greatest abundance of external points of contact, we are internally getting farther and farther apart, necessarily leads to inner isolation. Amid the stupendous driving-gear the individual sees himself left to his own resources and completely indifferent to everyone else. Such isolation is painful, yes, unbearable, especially for finer natures. All the fullness of human activity, highly as it is to be prized, cannot make good the lack of inner union and essential love. It affords no sufficient counterweight for self-seclusion of man in his special circle of interests, for the preponderance of selfishness. Yet this selfishness, which separates all from all, turns out to be too narrow for the man himself; irresistibly a longing arises for a greater harmony of our spirits and for a value for each individual that shall transcend himself. But how could such a longing push its way to victory against the indifference of nature and the corrupt doings of men, unless a kingdom of love, a world of love, come to man and lend him a value? But that is exactly what religion represented, and what it brought to mankind.

Soul, eternity, love—these are not brought to us quickly and painlessly by the world about us; they require an inner elevation, they demand a new world. And beyond these individual aspects doubts are also awakened and transformations made necessary by the totality of human nature. It was a main point of religion, especially of the Christian religion, not to accept and recognize man as experience presents him, but require of him a complete transformation, an inner re-birth. The modern age has more confidence in man, it awakens in him the consciousness of strength more than that of weakness, it summons him to the full development of all his slumbering powers. And in fact it has been shown that man is capable of far more than he used to be given credit for, that he can actively put his hand to the world, and successfully strive to realize the rational and rationalize the real. While, however, man in the past thought highly of himself and bravely undertook high things, he formerly felt himself to be still living in the spiritual association which he had inherited, as a member of the Kingdom of God or as sharer in a world of reason; and this consciousness disciplined and enlarged his power. But these associations have gradually vanished; the tendency toward man has gradually passed into a rude opposition to any superhuman world, and constantly takes a more hostile attitude toward religion and toward any visible order. Characteristic of this is the well-known saying of Ludwig Feuerbach: "God was my first, reason my second, man my third and last thought." The consequence of putting man into the highest place is that he holds himself in no esteem. For only with the consciousness that a higher being exists does man attain a standpoint which allows him true esteem.

It cannot be denied that by giving up all connection with an invisible world and by complete limitation to visible existence man has been growing smaller. First of all, his place in the sum of reality has been reduced. He is now a mere bit of nature, and cannot claim a superior position and a peculiar work. In contrast to the enormously expanded space and time which nature has opened to modern research, the whole human circle is shrinking into tiny littleness. Rightly did William James emphasize the fact that for one hundred and fifty years progress seems to have meant nothing but a continual magnifying of the material world and a steady diminution of the importance of man.

And not only has the external position of man grown worse, he has also retrograded internally. When man is limited to sensuous existence, he loses all motive and all capacity to raise substantially his spiritual level and to counteract with any vigor the petty, low, self-centered part of his own being. He has to accept what he finds in himself, and exclusively follow the impulses awakened in him by nature; all resistance to them necessarily seems folly. That was endurable while an optimistic point of view glorified man, and lent him greatness and dignity in his own eyes; it becomes intolerable as soon as a more candid consideration causes us to discern and recognize the limitations and defects of man, understood as a mere natural being. And it cannot be denied that the experiences of modern life have given decisive preponderance to this unfavorable estimate. Whereas the eighteenth century could not exert itself enough to exalt the dignity and greatness of man, we of today, when we picture man to ourselves, are far more inclined to think of what is petty, low, self-centered, the "all-too-human" (Nietzsche). And since we do not intend to yield without a struggle to this humiliation, we are developing a zealous endeavor to elevate man of himself, in his own sphere. Some hope to attain this by uniting individuals into great masses and considering those masses as the bearers of reason, in agreement with the doctrine set up by Aristotle of the accumulation of reason in the mass; such have a firm belief in the reason of the multitude. In exactly the opposite direction, others wish to exalt single eminent individuals as high as possible above the masses and to make them the center of gravity of intellectual creation. Thus the former through aggregation, the latter through isolation, hope to be able to make more out of man. But, whatever relative justification these two tendencies may have, they do not reach the main goal. For by no readjustment within the human circle can greatness be given to man, if human nature is not capable of elevation from within, if man is a mere natural being. So we continue to press on to a mere human culture and civilization; we see through its inadequacy, and yet cannot emancipate ourselves from it or lift ourselves above it; we can neither discover new aims nor develop new powers other than those which it supplies. The fact, however, that despite the vast amount of earnest work and the restless movement of today, we yet lack a satisfying aim for this work, an aim that ennobles and inspires the work itself—that fact makes the present state of civilization absolutely intolerable. Man can bear much hindrance and hurt and not lose his courage; but he cannot endure to have his whole life aimless and meaningless. Just because our life is ever growing more intense and more laborious, we must unconditionally demand that it be given an aim and a meaning.

Therefore in all deeper souls today is stirring a demand for inner uplift of human nature, for a new idealism. And this demand will necessarily have to seek an alliance with religion. No matter how many opponents religion may still encounter, nevertheless, stronger than all opponents, stronger even than all intellectual difficulties, is the necessity of the spiritual self-preservation of humanity and of man. Out of the very resistance to the menace of annihilation will proceed elemental forces—which are the strongest thing in the world.

Thus, though it be through a course of hard fights and radical upheavals (as history indirectly tends to prove), religion will surely come to new ascendancy. But the return to religion by no means signifies a return to the old forms of religion. Through modern culture, too much in the condition of life has been changed for us to resume these forms unchanged. Religion will win back men's souls so much the sooner, the more energetically it harks back to its original sources, the more sharply it separates the temporal and the eternal in their own spheres, and so brings the eternal to new effectiveness and sets it in close and fruitful relation to the real needs of the present. The superiority of the eternal consists not in that it persists unchanged within time, but in that it can enter all times without losing itself in them, and from them all can elicit that particular portion of truth which endeavor holds. "The old that ages, he must let go, who would hold fast the old that ages not," (Runeberg).

The fundamental mood of mankind today is essentially the reverse of what it was at the beginning of the modern world. At that time the freshness of new vital power lent a rose-colored hue to all reality, and it was possible to hope that an imminent culture would bring about the complete satisfaction of all man's spiritual needs. The experiences of the period have shown man his limitations; great complications have arisen, much unreason has become apparent in our circumstances, our ambition has encountered greater and greater obstacles. But the recognition of so much unreason in our world forces us to the following alternative: either we declare ourselves powerless against unreason—then all the courage and strength of life must collapse and we succumb to pessimism; or, on the other hand, wrestling manfully, we gain a connection with an invisible world and the depths of reality, draw thence new power of life, and take up with new courage the fight against all unreason. That course will result in a well-founded and serious optimism, radically different from the superficial optimism of the market-place. The false optimism ignores complication and unreason, and hence inevitably loses all depth of life; the true optimism knows and appreciates these, but is not warped and deterred by them. It possesses a resource superior to every hindrance, and from opposition only gains new might and courage. I should like to think that such a genuine and well-founded optimism corresponds to the intrinsic nature of the American people. But without Religion genuine optimism is impossible.

Rabindranath Tagore

EAST AND WEST

RABINDRANATH TAGORE, *the son of a wealthy Brahmin, was born in Calcutta in 1861. After studying law in London, he returned to India and embarked upon a prolific literary career, culminating in the Nobel Prize award in 1913. His first publication in 1878, a long narrative poem, was followed in time by numerous poem cycles and collections* (Gitanjali, 1912; Chitra, 1913; Songs of Kabir, 1915; Stray Birds, 1917). *His plays and stories, from* The Post Office (1914) *to* Broken Ties (1925), *are really poems cast in prose. In 1901, he founded a school in Bengal which later became the international university called Visva-Bharati, but he continued to write and translated many Hindu works, including his own, into English. Also a talented musician, he composed several thousand songs during his lifetime. In his sixties, he took up painting and his canvases were exhibited in the principal cities of the world. He was knighted in 1915, but later renounced the title in protest against the British suppression of the Punjab riots. Many years after his death in 1941 he remains, as the following essay indicates, an outstanding interpreter of Indian thought and feeling.*

I

It is not always a profound interest in man that carries travelers nowadays to distant lands. More often it is the facility for rapid movement. For lack of time and for the sake of convenience we generalize and crush our human facts into the packages within the steel trunks that hold our traveler's reports.

Our knowledge of our own countrymen and our feelings about them have slowly and unconsciously grown out of innumerable facts which are full of contradictions and subject to incessant change. They have the elusive mystery and fluidity of life. We cannot define to ourselves what we are as a whole, because we know too much; because our knowledge is more than knowledge. It is an immediate consciousness of personality, any evaluation of which carries some emotion, joy or sorrow, shame or exaltation. But in a foreign land we try to find our compensation for the meagerness of our data by the compactness of the generalization which our imperfect sympathy itself helps us to form. When a stranger from the West travels in the Eastern world he takes the facts that displease him and readily makes use of them for his rigid conclusions, fixed upon the unchallengeable authority of his personal experience. It is like a man who has his own boat for crossing his village stream, but, on being compelled to wade across some strange watercourse, draws angry comparisons as he goes from every patch of mud and every pebble which his feet encounter.

Our mind has faculties which are universal, but its habits are insular. There are men who become impatient and angry at the least discomfort when their habits are incommoded. In their idea of the next world they probably conjure up the ghosts of their slippers and dressing-gowns, and expect the latchkey that opens their lodging-house door on earth to fit their front door in the other world. As travelers they are a failure; for they have grown too accustomed to their mental easy-chairs, and in their intellectual nature love home comforts, which are of local make, more than the realities of life, which, like earth itself, are full of ups and downs, yet are one in their rounded completeness.

The modern age has brought the geography of the earth near to us, but made it difficult for us to come into touch with man. We go to strange lands and observe; we do not live there. We hardly meet men: but only specimens of knowledge. We are in haste to seek for general types and overlook individuals.

When we fall into the habit of neglecting to use the understanding that comes of sympathy in our travels, our knowledge of foreign people grows insensitive, and therefore easily becomes both unjust and cruel in its character, and also selfish and contemptuous in its application. Such has, too often, been the case with regard to the meeting of Western people in our days with others for whom they do not recognize any obligation of kinship.

It has been admitted that the dealings between different races of men are not merely between individuals; that our mutual understanding is either aided, or else obstructed, by the general emanations forming the social atmosphere. These emanations are our collective ideas and collective feelings, generated according to special historical circumstances.

For instance, the caste-idea is a collective idea in India. When we approach an Indian who is under the influence of this collective idea, he is no longer a pure individual with his conscience fully awake to the judging of the value of a human being. He is more or less a passive medium for giving expression to the sentiment of a whole community.

It is evident that the caste-idea is not creative; it is merely institutional. It adjusts human beings according to some mechanical arrangement. It emphasizes the negative side of the individual—his separateness. It hurts the complete truth in man.

In the West, also, the people have a certain collective idea that obscures their humanity. Let me try to explain what I feel about it.

II

Lately I went to visit some battlefields of France which had been devastated by war. The awful calm of desolation, which still bore wrinkles of pain—death-struggles stiffened into ugly ridges—brought before my mind the vision of a huge demon, which had no shape, no meaning, yet had two arms that could strike and break and tear, a gaping mouth that could devour, and bulging brains that could conspire and plan. It was a purpose, which had a living body, but no complete humanity to temper it. Because it was passion—belonging to life, and yet not having the wholeness of life—it was the most terrible of life's enemies.

Something of the same sense of oppression in a different degree, the same desolation in a different aspect, is produced in my mind when I realize the effect of the West upon Eastern life—the West which, in its relation to us, is all plan and purpose incarnate, without any superfluous humanity.

I feel the contrast very strongly in Japan. In that country the old world presents itself with some ideal of perfection, in which man has his varied opportunities of self-revelation in art, in ceremonial, in religious faith, and in customs expressing the poetry of social relationship. There one feels that deep delight of hospitality which life offers to life. And side by side, in the same soil, stands the modern world, which is stupendously big and powerful, but inhospitable. It has no simple-hearted welcome for man. It is living; yet the incompleteness of life's ideal within it cannot but hurt humanity.

The wriggling tentacles of a cold-blooded utilitarianism, with which the West has grasped all the easily yielding succulent portions of the East, are causing pain and indignation throughout the Eastern countries. The West comes to us, not with the imagination and sympathy that create and unite, but with a shock of passion—passion for power and wealth. This passion is a mere force, which has in it the principle of separation, of conflict.

I have been fortunate in coming into close touch with individual men and women of the Western countries, and have felt with them their sorrows and shared their aspirations. I have known that they seek the same God, who is my God—even those who deny Him. I feel certain that, if the great light of culture be extinct in Europe, our horizon in the East will mourn in darkness. It does not hurt my pride to acknowledge that, in the present age, Western humanity has received its mission to be the teacher of the world; that her science, through the mastery of laws of nature, is to liberate human souls from the dark dungeon of matter. For this very reason I have realized all the more strongly, on the other hand, that the dominant collective idea in the Western countries is not creative. It is ready to enslave or kill individuals, to drug a great people with soul-killing poison, darkening their whole future with the black mist of stupefaction, and emasculating entire races of men to the utmost degree of help-lessness. It is wholly wanting in spiritual power to blend and har-monize; it lacks the sense of the great personality of man.

The most significant fact of modern days is this, that the West has met the East. Such a momentous meeting of humanity, in or-der to be fruitful, must have in its heart some great emotional idea, generous and creative. There can be no doubt that God's choice has fallen upon the knights-errant of the West for the serv-ice of the present age; arms and armor have been given to them; but have they yet realized in their hearts the single-minded loyalty to their cause which can resist all temptations of bribery from the devil? The world to-day is offered to the West. She will destroy it, if she does not use it for a great creation of man. The mate-rials for such a creation are in the hands of science; but the crea-tive genius is in Man's spiritual ideal.

III

When I was young, a stranger from Europe came to Bengal. He chose his lodging among the people of the country, shared with them their frugal diet, and freely offered them his service. He found employment in the houses of the rich, teaching them French and German, and the money thus earned he spent to help poor students in buying books. This meant for him hours of walk-ing in the mid-day heat of a tropical summer; for, intent upon exercising the utmost economy, he refused to hire conveyances. He was pitiless in his exaction from himself of his resources, in money, time, and strength, to the point of privation; and all this for the sake of a people who were obscure, to whom he was not born, yet whom he dearly loved. He did not come to us with a professional mission of teaching sectarian creeds; he had not in his nature the least trace of that self-sufficiency of goodness, which humiliates by gifts the victims of its insolent benevolence. Though he did not know our language, he took every occasion to frequent our meetings and ceremonies; yet he was always afraid of intru-sion, and tenderly anxious lest he might offend us by his igno-rance of our customs. At last, under the continual strain of work in an alien climate and surroundings, his health broke down. He died, and was cremated at our burning ground, according to his express desire.

The attitude of his mind, the manner of his living, the object of his life, his modesty, his unstinted self-sacrifice for a people who had not even the power to give publicity to any benefaction bestowed upon them, were so utterly unlike anything we were accustomed to associate with the Europeans in India, that it gave rise in our mind to a feeling of love bordering upon awe.

We all have a realm, a private paradise, in our mind, where dwell deathless memories of persons who brought some divine light to our life's experience, who may not be known to others, and whose names have no place in the pages of history. Let me confess to you that this man lives as one of those immortals in the paradise of my individual life.

He came from Sweden, his name was Hammargren. What was most remarkable in the event of his coming to us in Bengal was the fact that in his own country he had chanced to read some works of my great countryman, Ram Mohan Roy, and felt an immense veneration for his genius and his character. Ram Mohan Roy lived in the beginning of the last century, and it is no exaggeration when I describe him as one of the immortal personalities of modern time. This young Swede had the unusual gift of a far-sighted intellect and sympathy, which enabled him even from his distance of space and time, and in spite of racial differences, to realize the greatness of Ram Mohan Roy. It moved him so deeply that he resolved to go to the country which produced this great man, and offer her his service. He was poor, and he had to wait some time in England before he could earn his passage money to India. There he came at last, and in reckless generosity of love utterly spent himself to the last breath of his life, away from home and kindred and all the inheritances of his motherland. His stay among us was too short to produce any outward result. He failed even to achieve during his life what he had in his mind, which was to found by the help of his scanty earnings a library as a memorial to Ram Mohan Roy, and thus to leave behind him a visible symbol of his devotion. But what I prize most in this European youth, who left no record of his life behind him, is not the memory of any service of goodwill, but the precious gift of respect which he offered to a people who are fallen upon evil times, and whom it is so easy to ignore or to humiliate. For the first time in the modern days this obscure individual from Sweden brought to our country the chivalrous courtesy of the West, a greeting of human fellowship.

The coincidence came to me with a great and delightful surprise when the Nobel prize was offered to me from Sweden. As a recognition of individual merit it was of great value to me, no doubt; but it was the acknowledgment of the East as a collaborator with the Western continents, in contributing its riches to the common stock of civilization, which had the chief significance for the present age. It meant joining hands in comradeship by the two great hemispheres of the human world across the sea.

IV

To-day the real East remains unexplored. The blindness of contempt is more hopeless than the blindness of ignorance; for contempt kills the light which ignorance merely leaves unignited. The East is waiting to be understood by the Western races, in order not only to be able to give what is true in her, but also to be confident of her own mission.

In Indian history, the meeting of the Mussulman and the Hindu produced Akbar, the object of whose dream was the unification of hearts and ideals. It had all the glowing enthusiasm of a religion, and it produced an immediate and a vast result even in his own lifetime.

But the fact still remains that the Western mind, after centuries of contact with the East, has not evolved the enthusiasm of a chivalrous ideal which can bring this age to its fulfillment. It is everywhere raising thorny hedges of exclusion and offering human sacrifices to national self-seeking. It has intensified the mutual feelings of envy among Western races themselves, as they fight over their spoils and display a carnivorous pride in their snarling rows of teeth.

We must again guard our minds from any encroaching distrust of the individuals of a nation. The active love of humanity and the spirit of martyrdom for the cause of justice and truth which I have met with in the Western countries have been a great lesson and inspiration to me. I have no doubt in my mind that the West owes its true greatness, not so much to its marvelous training of intellect, as to its spirit of service devoted to the welfare of man. Therefore I speak with a personal feeling of pain and sadness about the collective power which is guiding the helm of Western civilization. It is a passion, not an ideal. The more success it has brought to Europe, the more costly it will prove to her at last, when the accounts have to be rendered. And the signs are unmistakable, that the accounts have been called for. The time has come when Europe must know that the forcible parasitism which she has been practicing upon the two large Continents of the world—the two most unwieldy whales of humanity —must be causing to her moral nature a gradual atrophy and degeneration.

As an example, let me quote the following extract from the concluding chapter of *From the Cape to Cairo*, by Messrs. Grogan and Sharp, two writers who have the power to inculcate their doctrines by precept and example. In their reference to the African they are candid, as when they say, "We have stolen his land. Now we must steal his limbs." These two sentences, carefully articulated, with a smack of enjoyment, have been more clearly explained in the following statement, where some sense of that decency which is the attenuated ghost of a buried conscience, prompts the writers to use the phrase "compulsory labor" in place of the honest word "slavery"; just as the modern politician adroitly avoids the word "injunction" and uses the word "mandate." "Compulsory labor in some form," they say, "is the corollary of our occupation of the country." And they add: "It is pathetic, but it is history," implying thereby that moral sentiments have no serious effect in the history of human beings.

Elsewhere they write: "Either we must give up the country commercially, or we must make the African work. And mere abuse of those who point out the impasse cannot change the facts. We must decide, and soon. Or rather the white man of South Africa will decide." The authors also confess that they have seen too much of the world "to have any lingering belief that Western civilization benefits native races."

The logic is simple—the logic of egoism. But the argument is simplified by lopping off the greater part of the premise. For these writers seem to hold that the only important question for the white men of South Africa is, how indefinitely to grow fat on ostrich feathers and diamond mines, and dance jazz dances over the misery and degradation of a whole race of fellow-beings of a different color from their own. Possibly they believe that moral laws have a special domesticated breed of comfortable concessions for the service of the people in power. Possibly they ignore the fact that commercial and political cannibalism, profitably practiced upon foreign races, creeps back nearer home; that the cultivation of unwholesome appetites has its final reckoning with the stomach which has been made to serve it. For, after all, man is a spiritual being, and not a mere living money-bag jumping from profit to profit, and breaking the backbone of human races in its financial leapfrog.

Such, however, has been the condition of things for more than a century; and to-day, trying to read the future by the light of the European conflagration, we are asking ourselves everywhere in the East: "Is this frightfully overgrown power really great? It can bruise us from without, but can it add to our wealth of spirit? It can sign peace treaties, but can it give peace?"

It was about two thousand years ago that all-powerful Rome in one of its eastern provinces executed on a cross a simple teacher of an obscure tribe of fishermen. On that day the Roman governor felt no falling off of his appetite or sleep. On that day there was, on the one hand, the agony, the humiliation, the death; on the other, the pomp of pride and festivity in the Governor's palace.

And to-day? To whom, then, shall we bow the head?

> *Kasmai devaya havisha vidhema?*
> (To which God shall we offer oblation?)

We know of an instance in our own history of India, when a great personality, both in his life and voice, struck the keynote of the solemn music of the soul—love for all creatures. And that music crossed seas, mountains, and deserts. Races belonging to different climates, habits, and languages were drawn together, not in the clash of arms, not in the conflict of exploitation, but in harmony of life, in amity and peace. That was creation.

When we think of it, we see at once what the confusion of thought was to which the Western poet, dwelling upon the difference between East and West, referred when he said, "Never the twain shall meet." It is true that they are not yet showing any real sign of meeting. But the reason is because the West has not sent out its humanity to meet the man in the East, but only its machine. Therefore the poet's line has to be changed into something like this:

> *Man is man, machine is machine,*
> *And never the twain shall wed.*

You must know that red tape can never be a common human bond; that official sealing-wax can never provide means of mutual attachment; that it is a painful ordeal for human beings to have to receive favors from animated pigeonholes, and condescensions from printed circulars that give notice but never speak. The presence of the Western people in the East is a human fact. If we are to gain anything from them, it must not be a mere sum-total of legal codes and systems of civil and military services. Man is a great deal more to man than that. We have our human birthright to claim direct help from the man of the West, if he has anything great to give us. It must come to us, not through mere facts in a juxtaposition, but through the spontaneous sacrifice made by those who have the gift, and therefore the responsibility.

Earnestly I ask the poet of the Western world to realize and sing to you with all the great power of music which he has, that the East and the West are ever in search of each other, and that they must meet not merely in the fullness of physical strength, but in fullness of truth; that the right hand, which wields the sword, has the need of the left, which holds the shield of safety.

The East has its seat in the vast plains watched over by the snow-peaked mountains and fertilized by rivers carrying mighty volumes of water to the sea. There, under the blaze of a tropical sun, the physical life has bedimmed the light of its vigor and lessened its claims. There man has had the repose of mind which has ever tried to set itself in harmony with the inner notes of existence. In the silence of sunrise and sunset, and on the star-crowded nights, he has sat face to face with the Infinite, waiting for the revelation that opens up the heart of all that there is. He has said, in a rapture of realization:

"Hearken to me, ye children of the Immortal, who dwell in the Kingdom of Heaven. I have known, from beyond darkness, the Supreme Person, shining with the radiance of the sun."

The man from the East, with his faith in the eternal, who in his soul had met the touch of the Supreme Person—did he never come to you in the West and speak to you of the Kingdom of Heaven? Did he not unite the East and the West in truth, in the unity of one spiritual bond between all children of the Immortal, in the realization of one great Personality in all human persons?

Yes, the East did once meet the West profoundly in the growth of her life. Such union became possible, because the East came to the West with the ideal that is creative, and not with the passion that destroys moral bonds. The mystic consciousness of the Infinite, which she brought with her, was greatly needed by the man of the West to give him his balance.

On the other hand, the East must find her own balance in Science—the magnificent gift that the West can bring to her. Truth has its nest as well as its sky. That nest is definite in structure, accurate in law of construction; and though it has to be changed and rebuilt over and over again, the need of it is never-ending and its laws are eternal. For some centuries the East has neglected the nest-building of truth. She has not been attentive to learn its secret. Trying to cross the trackless infinite, the East has relied solely upon her wings. She has spurned the earth, till, buffeted by storms, her wings are hurt and she is tired, sorely needing help. But has she then to be told that the messenger of the sky and the builder of the nest shall never meet?

Romain Rolland

THE PLACE OF MUSIC IN
GENERAL HISTORY

ROMAIN ROLLAND, *born in a small Burgundian town in 1866, was schooled in Paris as a "docteur en lettre." He became professor of music history at the Sorbonne, and much of his illustrious writing career was devoted to music and musicians. He recreated the life of Beethoven both in a biography and in the fiction of his monumental novel,* Jean Christophe *(1904-12) for which he received the Nobel Prize in 1915. The diversity of his interests is reflected in his biographies of Michelangelo, Tolstoy, and Ghandi, his works on and for the stage (*Danton, *1901 and* The People's Theater, *1903), and his critical studies and tracts. At the outbreak of World War I, Rolland insisted upon remaining neutral and took up self-imposed exile in Switzerland, where he worked with the International Red Cross for peace. His idealistic outlook is perhaps best summed up in his dedication of* Jean Christophe *to "tous les âmes libres du mond entier." In his later years, he showed sympathy for the ideas advanced by the Third International. In 1938, he returned to France, where he died six years later.*

Music is only now beginning to take the place due to it in general history. It seems a strange thing that concepts of the evolution of man's soul should have been formed while one of the strongest expressions of that soul has been ignored. But we know what difficulty the other arts have had in obtaining recognition in general history, even when they were more favored and easier of approach by the French mind. Is it so long ago that this did not apply to the history of literature and science and philosophy and, indeed, the whole of human thought? Yet the political life of a nation is only a superficial part of its being; in order to learn its inner life—the source of its actions—we must penetrate to its very soul by way of its literature, its philosophy, and its art, where the ideas, the passions, and the dreams of its people are reflected.

We know that history may find resources in literature; we know the kind of help, for example, that Corneille's poetry and Descartes' philosophy may bring to the understanding of the Treaty of Westphalia; or, again, what a dead letter the Revolution of '89 might be if we were not acquainted with the thought of the Encyclopedists and eighteenth-century salons.

Nor do we forget the valuable information that the plastic arts give us about different epochs, for in them we behold an age's very countenance—its type, its gestures, its dress, its fashions, indeed its whole daily life. What a storehouse for history! One thing hangs to another: political revolutions have their counterpart in artistic revolutions; the life of a nation is an organism in which all is bound together—economic phenomena and artistic phenomena alike. In the resemblances and differences of Gothic monuments a Viollet-le-Duc could trace the great highways of commerce in the twelfth century. The study of some detail of architecture—a belfry, for instance—would show the progress of royalty in France, the thought of the Île-de-France imposing a peculiar construction upon provincial schools from the time of Philip Augustus onward. But the great service that art renders history is to bring it close to the soul of an epoch and so let it touch the springs of emotion. On the surface, literature and philosophy may seem to give us more definitive information by reducing the characteristics of an age to precise formulas. On the other hand, this artificial simplification may leave us with inelastic and impoverished ideas. Art is modeled on life, and it has an almost greater value than literature because its domain is infinitely more extended. We have six centuries of art in France, and yet we are often content to judge the French spirit by four centuries of literature. Further, our medieval art, for example, can show us the life of the provinces, about which our classical literature has hardly anything to say. Few countries are composed of elements more disparate than ours. Our races, traditions, and social life are varied and show evidence of the influence of Italians, Spanish, Germans, Swiss, English, Flemish, and inhabitants of other countries. A strong political unity has dissolved these antagonistic elements and established an average and an equilibrium in the civilizations that clashed about us. But if such a unity is apparent in our literature, the multiple nuances of our personality have become very blurred. Art gives us a much richer image of French genius. It is not like a grisaille but like a cathedral window where all the colors of earth and sky blend. It is not a simple picture but like those rose windows which are the product of the purely French art of the Île-de-France and Champagne. And I say to myself: Here is a people whose characteristics are said to be reason and not imagination, common sense and not fancy, drawing and not coloring; yet this is the people who created those mystical east-windows!

And so it is that acquaintance with the arts enlarges and gives life to the image one has formed of a people from their literature alone.

Now by turning to music we may extend this idea still futher.

Music perplexes those who have no feeling for it; it seems to them an incomprehensible art, beyond reasoning and having no connection with reality. What help can history possibly draw from that which is outside ordinary matter and therefore outside history?

Well, first of all it is not true that music has so abstract a character, for she has an undoubted relationship with literature, with the theater, and with the life of an epoch. Thus no one can fail to see that a history of opera will throw light on the ways and manners of society. Indeed, every form of music is allied with some form of society and makes it easier to understand; also, in many cases, the history of music is closely connected with that of other arts.

It constantly happens that the arts influence one another, that they intermingle, or that, as a result of their natural evolution, they overflow their boundaries and invade the domains of neighboring arts. Now it is music that would become painting, now painting that would be music. "Good painting is music, a melody," said Michelangelo, at a time when painting was giving precedence to music, when Italian music was extricating itself, so to speak, from the very decadence of other arts. The doors between the arts are not closely shut as many theorists would pretend, and one art is constantly opening upon another. Arts may extend and find their consummation in other arts; when the mind has exhausted one form, it seeks and finds a more complete expression in another. Thus is a knowledge of the history of music often necessary to the history of the plastic arts.

But the essence of the great interest of art lies in the way it reveals the true feeling of the soul, the secrets of its inner life, and the world of passion that has long accumulated and fermented there before surging up to the surface. Very often, thanks to its depth and spontaneity, music is the first indication of tendencies which later translate themselves into words, and afterward into deeds. The *Eroica* Symphony anticipated by more than ten years the awakening of the German nation. The *Meistersinger* and *Siegfried* proclaimed ten years beforehand the imperial triumph of Germany. There are even cases where music is the only witness of a whole inner life which never reaches the surface.

What does the political history of Italy and Germany in the seventeenth century teach us? A series of court intrigues, of military defeats, of princely weddings, of feastings, of miseries, and of one ruin after another. How is one, then, to account for the miraculous resurrection of these two nations in the eighteenth and nineteenth centuries? The work of their musicians gives us an insight. It shows in Germany the treasures of faith and activity which were silently accumulating; it shows simple and heroic characters like Heinrich Schütz who, during the Thirty Years' War, in the midst of the worst disasters that ever devastated a country, quietly went his way, singing his own robust and resolute faith. About him were Johann Christoph Bach and Michæl Bach (ancestors of the great Bach), who seemed to carry with them the quiet presentiment of the genius who followed them. Besides these were Pachelbel, Kuhnau, Buxtehude, Zachau, and Erlebach—great souls who were shut up all their lives in the narrow sphere of a little provincial town, known only to a few men, without worldly ambition, without hope of leaving anything to posterity, singing for themselves alone and for their God; and who, among all their sorrows of home life and public life, slowly and persistently gathered reserves of strength and moral well-being, building stone by stone the great future of Germany. In Italy there was, at the same time, a perfect ebullition of music which streamed all over Europe. It flooded France, Austria, and England, showing that Italian genius in the seventeenth century was still supreme; and in this splendid exuberance of musical production a succession of thoughtful geniuses like Monteverdi at Mantua, Carissimi at Rome, and Provenzale at Naples gave evidence of the loftiness of soul and purity of heart which was preserved among the frivolities and dissoluteness of Italian courts.

Here is a still more striking example. It is scarcely likely that there has ever been seen a more terrible age than that of the end of the old world—the time of the decomposition of the Roman Empire and the great Invasions. The flame of art, however, continued to burn under that heap of smoking rubbish. A passion for music served to reconcile the Gallic Romans with their barbarian conquerors, for the detestable Cæsars of Rome's waning empire and the Visigoths of Toulouse had an equal relish for concerts; and both the Roman houses and the half-savage camps resounded with the noise of instruments. Clovis had musicians brought from Constantinople. And the remarkable fact was not that art was still loved but that the age created a new kind of art. From this upheaval of humanity sprang an art as perfect and as pure as that of the most finished products of happier times. According to Gevært, the Gregorian chant made its first appearance in the fourth century in the *Alleluia* song—"the cry of the victory of Christianity after two and a half centuries of persecution." The musical masterpieces of the early church seem to have been produced in the sixth century, between 540 and 600; that is to say, between the invasions of the Goths and the invasions of the Lombards, "at a time which we imagine was represented by an uninterrupted series of wars, massacres, pillages, plagues, famines, and cataclysms of such a kind that St. Gregory saw in them evidence of the decrepitude of the world and premonitory signs of the Last Judgment." In these chants, however, everything breathes of peace and hope in the future. Out of barbarity sprang a gentle art, in which we find pastoral simplicity, clear and sober outlines like those of Greek bas-reliefs, free poetry filled with love of nature, and a touching sweetness of disposition—"a speaking witness of the soul of those who lived amid such terrible disturbance." Nor was this an art of cloisters and convents, shut away in confinement. It was a popular art which prevailed through the whole of the ancient Roman world. From Rome it went to England, to Germany, and to France; and no art was more representative of its time. Under the reign of the Carolingians it had its golden age, for the princes were enamored of it. Charlemagne and Louis the Pious spent whole days in singing or listening to chants and were absorbed by their charm. Charles the Bald, in spite of the troubles of his empire, kept up a correspondence about music and composed music in collaboration with the monks of the monastery of Saint-Gall, the musical center of the world in the ninth century. Few occurrences have been more striking than this harvest of art, this smiling efflorescence of music which was gathered, in spite of everything, amid the convulsions of society.

Thus music shows us the continuity of life in apparent death, the flowering of an eternal spirit amidst the ruin of the world. How then should one write the history of these times if one neglected some of their essential characteristics? How should one understand them if one ignored their true inner force? And who knows but that such an omission might falsify not only the aspect of one period of history but the whole of history itself? Who knows if the words "Renaissance" and "Decadence" do not arise, as in the preceding example, from our limited view of a single aspect of things? An art may decline, but does Art itself ever die? Does it not rather have its metamorphoses and its adaptations to environment? It is quite evident, at any rate, that in a ruined kingdom, wrecked by war or revolution, creative force could express itself in architecture only with difficulty; for architecture needs money and new structures, besides prosperity and confidence in the future. One might even say that the plastic arts in general have need of luxury and leisure, of refined society, and of a certain equilibrium in civilization, in order to develop themselves fully. But when material conditions are harder, when life is bitter, starved, and harassed with care, when the opportunity of outside development is withheld, then the spirit is forced back upon itself, and its eternal need of happiness drives it to other outlets; its expression of beauty is changed and takes a less external character, and it seeks refuge in more intimate arts, such as poetry and music. It never dies—that I believe with all my heart. There is no death or new birth of the spirit there, for its light has never been extinguished; it has died down only to blaze anew somewhere else. And so it goes from one art to another, as from one people to another. If you study only one art you will naturally be led to think that there are interruptions in its life, a cessation of its heartbeats. On the other hand, if you look at art as a whole, you will feel the stream of its eternal life.

That is why I believe that for the foundation of all general history we need a sort of comparative history of all forms of art; the omission of a single form risks the blurring of the whole picture. History should have the living unity of the spirit of humanity for its object and should maintain the cohesion of all its thought.

Let us try to sketch the place of music in the course of history. That place is far more important than is generally thought, for music goes back to the far distances of civilization. To those who would date it from yesterday, one would recall Aristoxenus of Tarentum, who made the decadence of music begin with Sophocles; and Plato who, with sounder judgment, found that no progress had been made since the seventh century and the melodies of Olympus. From one age to another people have said that music had reached its apogee and that nothing but its decline could follow. There are no epochs in the world without their music, and there has been no civilized people without its musicians at some time in its history—even those whom we are accustomed to regard as least endowed with the gift of music, as for example, England, which was a great musical nation until the Revolution of 1688.

There are historical conditions more favorable than others to the development of music, and it seems natural, in some respects, that a musical efflorescence should coincide with the decadence of other arts and even with a country's misfortunes. The examples which we have quoted from the time of the Invasions and from the seventeenth century in Italy or Germany incline our belief that way. And this would seem quite logical, since music is an individual form of thought and for its expression demands nothing but a soul and a voice. An unhappy person, surrounded by ruin and misery, may nevertheless achieve a masterpiece in music or poetry.

But we have been speaking of only one form of music. Music, although it may be an individual art, is also a social art; it may be the offspring of meditation and sorrow, but it may also be that of joy and even frivolity. It accommodates itself to the characters of all people and all time; when one knows its history and the diverse forms it has taken throughout the centuries, one is no longer astonished at the contradictory definitions given to it by lovers of beauty. One man may call it architecture in motion, another poetical psychology; one man sees it as a plastic and well-defined art, another as an art of purely spiritual expression; for one theorist melody is the essence of music, for another this same essence is harmony. And, in truth, it is so; they are all right.

So history leads us, not to doubt everything—far from it—but to believe a little of everything; to test general theories by opinions that are true for this particular group of facts and that particular hour in history; to use fragments of the truth. It is perfectly right to give music every possible kind of name, for it is an architecture of sound in certain centuries of architecture and with certain architectural people, such as the Franco-Flemings of the fifteenth and sixteenth centuries. It is also drawing, line, melody, and plastic beauty, with people who have an appreciation and admiration for form, with painter and sculptor people like the Italians. It is inner poetry, lyrical outpouring, and philosophic meditation with poets and philosophers like the Germans. It adapts itself to all conditions of society. It is a courtly and poetic art under Francis I and Charles IX; an art of faith and fighting with the Reformation; an art of affectation and princely pride under Louis XIV; an art of the salon in the eighteenth century. Then it becomes the lyric expression of revolutionaries, and it will be the voice of the democratic societies of the future, as it was the voice of the aristocratic societies of the past. No formula will hold it. It is the song of centuries and the flower of history; its growth pushes upward from the griefs as well as from the joys of humanity.

We know the important place that music took in ancient civilizations. Greek philosophy testifies to this by the part assigned to music in education, by its close connection with the other arts, science, literature, and drama especially. We find in classic times hymns sung and danced by whole nations, Bacchic dithyrambs, and tragedies and comedies steeped in music; indeed, music enveloped all literary forms, it was everywhere, and it reached from one end to the other of Greek history. It was a world that never ceased to evolve, and its development offered as many varieties of form and style as our modern music. Little by little, pure music, instrumental music, played an almost extravagant part in the social life of the Greek world. It shone with all magnificence at the court of the Roman emperors, among whom were Nero, Titus, Hadrian, Caracalla, Helagabal, Alexander Severus, Gordian III, Carinus, and Numerian, who were all keen musicians and even composers and virtuosos of remarkable ability.

Christianity, as it grew, took into its service the force of music and used it to conquer souls. St. Ambrose fascinated the people, he said, by the melodic charm of his hymns; and one perceives that of all the artistic heritage of the Roman world, music was the only art which was not only preserved intact at the time of the Invasions but even blossomed forth more vigorously. In the years that followed, in the Romance and Gothic periods, music kept its high place. St. Thomas Aquinas said that music occupied the first rank among the seven fine arts, that it was the noblest of civilized sciences. It was taught everywhere. At Chartres from the eleventh to the sixteenth century there flourished a great school of music, of a sort both practical and theoretical. At the University of Toulouse there was a Chair of Music in the thirteenth century. At Paris, the center of the musical world in the thirteenth and fourteenth centuries, one may read in the list of professors of the University the names of the most famous theorists of music of that time. Music had its place in the quadrivium, with arithmetic, geometry, and astronomy. For it was then a study like science and logic, or at any rate pretended to be so. A quotation from Jerome of Moravia at the end of the thirteenth century shows well enough how the esthetics of that time differed from ours: "The principal difficulty," he says, "in the way of making beautiful notes is sadness of heart." What would Beethoven have thought of that? To the artists of that time individual feeling

seemed a hindrance rather than a stimulus to art; for music was
to them something impersonal, demanding first of all the calm of
a well-ordered mind. Yet its power was never more mighty than in
this age when it was most academic. Besides the tyrannical
authority of Pythagoras, which was transmitted to the Middle
Ages by Bœthius, there were many reasons for this musical intel-
lectualism: moral reasons belonging to the spirit of a time which
was much more rationalistic than mystical, more polemical than
inspired; social reasons coming from the habitual association of
thought and power which linked any man's thought, if it were
original, to the thought of all men—as in the motets, where different airs with different words were bound together without concern; and lastly, there were technical reasons connected with the
heavy labor which had to be undergone in order to shape the unformed mass of modern polyphony, then fashioned like a statue
ready for the life and thought that were afterward to enter into it.
But this academic art was soon followed by the exquisite art of
chivalrous poetry with its amorous lyricism, its glowing life, and its
well-defined popular feeling.

At the beginning of the fourteenth century a breath blown from
Provence, a first intimation of the Renaissance, made itself felt
in Italy. Already the dawn was breaking upon the Florentine
composers of madrigals, *cascie* (chassés), and *ballate*, of the time
of Dante, Petrarch, and Giotto. Through Florence and Paris the
new art, *ars nova*, was disseminated in Europe and produced at
the beginning of the fifteenth century that harvest of rich vocal
music and its accompaniments which are now gradually being
brought to light. The spirit of liberty, originating in profane
music, began to be assimilated by church art; by the end of the
fifteenth century there was a glory of music equal in brilliance
to that of other arts in that happy age. The musical literature of
the Renaissance is of perhaps unparalleled richness in history.
Flemish supremacy, so marked in painting, asserted itself even
more in music. The Flemish masters of counterpoint spread over
Europe and were leaders in music over all other people. French
and Flemish dominated in Germany and in Italy at Rome. Their
works are magnificent structures of sound, with branching outlines
and rhythms and of an abundant beauty, though at first sight

they may seem more formal than expressive. But after the second half of the fifteenth century, individualism, which was making itself felt in other arts, began to awake everywhere in music; personal feeling shook itself free; there was a return to nature. Glarean wrote concerning Josquin: "No one has rendered better the passions of the soul in music." And Vincenzo Galilei called Palestrina "that great imitator of nature."

The representation of nature and the expression of passion were in the eyes of contemporaries characteristics of the musical renaissance of the sixteenth century; such appeared to be the distinctive traits of that art. It does not strike ourselves so much, for since that time music's endeavor to reach spiritual truth has been unceasing and has brought about a continual advance. But what does stir our imagination for the art of that period is the beauty of its form, which has never been surpassed, perhaps never even equaled except in certain pages of Handel or Mozart. It was an age of pure beauty, for beauty flourished everywhere, was intermingled with every form of social life, and was united to every art. At no time were music and poetry more intimately bound together than in the time of Charles IX; music was hymned by Dorat, Jodelle, and Belleau. Ronsard called music "the younger sister of poetry," and said also that without music, poetry almost lacked grace, just as music without the melodiousness of poetry was dull and lifeless. Baïf founded an academy of poetry and music and endeavored to create in France a language adapted for song, giving as models metrical verses written after the manner of the Greeks and Latins—treasures whose rich boldness is hardly guessed by the poets and musicians of today. Never had France been so truly musical; for music then was not the property of a class but the possession of the whole nation, of the nobility, the intellectual few, the middle classes, the people, and both Catholic and Protestant churches. The same rich rising of musical sap was evident in England under Henry VIII and Elizabeth, in the Germany of Luther, in the Geneva of Calvin, and in the Rome of Leo X. Music was the last branch of the Renaissance, but perhaps it was the biggest, for it covered the whole of Europe.

The striving for more and more exact expression of feeling in music, during the whole of the sixteenth century, in a series of picturesque and descriptive madrigals, culminated in Italy in the creation of musical tragedy. The influence of former ages intervened at the birth of opera as it did in the formation and development of the other Italian arts. Opera, in the mind of its founders, was a resurrection of classical tragedy and was thus more literary than musical. Indeed, even after the dramatic principles of the first Florentine masters had fallen into oblivion, even after music had profitably broken the bonds which attached it to poetry, opera continued to exercise an influence on the spirit of the theater, especially at the end of the seventeenth century, in a way that has not been fully realized. It would be wrong to regard the triumph of opera in Europe and the morbid enthusiasm it excited as something of small account. We may affirm that without it we should scarcely be acquainted with half the artistic mind of the century, for we should see only the intellectual side of it. It is through opera that we best reach the depth of the sensuality of that time, with its voluptuous imagination, its sentimental materialism, and, in short, if I may so put it, the tottering foundations on which the reason, the will, and the serious business of French society of that great century rested. On the other hand, the spirit of the Reformation was putting out strong roots in German music. English music was also kindled but died out after the expulsion of the Stuarts and the conquest of the Puritan spirit. Toward the end of the century the thought of Italy was lulled to sleep in the cult of admirable but empty form.

In the eighteenth century Italian music continued to reflect the sweetness and ease and futility of life. In Germany the springs of inner harmony which had been gathering for a century began to flow like a swift stream in Handel and Bach. France was working at the foundations of a musical theater which had been sketched out by the Florentines and by Lully with the idea of building up a great tragic art after the likeness of Greek drama; and Paris was a kind of workshop where the finest musicians of Europe met together and vied with one another—French, Italians, Germans, and Belgians, all striving to create a style for tragedy and lyric comedy. The whole of French society took an eager part in these productive struggles, which carved the way for the musical revolutionaries of the nineteenth century. The best genius of Germany and Italy in the eighteenth century was perhaps their musicians. France was really more fruitful in other arts than in music; nevertheless, in that direction she climbed higher, I think, than in other arts; for among the fine painters and sculptors in the reign of Louis XV, I cannot find a genius comparable to Rameau. Rameau was much more than Lully's successor, for he founded French dramatic art in music, both on a basis of harmonic learning and on the observation of nature. Lastly, the whole French theater of the eighteenth century, and indeed the whole theater of Europe, was put into the background by the genius of Gluck, whose works are not only masterpieces in music but, to my mind, the masterpieces of French tragedy of the eighteenth century.

At the end of the century, music was expressing the awakening of a revolutionary individualism which roused the whole world. The enormous growth of its power of expression, due to the researches of French and German musicians and the sudden development of symphonic music, put at its disposition a richness of means without equal and a means which was almost new. In thirty years' time, the orchestral symphony and chamber music had produced their masterpieces. The old world, which was then dying, found there its last portraits, and perhaps the most perfect of these were painted by Haydn and Mozart. Then came the Revolution, which after being expressed by the French musicians of the Convention—Gossec, Méhul, Lesueur, and Cherubini—found its most heroic voice in Beethoven—Beethoven, the greatest composer-poet of the Revolution and the Empire, the artist who has most vividly painted the tempests of Napoleonic times, with their anguish and sorrow, the strenuousness of war and the intoxicated transports of a free spirit.

Then streamed out a wave of romantic poetry—the melodies of Weber, Schubert, Chopin, Mendelssohn, Schumann, and Berlioz—those great lyricists of music, the poets and youthful dreamers of a new age, waking with the dawn in strange disquietude. The ancient world of Italy in voluptuous idleness had sung its last song with Rossini and Bellini; the new Italy, the brilliant, noisy Piedmont, made its appearance with Verdi, a singer of the struggles of *Il Risorgimento*. Germany, whose empire had been forming for the past two centuries, found a genius to incarnate its victory in the person of Wagner, the herald who sounded the advent of this military and mysterious empire, the despotic and dangerous master who brought the wild romanticism of Beethoven and Berlioz, the tragedy of the century, to the foot of the Cross, to the mysticism of *Parsifal*. After Wagner this atmosphere of mysticism was spread over all Europe by the help of César Franck and his disciples, by Italian and Belgian masters of oratorio, and by a return to classicism and the art of Palestrina and Bach. And while one side of contemporary music used the wonderful means at hand that had been elaborated by nineteenth-century geniuses in painting the subtle soul of a decadent society, on the other side were the signs of a popular movement which was giving fresh life to art by seeking inspiration from popular melodies and by translating into music popular feelings, among the earlier protagonists of which were Bizet and Mussorgsky.

I hope my readers will forgive this rather rough sketch. I have tried to present only a panoramic view of this vast history by showing how much music is intermingled with the rest of social life.

The thought of the eternal efflorescence of music is a comforting one, and comes like a messenger of peace in the midst of universal disturbance. Political and social history is a never-ending conflict, a thrusting of humanity forward to a doubtful issue, with obstacles at every step which have to be conquered one by one with desperate persistence. But from the history of art we may disengage a character of fullness and peace. In art, there is no thought of progress, for however far we look behind, we see that perfection has already been attained; and that man is absurd who thinks the efforts of the centuries have advanced us a step nearer beauty since the days of St. Gregory and Palestrina. There is nothing sad or humiliating in the idea; on the contrary, art is humanity's dream—a dream of light and liberty and quiet power. It is a dream whose thread is never broken, and there is no fear for the future. In our anxiety and pride we tell ourselves that we have reached the pinnacle of art and are on the eve of a decline. That has been said since the beginning of the world. In every century people have sighed, "All has been said; we have come too late."

Well, everything may have been said; yet everything is still to say. Art, like life, is inexhaustible; and nothing makes us feel the truth of this better than music's ever-welling spring, which has flowed through the centuries until it has become an ocean.

Henri Bergson

WHY DO WE LAUGH?

HENRI BERGSON, *French philosopher and teacher, received the Nobel Prize for Literature in 1927 in "recognition of his rich and life-giving ideas and the resplendent art with which they are presented." Born in 1859 in Paris, he attended the Ecole Normale Superieur and in 1900 joined the faculty of the College de France, where as professor of philosophy his lectures were soon jammed with enthusiastic auditors. At first an advocate of materialism, Bergson later developed a philosophy which emphasized the spiritual and the intuitive in man. His concept that "real" time is not measurable like space, but is of variable duration "as revealed by our consciousness" had a profound influence upon the novels of James Joyce, Virginia Woolf, and others. His interest in the functioning of the human mind led him to study the nature of dreams and of humor.* Laughter (1900), *from which this essay comes, stands right behind* Creative Evolution (1906) *and* Time and Free Will (1922) *as his best-known book. His simple clear style in his philosophical writing attracted wide readership, and when he died in 1941, he was revered as France's greatest philosopher of the century.*

What does laughter mean? What is the basal element in the laughable? What common ground can we find between the grimace of a merry-andrew, a play upon words, an equivocal situation in a burlesque and a scene of high comedy? What method of distillation will yield us invariably the same essence from which so many different products borrow either their obtrusive odor or their delicate perfume? The greatest of thinkers, from Aristotle downwards, have tackled this little problem, which has a knack of baffling every effort, of slipping away and escaping only to bob up again, a pert challenge flung at philosophic speculation.

Our excuse for attacking the problem in our turn must lie in the fact that we shall not aim at imprisoning the comic spirit within a definition. We regard it, above all, as a living thing. However trivial it may be, we shall treat it with the respect due to life. We shall confine ourselves to watching it grow and expand. Passing by imperceptible gradations from one form to another, it will be seen to achieve the strangest metamorphoses. We shall disdain nothing we have seen. Maybe we may gain from this prolonged contact, for the matter of that, something more flexible than an abstract definition,—a practical, intimate acquaintance, such as springs from a long companionship. And maybe we may also find that, unintentionally, we have made an acquaintance that is useful. For the comic spirit has a logic of its own, even in its wildest eccentricities. It has a method in its madness. It dreams, I admit, but it conjures up in its dreams visions that are at once accepted and understood by the whole of a social group. Can it then fail to throw light for us on the way that human imagination works, and more particularly social, collective, and popular imagination? Begotten of real life and akin to art, should it not also have something of its own to tell us about art and life?

At the outset we shall put forward three observations which we look upon as fundamental. They have less bearing on the actually comic than on the field within which it must be sought.

The first point to which attention should be called is that the comic does not exist outside the pale of what is strictly *human*. A landscape may be beautiful, charming and sublime, or insignificant and ugly; it will never be laughable. You may laugh at an animal, but only because you have detected in it some human attitude or expression. You may laugh at a hat, but what you are making fun of, in this case, is not the piece of felt or straw, but the shape that men have given it,—the human caprice whose mold it has assumed. It is strange that so important a fact, and such a simple one too, has not attracted to a greater degree the attention of philosophers. Several have defined man as "an animal which laughs." They might equally well have defined him as an animal which is laughed at; for if any other animal, or some lifeless object, produces the same effect, it is always because of some resemblance to man, of the stamp he gives it or the use he puts it to.

Here I would point out, as a symptom equally worthy of notice, the *absence of feeling* which usually accompanies laughter. It seems as though the comic could not produce its disturbing effect unless it fell, so to say, on the surface of a soul that is thoroughly calm and unruffled. Indifference is its natural environment, for laughter has no greater foe than emotion. I do not mean that we could not laugh at a person who inspires us with pity, for instance, or even with affection, but in such a case we must, for the moment, put our affection out of court and impose silence upon our pity. In a society composed of pure intelligences there would probably be no more tears, though perhaps there would still be laughter; whereas highly emotional souls, in tune and unison with life, in whom every event would be sentimentally prolonged and re-echoed, would neither know nor understand laughter. Try, for a moment, to become interested in everything that is being said and done; act, in imagination, with those who act, and feel with those who feel; in a word, give your sympathy its widest expansion: as though at the touch of a fairy wand you will see the flimsiest of objects assume importance, and a gloomy hue spread over everything. Now step aside, look upon life as a disinterested spectator: many a drama will turn into a comedy. It is enough for us to stop our ears to the sound of music in a room, where dancing is going on, for the dancers at once to appear ridiculous. How many human actions would stand a similar test? Should we not see many of them suddenly pass from grave to gay, on isolating them from the accompanying music of sentiment? To produce the whole of its effect, then, the comic demands something like a momentary anesthesia of the heart. Its appeal is to intelligence, pure and simple.

This intelligence, however, must always remain in touch with other intelligences. And here is the third fact to which attention should be drawn. You would hardly appreciate the comic if you felt yourself isolated from others. Laughter appears to stand in need of an echo. Listen to it carefully: it is not an articulate, clear, well-defined sound; it is something which would fain be prolonged by reverberating from one to another, something beginning with a crash, to continue in successive rumblings, like thunder in a mountain. Still, this reverberation cannot go on forever. It can travel within as wide a circle as you please: the circle remains, none the less, a closed one. Our laughter is always the laughter of a group. It may, perchance, have happened to you, when seated in a railway carriage or at *table d'hôte*, to hear travelers relating to one another stories which must have been comic to them, for they laughed heartily. Had you been one of their company, you would have laughed like them, but, as you were not, you had no desire whatever to do so. A man who was once asked why he did not weep at a sermon when everybody else was shedding tears replied: "I don't belong to the parish!" What that man thought of tears would be still more true of laughter. However spontaneous it seems, laughter always implies a kind of secret freemasonry, or even complicity, with other laughers, real or imaginary. How often has it been said that the fuller the theater, the more uncontrolled the laughter of the audience! On the other hand, how often has the remark been made that many comic effects are incapable of translation from one language to another, because they refer to the customs and ideas of a particular social group! It is through not understanding the importance of this double fact that the comic has been looked upon as a mere curiosity in which the mind finds amusement, and laughter itself as a strange, isolated phenomenon, without any bearing on the rest of human activity. Hence those definitions which tend to make the comic into an abstract relation between ideas: "an intellectual contrast," "a patent absurdity," etc., definitions which, even were they really suitable to every form of the comic, would not in the least explain why the comic makes us laugh. How, indeed, should it come about that this particular logical relation, as soon as it is perceived, contracts, expands and shakes our limbs, whilst all other relations leave the body unaffected? It is not from this point of view that we shall approach the problem. To understand laughter, we must put it back into its natural environment, which is society, and above all must we determine the utility of its function, which is a social one. Such, let us say at once, will be the leading idea of all our investigations. Laughter must answer to certain requirements of life in common. It must have a *social* signification.

Let us clearly mark the point towards which our three preliminary observations are converging. The comic will come into being, it appears, whenever a group of men concentrate their attention on one of their number, imposing silence on their emotions and calling into play nothing but their intelligence. What, now, is the particular point on which their attention will have to be concentrated, and what will here be the function of intelligence? To reply to these questions will be at once to come to closer grips with the problem. But here a few examples have become indispensable.

II

A man, running along the street, stumbles and falls; the passers-by burst out laughing. They would not laugh at him, I imagine, could they suppose that the whim had suddenly seized him to sit down on the ground. They laugh because his sitting down is involuntary. Consequently, it is not his sudden change of attitude that raises a laugh, but rather the involuntary element in this change,—his clumsiness, in fact. Perhaps there was a stone on the road. He should have altered his pace or avoided the obstacle. Instead of that, through lack of elasticity, through absentmindedness and a kind of physical obstinacy, *as a result, in fact, of rigidity or of momentum*, the muscles continued to perform the same movement when the circumstances of the case called for something else. That is the reason of the man's fall, and also of the people's laughter.

Now, take the case of a person who attends to the petty occupations of his everyday life with mathematical precision. The objects around him, however, have all been tampered with by a mischievous wag, the result being that when he dips his pen into the inkstand he draws it out all covered with mud, when he fancies he is sitting down on a solid chair he finds himself sprawling on the floor, in a word his actions are all topsy-turvy or mere beating the air, while in every case the effect is invariably one of momentum. Habit has given the impulse: what was wanted was to check the movement or deflect it. He did nothing of the sort, but continued like a machine in the same straight line. The victim, then, of a practical joke is in a position similar to that of a runner who falls—he is comic for the same reason. The laughable element in both cases consists of a certain *mechanical inelasticity*, just where one would expect to find the wideawake adaptability and the living pliableness of a human being. The only difference in the two cases is that the former happened of itself, whilst the latter was obtained artificially. In the first instance, the passer-by does nothing but look on, but in the second the mischievous wag intervenes.

All the same, in both cases the result has been brought about by an external circumstance. The comic is therefore accidental: it remains, so to speak, in superficial contact with the person. How is it to penetrate within? The necessary conditions will be fulfilled when mechanical rigidity no longer requires for its manifestation a stumbling-block which either the hazard of circumstance or human knavery has set in its way, but extracts by natural processes, from its own store, an inexhaustible series of opportunities for externally revealing its presence. Suppose, then, we imagine a mind always thinking of what it has just done and never of what it is doing, like a song which lags behind its accompaniment. Let us try to picture to ourselves a certain inborn lack of elasticity of both senses and intelligence, which brings it to pass that we continue to see what is no longer visible, to hear what is no longer audible, to say what is no longer to the point: in short, to adapt ourselves to a past and therefore imaginary situation, when we ought to be shaping our conduct in accordance with the reality which is present. This time the comic will take up its abode in the person himself; it is the person who will supply it with everything—matter and form, cause and opportunity. Is it then surprising that the absent-minded individual—for this is the character we have just been describing—has usually fired the imagination of comic authors? When La Bruyère came across this particular type, he realized, on analyzing it, that he had got hold of a recipe for the wholesale manufacture of comic effects. As a matter of fact he overdid it, and gave us far too lengthy and detailed a description of *Ménalque,* coming back to his subject, dwelling and expatiating on it beyond all bounds. The very facility of the subject fascinated him. Absentmindedness, indeed, is not perhaps the actual fountain-head of the comic, but surely it is contiguous to a certain stream of facts and fancies which flows straight from the fountain-head. It is situated, so to say, on one of the great natural watersheds of laughter.

Now, the effect of absentmindedness may gather strength in its turn. There is a general law, the first example of which we have just encountered, and which we will formulate in the following terms: when a certain comic effect has its origin in a certain cause, the more natural we regard the cause to be, the more comic shall we find the effect. Even now we laugh at absentmindedness when presented to us as a simple fact. Still more laughable will be the absentmindedness we have seen springing up and growing before our very eyes, with whose origin we are acquainted and whose life-history we can reconstruct. To choose a definite example: suppose a man has taken to reading nothing but romances of love and chivalry. Attracted and fascinated by his heroes, his thoughts and intentions gradually turn more and more towards them, till one fine day we find him walking among us like a somnambulist. His actions are distractions, But then his distractions can be traced back to a definite, positive cause. They are no longer cases of *absence* of mind, pure and simple; they find their explanation in the *presence* of the individual in quite definite, though imaginary, surroundings. Doubtless a fall is always a fall, but it is one thing to tumble into a well because you were looking anywhere but in front of you, it is quite another thing to fall into it because you were intent upon a star. It was certainly a star at which Don Quixote was gazing. How profound is the comic element in the overromantic, Utopian bent of mind! And yet, if you reintroduce the idea of absentmindedness, which acts as a go-between, you will see this profound comic element uniting with the most superficial type. Yes, indeed, these whimsical wild enthusiasts, these madmen who are yet so strangely reasonable, excite us to laughter by playing on the same chords within ourselves, by setting in motion the same inner mechanism, as does the victim of a practical joke or the passer-by who slips down in the street. They, too, are runners who fall and simple souls who are being hoaxed—runners after the ideal who stumble over realities, childlike dreamers for whom life delights to lie in wait. But, above all, they are past-masters in absentmindedness, with this superiority over their fellows that their absentmindedness is systematic and organized around one central idea, and that their mishaps are also quite coherent, thanks to the inexorable logic which reality applies to the correction of dreams, so that they kindle in those around them, by a series of cumulative effects, a hilarity capable of unlimited expansion.

Now, let us go a little further. Might not certain vices have the same relation to character that the rigidity of a fixed idea has to intellect? Whether as a moral kink or a crooked twist given to the will, vice has often the appearance of a curvature of the soul. Doubtless there are vices into which the soul plunges deeply with all its pregnant potency, which it rejuvenates and drags along with it into a moving circle of reincarnations. Those are tragic vices. But the vice capable of making us comic is, on the contrary, that which is brought from without, like a ready-made frame into which we are to step. It lends us its own rigidity instead of borrowing from us our flexibility. We do not render it more complicated; on the contrary, it simplifies us. Here, as we shall see later on in the concluding section of this study, lies the essential difference between comedy and drama. A drama, even when portraying passions or vices that bear a name, so completely incorporates them in the person that their names are forgotten, their general characteristics effaced, and we no longer think of them at all, but rather of the person in whom they are assimilated; hence, the title of a drama can seldom be anything else than a proper noun. On the other hand, many comedies have a common noun as their title: *l'Avare, le Joueur*, etc. Were you asked to think of a play capable of being called *le Jaloux*, for instance, you would find that *Sganarelle* or *George Dandin* would occur to your mind, but not *Othello: le Jaloux* could only be the title of a comedy. The reason is that, however intimately vice, when comic, is associated with persons, it none the less retains its simple, independent existence, it remains the central character, present though invisible, to which the characters in flesh and blood on the stage are attached. At times it delights in dragging them down with its own weight and making them share in its tumbles. More frequently, however, it plays on them as on an instrument or pulls the strings as though they were puppets. Look closely: you will find that the art of the comic poet consists in making us so well acquainted with the particular vice, in introducing us, the spectators, to such a degree of intimacy with it, that in the end we get hold of some of the strings of the marionette with which he is playing, and actually work them ourselves; this it is that explains part of the pleasure we feel. Here, too, it is really a kind of automatism that makes us laugh—an automatism, as we have already remarked, closely akin to mere absentmindedness. To realize this more fully, it need only be noted that a comic character is generally comic in proportion to his ignorance of himself. The comic person is unconscious. As though wearing the ring of Gyges with reverse effect, he becomes invisible to himself while remaining visible to all the world. A character in a tragedy will make no change in his conduct because he will know how it is judged by us; he may continue therein even though fully conscious of what he is and feeling keenly the horror he inspires in us. But a defect that is ridiculous, as soon as it feels itself to be so, endeavors to modify itself or at least to appear as though it did. Were Harpagon to see us laugh at his miserliness, I do not say that he would get rid of it, but he would either show it less or show it differently. Indeed, it is in this sense only that laughter "corrects men's manners." It makes us at once endeavor to appear what we ought to be, what some day we shall perhaps end in being.

It is unnecessary to carry this analysis any further. From the runner who falls to the simpleton who is hoaxed, from a state of being hoaxed to one of absentmindedness, from absentmindedness to wild enthusiasm, from wild enthusiasm to various distortions of character and will, we have followed the line of progress along which the comic becomes more and more deeply imbedded in the person, yet without ceasing, in its subtler manifestations, to recall to us some trace of what we noticed in its grosser forms, an effect of automatism and of inelasticity. Now we can obtain a first glimpse—a distant one, it is true, and still hazy and confused—of the laughable side of human nature and of the ordinary function of laughter.

What life and society require of each of us is a constantly alert attention that discerns the outlines of the present situation, together with a certain elasticity of mind and body to enable us to adapt ourselves in consequence. *Tension,* and *elasticity* are two forces, mutually complementary, which life brings into play. If these two forces are lacking in the body to any considerable extent, we have sickness and infirmity and accidents of every kind. If they are lacking in the mind, we find every degree of mental deficiency, every variety of insanity. Finally, if they are lacking in the character, we have cases of the gravest inadaptability to social life, which are the sources of misery and at times the causes of crime. Once these elements of inferiority that affect the serious side of existence are removed—and they tend to eliminate themselves in what has been called the struggle for life—the person can live, and that in common with other persons. But society asks for something more; it is not satisfied with simply living, it insists on living well. What it now has to dread is that each one of us, content with paying attention to what affects the essentials of life, will, so far as the rest is concerned, give way to the easy automatism of acquired habits. Another thing it must fear is that the members of whom it is made up, instead of aiming after an increasingly delicate adjustment of wills which will fit more and more perfectly into one another, will confine themselves to respecting simply the fundamental conditions of this adjustment: a cut-and-dried agreement among the persons will not satisfy it, it insists on a constant striving after reciprocal adaptation. Society will therefore be suspicious of all *inelasticity* of character, of mind and even of body, because it is the possible sign of a slumbering activity as well as of an activity with separatist tendencies, that inclines to swerve from the common center round which society gravitates: in short, because it is the sign of an eccentricity. And yet, society cannot intervene at this stage by material repression, since it is not affected in a material fashion. It is confronted with something that makes it uneasy, but only as a symptom—scarcely a threat, at the very most a gesture. A gesture, therefore, will be its reply. Laughter must be something of this kind, a sort of *social gesture*. By the fear which it inspires, it restrains eccentricity, keeps constantly awake and in mutual contact certain activities of a secondary order which might retire into their shell and go to sleep, and in short, softens down whatever the surface of the social body may retain of mechanical inelasticity. Laughter, then, does not belong to the province of esthetics alone, since unconsciously (and even immorally in many particular instances) it pursues a utilitarian aim of general improvement. And yet there is something esthetic about it, since the comic comes into being just when society and the individual, freed from the worry of self-preservation, begin to regard themselves as works of art. In a word, if a circle be drawn round those actions and dispositions—implied in individual or social life—to which their natural consequences bring their own penalties, there remains outside this sphere of emotion and struggle—and within a neutral zone in which man simply exposes himself to man's curiosity—a certain rigidity of body, mind and character that society would still like to get rid of in order to obtain from its members the greatest possible degree of elasticity and sociability. This rigidity is the comic, and laughter is its corrective.

Still, we must not accept this formula as a definition of the comic. It is suitable only for cases that are elementary, theoretical and perfect, in which the comic is free from all adulteration. Nor do we offer it, either, as an explanation. We prefer to make it, if you will, the *leitmotiv* which is to accompany all our explanations. We must ever keep it in mind, though without dwelling on it too much, somewhat as a skillful fencer must think of the discontinuous movements of the lesson whilst his body is given up to the continuity of the fencing-match. We will now endeavor to reconstruct the sequence of comic forms, taking up again the thread that leads from the horse-play of a clown up to the most refined effects of comedy, following this thread in its often unforeseen windings, halting at intervals to look around, and finally getting back, if possible, to the point at which the thread is dangling and where we shall perhaps find—since the comic oscillates between life and art—the general relation that art bears to life.

III

Let us begin at the simplest point. What is a comic physiognomy? Where does a ridiculous expression of the face come from? And what is, in this case, the distinction between the comic and the ugly? Thus stated, the question could scarcely be answered in any other than an arbitrary fashion. Simple though it may appear, it is, even now, too subtle to allow of a direct attack. We should have to begin with a definition of ugliness, and then discover what addition the comic makes to it; now, ugliness is not much easier to analyze than is beauty. However, we will employ an artifice which will often stand us in good stead. We will exaggerate the problem, so to speak, by magnifying the effect to the point of making the cause visible. Suppose, then, we intensify ugliness to the point of deformity, and study the transition from the deformed to the ridiculous.

Now, certain deformities undoubtedly possess over others the sorry privilege of causing some persons to laugh; some hunchbacks, for instance, will excite laughter. Without at this point entering into useless details, we will simply ask the reader to think of a number of deformities, and then to divide them into two groups: on the one hand, those which nature has directed towards the ridiculous; and on the other, those which absolutely diverge from it. No doubt he will hit upon the following law: A *deformity that may become comic is a deformity that a normally built person could successfully imitate.*

Is it not, then, the case that the hunchback suggests the appearance of a person who holds himself badly? His back seems to have contracted an ugly stoop. By a kind of physical obstinacy, by *rigidity*, in a word, it persists in the habit it has contracted. Try to see with your eyes alone. Avoid reflection, and above all, do not reason. Abandon all your prepossessions; seek to recapture a fresh, direct and primitive impression. The vision you will reacquire will be one of this kind. You will have before you a man bent on cultivating a certain rigid attitude whose body, if one may use the expression, is one vast grin.

Now, let us go back to the point we wished to clear up. By

toning down a deformity that is laughable, we ought to obtain an ugliness that is comic. A laughable expression of the face, then, is one that will make us think of something rigid and, so to speak, coagulated, in the wonted mobility of the face. What we shall see will be an ingrained twitching or a fixed grimace. It may be objected that every habitual expression of the face, even when graceful and beautiful, gives us this same impression of something stereotyped? Here an important distinction must be drawn. When we speak of expressive beauty or even expressive ugliness, when we say that a face possesses expression, we mean expression that may be stable, but which we conjecture to be mobile. It maintains, in the midst of its fixity, a certain indecision in which are obscurely portrayed all possible shades of the state of mind it expresses, just as the sunny promise of a warm day manifests itself in the haze of a spring morning. But a comic expression of the face is one that promises nothing more than it gives. It is a unique and permanent grimace. One would say that the person's whole moral life has crystallized into this particular cast of features. This is the reason why a face is all the more comic, the more nearly it suggests to us the idea of some simple mechanical action in which its personality would for ever be absorbed. Some faces seem to be always engaged in weeping, others in laughing or whistling, others, again, in eternally blowing an imaginary trumpet, and these are the most comic faces of all. Here again is exemplified the law according to which the more natural the explanation of the cause, the more comic is the effect. Automatism, *inelasticity*, habit that has been contracted and maintained, are clearly the causes why a face makes us laugh. But this effect gains in intensity when we are able to connect these characteristics with some deep-seated cause, a certain *fundamental absentmindedness*, as though the soul had allowed itself to be fascinated and hypnotized by the materiality of a simple action.

We shall now understand the comic element in caricature. However regular we may imagine a face to be, however harmonious its lines and supple its movements, their adjustment is never altogether perfect: there will always be discoverable the signs of some impending bias, the vague suggestion of a possible grimace, in short, some favorite distortion towards which nature seems to be particularly inclined. The art of the caricaturist consists in detecting this, at times, imperceptible tendency, and in rendering it visible to all eyes by magnifying it. He makes his models grimace, as they would do themselves if they went to the end of their tether. Beneath the skin-deep harmony of form, he divines the deep-seated recalcitrance of matter. He realizes disproportions and deformations which must have existed in nature as mere inclinations, but which have not succeeded in coming to a head, being held in check by a higher force. His art, which has a touch of the diabolical, raises up the demon who had been overthrown by the angel. Certainly, it is an art that exaggerates, and yet the definition would be very far from complete were exaggeration alone alleged to be its aim and object, for there exist caricatures that are more lifelike than portraits, caricatures in which the exaggeration is scarcely noticeable, whilst, inversely, it is quite possible to exaggerate to excess without obtaining a real caricature. For exaggeration to be comic, it must not appear as an aim, but rather as a means that the artist is using in order to make manifest to our eyes the distortions which he sees in embryo. It is this process of distortion that is of moment and interest. And that is precisely why we shall look for it even in those elements of the face that are incapable of movement, in the curve of a nose or the shape of an ear. For, in our eyes, form is always the outline of a movement. The caricaturist who alters the size of a nose, but respects its ground plan, lengthening it, for instance, in the very direction in which it was being lengthened by nature, is really making the nose indulge in a grin. Henceforth, we shall always look upon the original as having determined to lengthen itself and start grinning. In this sense, one might say that Nature herself often meets with the successes of a caricaturist. In the movement through which she has slit that mouth, curtailed that chin and bulged out that cheek, she would appear to have succeeded in completing the intended grimace, thus outwitting the restraining supervision of a more reasonable force. In that case, the face we laugh at is, so to speak, its own caricature.

To sum up, whatever be the doctrine to which our reason assents, our imagination has a very clear-cut philosophy of its own: in every human form it sees the effort of a soul which is shaping matter, a soul which is infinitely supple and perpetually in motion, subject to no law of gravitation, for it is not the earth that attracts it. This soul imparts a portion of its winged lightness to the body it animates: the immateriality which thus passes into matter is what is called gracefulness. Matter, however, is obstinate and resists. It draws to itself the ever-alert activity of this higher principle, would fain convert it to its own inertia and cause it to revert to mere automatism. It would fain immobilize the intelligently varied movements of the body in stupidly contracted grooves, stereotype in permanent grimaces the fleeting expressions of the face, in short imprint on the whole person such an attitude as to make it appear immersed and absorbed in the materiality of some mechanical occupation instead of ceaselessly renewing its vitality by keeping in touch with a living ideal. Where matter thus succeeds in dulling the outward life of the soul, in petrifying its movements and thwarting its gracefulness, it achieves, at the expense of the body, an effect that is comic. If, then, at this point we wish to define the comic by comparing it with its contrary, we should have to contrast it with gracefulness even more than with beauty. It partakes rather of the unsprightly than of the unsightly, of *rigidness* rather than of *ugliness*.

IV

We will now pass from the comic element in *forms* to that in *gestures* and *movements*. Let us at once state the law which seems to govern all the phenomena of this kind. It may indeed be deduced without any difficulty from the considerations stated above.

The attitudes, gestures and movements of the human body are laughable in exact proportion as that body reminds us of a mere machine.

There is no need to follow this law through the details of its immediate applications, which are innumerable. To verify it directly, it would be sufficient to study closely the work of comic artists, eliminating entirely the element of caricature, and omitting that portion of the comic which is not inherent in the drawing itself. For, obviously, the comic element in a drawing is often a borrowed one, for which the text supplies all the stock-in-trade.

I mean that the artist may be his own understudy in the shape of a satirist, or even a playwright, and that then we laugh far less at the drawings themselves than at the satire or comic incident they represent. But if we devote our whole attention to the drawing with the firm resolve to think of nothing else, we shall probably find that it is generally comic in proportion to the clearness, as well as the subtleness, with which it enables us to see a man as a jointed puppet. The suggestion must be a clear one, for inside the person we must distinctly perceive, as though through a glass, a set-up mechanism. But the suggestion must also be a subtle one, for the general appearance of the person, whose every limb has been made rigid as a machine, must continue to give us the impression of a living being. The more exactly these two images, that of a person and that of a machine, fit into each other, the more striking is the comic effect, and the more consummate the art of the draughtsman. The originality of a comic artist is thus expressed in the special kind of life he imparts to a mere puppet.

We will, however, leave on one side the immediate application of the principle, and at this point insist only on the more remote consequences. The illusion of a machine working in the inside of the person is a thing that only crops up amid a host of amusing effects; but for the most part it is a fleeting glimpse, that is immediately lost in the laughter it provokes. To render it permanent, analysis and reflection must be called into play.

In a public speaker, for instance, we find that gesture vies with speech. Jealous of the latter, gesture closely dogs the speaker's thought, demanding also to act as interpreter. Well and good; but then it must pledge itself to follow thought through all the phases of its development. An idea is something that grows, buds, blossoms and ripens from the beginning to the end of a speech. It never halts, never repeats itself. It must be changing every moment, for to cease to change would be to cease to live. Then let gesture display a like animation! Let it accept the fundamental law of life, which is the complete negation of repetition! But I find that a certain movement of head or arm, a movement always the same, seems to return at regular intervals. If I notice it and it succeeds in diverting my attention, if I wait for it to occur and it occurs when I expect it, then involuntarily I laugh. Why? Because

I now have before me a machine that works automatically. This is no longer life, it is automatism established in life and imitating it. It belongs to the comic.

This is also the reason why gestures, at which we never dreamt of laughing, become laughable when imitated by another individual. The most elaborate explanations have been offered for this extremely simple fact. A little reflection, however, will show that our mental state is ever changing, and that if our gestures faithfully followed these inner movements, if they were as fully alive as we, they would never repeat themselves, and so would keep imitation at bay. We begin, then, to become imitable only when we cease to be ourselves. I mean our gestures can only be imitated in their mechanical uniformity, and therefore exactly in what is alien to our living personality. To imitate any one is to bring out the element of automatism he has allowed to creep into his person. And as this is the very essence of the ludicrous, it is no wonder that imitation gives rise to laughter.

Still, if the imitation of gestures is intrinsically laughable, it will become even more so when it busies itself in deflecting them, though without altering their form, towards some mechanical occupation, such as sawing wood, striking on an anvil, or tugging away at an imaginary bell-rope. Not that vulgarity is the essence of the comic,—although certainly it is to some extent an ingredient,—but rather that the incriminated gesture seems more frankly mechanical when it can be connected with a simple operation, as though it were intentionally mechanical. To suggest this mechanical interpretation ought to be one of the favorite devices of parody. We have reached this result through deduction, but I imagine clowns have long had an intuition of the fact.

This seems to me the solution of the little riddle propounded by Pascal in one passage of his *Thoughts:* "Two faces that are alike, although neither of them excites laughter by itself, make us laugh when together, on account of their likeness." It might just as well be said: "The gestures of a public speaker, no one of which is laughable by itself, excite laughter by their repetition." The truth is that a really living life should never repeat itself. Wherever there is repetition or complete similarity, we always suspect some mechanism at work behind the living. Analyze the impression you get from two faces that are too much alike, and you will find that you are thinking of two copies cast in the same mold, or two impressions of the same seal, or two reproductions of the same negative,—in a word, of some manufacturing process or other. This deflection of life towards the mechanical is here the real cause of laughter.

And laughter will be more pronounced still, if we find on the stage not merely two characters, as in the example from Pascal, but several, nay, as great a number as possible, the image of one another, who come and go, dance and gesticulate together, simultaneously striking the same attitudes and tossing their arms about in the same manner. This time, we distinctly think of marionettes. Invisible threads seem to us to be joining arms to arms, legs to legs, each muscle in one face to its fellow-muscle in the other: by reason of the absolute uniformity which prevails, the very litheness of the bodies seems to stiffen as we gaze, and the actors themselves seem transformed into lifeless automata. Such, at least, appears to be the artifice underlying this somewhat obvious form of amusement. I daresay the performers have never read Pascal, but what they do is merely to realize to the full the suggestions contained in Pascal's words. If, as is undoubtedly the case, laughter is caused in the second instance by the hallucination of a mechanical effect, it must already have been so, though in more subtle fashion, in the first.

Continuing along this path, we dimly perceive the increasingly important and far-reaching consequences of the law we have just stated. We faintly catch still more fugitive glimpses of mechanical effects, glimpses suggested by man's complex actions, no longer merely by his gestures. We instinctively feel that the usual devices of comedy, the periodical repetition of a word or a scene, the systematic inversion of the parts, the geometrical development of a farcical misunderstanding and many other stage contrivances must derive their comic force from the same source,—the art of the playwright probably consisting in setting before us an obvious clockwork arrangement of human events, while carefully preserving an outward aspect of probability and thereby retaining something of the suppleness of life.

Johannes V. Jensen

JOHANNES V. JENSEN, *Denmark's most virile and challenging writer, was born in the northern village of Forsö in 1873. The son of a veterinarian, he went to Copenhagen to study medicine, but never practiced this profession. His studies, however, created an interest in science which was expressed later in many essays. He completed two novels early in his literary career, but first won attention with* Himmerland Stories (1898), *simple yet spirited tales about his native region. Two trips to the United States made Jensen an articulate admirer of America and resulted in two more novels, additional stories, and a volume of poetry. His major work, for which he received the Nobel Prize in 1944, is an ambitious achievement entitled* The Longest Journey, *from which the following selection is drawn as an example of narrative skillfully combined with exposition. This six-part epic traces the development of man from a brute superanthropoid with a gradually awakening intelligence, down to the discovery of America, when man emerges as a builder, inventor, and visionary. Jensen died in 1950 in the city where he had studied and settled.*

The most ancient symbol of the Aztecs, which was connected with the founding of Tenochtitlan, the place of the cactus rock, was a rock on which just enough mold had collected for the cactus to grow; on the cactus sat an eagle, and in its beak it held a serpent: the natural features of the Mexican plateau summed up in an image.

On the spot where the first Aztecs saw this sign they had built their pueblo. After the arrival of the Spaniards they might have extended this totem to signify their fate, in a dramatic sense, a duel to the death. To this day it is the national standard of Mexico: the Eagle and the Serpent united and combining their forces.

But the epoch of Cortes was typified by the eagle swooping down upon the rattlesnake with beak and claw.

The conquest of Mexico is known to all, in its several data: how Cortes advanced on to the plateau, the conspiracy of Cholula, Malina's service and the massacre, the entrance into Mexico and Montezuma's captivity in his own city, the parenthesis with Narvaez and Alvarado's doubtful conduct in Mexico during the absence of Cortes, the revolt, Montezuma's death and the disastrous retreat from Mexico, the return and the siege, the sacrifice of the Spanish prisoners, the famine among the natives, and finally their surrender. All this we have in lengthy descriptions, losing in rapidity of action the more they are detailed.

With due respect to the true sequence of events, our memory, our inner eye, pictures the conquest of Mexico in foreshortening, a free consideration of the characters as they develop in one place, no matter whether events chanced to come before or after, the law of the drama; we see these protagonists before us, Cortes and Montezuma, Malina, Alvarado, Sandoval and other heroes, Huitzilopochtli and his repulsive priests, the harrowing night when Spaniards and Mexicans fought together in the gloomy cannibal city floating on causeways in a salt lake like a Venice of the Underworld—the threescore naked, shivering Europeans who were sacrificed up on Huitzilopochtli's teocalli, in full view of all the survivors—what a panopticon! Burning altars, burning houses, the whole scene shown up by fire, and in the background Popocatepetl in the burning sky, fire above fire!

And the piece may begin quite chronologically with the conspiracy, with Montezuma in the foreground, in person, not hiding in the wings, and the scene Tenochtitlan; the massacre we can lump together with Alvarado's massacre, and assign the butcheries, multiplied by two, to the great spring festival, historically enough as regards the second; the rest, the great fight in the city, the storming of the temples, the retreat, the sacrifices, the investment and starvation, we can present in rapid acts succeeding or jostling one another.

Well then: the Spring Festival. It was celebrated with remarkable ancient rites, a young Aztec being chosen for his strength and beauty, proclaimed as a god and married to four of the most beautiful maidens in the country, whereafter the honeymoon was solemnized with all possible luxury and magnificence for twenty days, a symbol of fertility and of the return of spring with all its gifts. On the twenty-first day the festival took on a more general character; all the young men and maidens dressed themselves in holiday attire, gorgeous cloaks of quetzal-feathers with jewels and gold on their limbs, spring made visible, and in a great solemn procession, so sacred that no other public act, not even war, might take place on that day, they accompanied the young family, the god and his brides, across the great square in the center of Tenochtitlan and up all the steps to the top of the great temple. Here all knelt and worshiped the young god, in whose form Tezcatlipoca himself was presumed to have taken up his abode. Thereupon he was handed over to the priests, sacrificed and slain; his heart was thrown into the golden incense-bowl before the image of the god, and his limbs were delivered to the congregation, to be devoured amid dancing and song.

But all is not as it should be at this festival, it is destined to be interrupted before it can be brought to a harmonious conclusion. The young caciques marching in the procession, the flower of the Aztec nobility, in precious garments of feathers, and with old hereditary emeralds, do they look as unconcerned and innocent as is fitting at a festival of joy? Put your hand on their hearts and perhaps you will feel something hard; for what purpose do they carry the macquauitl under the very raiment of innocence? Dark is the Mexican by nature, but if you look around in the teeming streets of the pueblo, you will notice perhaps that to-day they are more than usually dark, with lips drawn in and eyes like their own muddy lake.

There is one who reads all these faces like an open book, Cortes; for he knows the cipher, and it is Malina who has given it him. She has been quietly at work, at night, naked as a snake round all the holes and corners of the pueblo, using her ears here, playing the wide-mouthed native woman there, within hearing of a couple of distinguished old caciques; all the disguise she needs is to make herself suitably ugly, not an easy thing for this glaring flame of a woman, but she manages it; in the likeness of a per-

fectly doltish slave she carries water in and out of the inner sanc-
tuaries of the highest priestly initiates; she is with Montezuma
without his suspecting it, a meeting more secret than the abyss;
therefore it is that Cortes is so all-knowing, and his lip curls so
grimly under the mustache, inscrutable to all . . . what prep-
arations has not *he* been making in the profoundest secrecy!

A notable trio indeed, as they stand there in a mannerly group
to watch the spring-time pass in gay and joyous procession—Cortes, Montezuma and Malina. Cortes iron-clad from head to foot
in honor of the feast, full dress, with his sweaty soldier's nose
sniffing out of his helmet; Montezuma plainly dressed with only a
few jewels; as the chief man of the realm he has no need of magnificence, and he is in mourning, for though, of course, he stands
here as a free man, the object of the deepest obeisances, he knows
he is a prisoner; finally Malina, with feathers on her head and a
little apron of humming-bird feathers in open-work. The three
can only bestow courtly smiles on one another, gracious and minc-
ing, as they stand there knowing what the other knows; that is to
say, Cortes and Malina know what Montezuma knows, and look
him in the face when he speaks with an air of frankness—but *he*
doesn't know that artillery is posted all round the square, and
grimy gunners match in hand, and that cavalry, men in the saddle, drawn swords and all, are waiting behind the doors, which are
ready to swing open. . . .

Then it is that the three princely spectators, around whom a
courteous distance has hitherto been preserved, seem to become
the center of a circle which draws ever closer, composed as it happens entirely of very tall Aztecs, warlike in appearance, but, of
course, unarmed, only in long, voluminous cloaks. . . .

How pleasant on a festal day like this to be able to put away all
thoughts of bloodshed and abandon oneself entirely to the confidence one feels in an honorable prince, says Cortes with a bow,
as he looks Montezuma in the face, purring through his mustache. He puts his face so close to Montezuma's that the Emperor
shrinks back a little as he nods confirming the truth of the remark.

But Cortes comes still closer with his big, sweaty face, and there
is a glint of steel in those prominent, audacious blue eyes. He

drops his voice and adds another sentence or two, which appear to have a deadly effect upon Montezuma. The life ebbs out of him, his eyes, his features, his frame; he is a dead man, as one is who has betrayed and failed, and is told it to his face by his enemy.

Yes, Cortes tells him in a few dry words that he knows all his schemes, the conspiracy against his life which is ripe for this very moment . . . and by his side Malina crouches, leaning forward so that Montezuma may see her face. He turns yet grayer, for now he knows her, by a gleam she puts into her eyes, so that he remembers her and the night, and how he disclosed all, and in an instant he sees the whole wretchedness of his situation.

Cortes still holds him as though spitted on his gaze, with his face close to his—Eagle and Serpent!—but then he gives over his features entirely to cruelty, draws himself up and throws his gloved hand in the air. A band of disguised Tlascalans, his allies, who have been spread about among the crowd, fall upon certain of the Aztecs, the conspiring caciques and high chieftains, eloquently disclosing the weapons concealed beneath their cloaks— within an hour they are burnt alive at the stake, with a fire of native arrows and spears, a very brisk blaze, under them.

But Cortes' raised hand is a sign for more than that—all at once the cannons thunder from every side, the houses open like yawning mouths, and slowly Alvarado rides out, like a shining tower of steel, man and horse in one, swaying rhythmically up and down, and behind him all the cavalry with closed visors and bright gleaming swords in the air. And now the soldier in Cortes takes fire, now the general is ready for action; with his left hand he closes his helm, and with his right he draws his long singing sword from its sheath, spitting between hand and hilt—*Iago!* A loud, piercing scream is heard at his side, like a leaping ocelot; it is Malina giving vent to her rapacious heart.

Alarum. Volleys of guns and muskets, the twang of cross-bows, cavalry charges, and all the daintily adorned spring procession, the pick of the country's youth, lies swimming in its blood; the god who was to be sacrificed so prettily to himself is knocked down with his flowery wreaths about his head and trodden out of recognition under the horses' hoofs; bloody furrows are ploughed through the tightly packed crowds in the streets, so easily swept from the square; shrieks, curses and death.

And then an ominous pause, a hundred thousand souls hold their breath in horror at what has happened and what there may be to come.

The results: the revolt, the rising of the whole of Mexico, not the nobles this time but the people, whipped up by the priests, the holy war of extermination against this vermin that pretended to be gods and had seized upon the pueblo in order to snatch up all the gold and run away with it. Until now they had put up with all their shamelessness, their desecration of the gods' holy places where they had raised their own torture stake, for no other reason but that Montezuma in his indulgence had taken their part, he whom they had treated like an Indian, and in whose person they had for ever violated the ancient sacred royal house of the Aztecs root and branch, the dignity of the divine king; now there should be an end of that.

The gods were exasperated to the utmost, Huitzilopochtli sweated cold fire at night in his sanctuary, the priests said; he was phosphorescent, and the sacrificial blood on his flanks was alive; Popocatepetl himself, as every one could see, was moved and would soon destroy the world. The omens pointed to the last day being at hand: a three-year-old child which had been sacrificed had babbled prophecies before its death in a language nobody understood; in the stomach of another victim they had found a stone shaped like many-branched lightning; a condor flying from the east had dropped carrion on Huitzilopochtli's teocalli . . . was further evidence required? Mexico's fate was uncertain—but these foreign impostors who had stolen the thunder and in whom everything was false, even to the color of their skins, should die, even if it cost a thousand Mexicans for every one of the palefaces they made an end of!

The rising came at dawn; notwithstanding all other Powers, they would now have the Sun himself in their company; before sunrise a sound as of cockchafers in a sack arose from Mexico, the ardent whispering of a whole population—and that day, when the sun had reached the zenith, a vast pillar of dust and roaring seemed to rise up towards it, broad as the whole city of Mexico; all the countless hosts of the city attacked the palace, where the few whites had at once barricaded themselves—a rain of stones, obsidian arrows, fire-hardened stakes and spears, bare hands, teeth if they got near enough; thousands dropped before the cannons and the tireless Toledo blades, forming heaps in front of the palace, but other thousands came on, and that with a ceaseless shouting, roaring and howling from a multitude of throats, from the moment the sun rose, without cessation all through the day, calculated to scare the enemy—and it scared them.

The situation of the invested Spanish force, now with Narvaez' troops fully 1200 men, 6000 Tlascalans and 80 horses, was indeed desperate; the whole country rose against them, it was as though the earth opened wherever they looked and gave forth Mexicans, in black waves, host upon host of death-defying savages dressed like devils in the skins of beasts and feathers, rolling on towards the palace, howling, yelling and with a devilish ear-splitting noise behind them of terrifying instruments, drums, an inferno of pipes with four holes which screeched uninterruptedly hour after hour, grooved antelope-horns which were scraped with mussel-shells, a music invented by Satan.

Blood ran that day in rivers through the streets of Mexico. Flaming arrows penetrated the palace and set fire to the woodwork, many Spaniards fell, however many lives they took themselves. The howling and the infernal music exhausted the brain, not every one kept up his heroic spirit; the soldiers of Narvaez sat idly and began to ask why they should die to make Cortes' fortune —disorder even in their own lines.

When the position became untenable Cortes made a sally with his bravest,—Alvarado, Sandoval, Olid, all sportsmen to whom fighting was an art,—and together they stormed Huitzilopochtli's temple, an impossible thing, seeing that the pyramid was black from top to bottom, on all its hundred and fourteen terraces, with Mexican warriors, who flung down blazing timbers upon the attackers; they *took* the temple, after three hours of acrobatics and slaughter, set fire to the towers on the top, and—then Huitzilopochtli came!

The Mexicans saw him come out of his sanctuary like a toad out of its hole, but in a recumbent position, how now—the Spaniards were behind him, rolling him along; out he came in his square block over the edge of the topmost platform, and down he thundered squarely over all the steps, taking a dozen at a jump, knocking holes in the masonry and a corner off himself, smoking with a breath of thunder, and finally crushing a group of redjerkined priests who stood howling at the foot of the pyramid!

A mighty exploit, the fall of Mexico underlined—but a piece of bravado; the Mexicans themselves were not dead yet, they came and continued to come, one black wave out of another like the smoke of a conflagration, shooting, stabbing, yelling, not a Spaniard but was wounded; what could be done?

An appeal to the people, through Montezuma himself, was attempted; he had power over them after all, and was induced to go out on the roof and get them to listen to reason. A great moment; the noise actually stopped for a few minutes and gave place to a stillness never known before, when Montezuma showed himself and the crowds saw him they had regarded as the highest and most dignified of all men. He spoke, a single thin human voice was heard amid the ocean of silence, with thousands of lowering eyes directed upon him.

But he had no answer. Stones answered him, arrows and stones; wounded and bleeding, Montezuma staggered and had to be led away.

No, he had no answer. For he was no longer Montezuma. They had torn him out of their hearts. The Council, the ancient power in the land, had met and declared his hereditary rights forfeit; he was a nobody now, and in his stead Guatemozin, the next-of-kin, had been proclaimed God's deputy and leader of the armies.

Then Cortes himself tried to appeal to the people. After the fall of the temple he went up on to the roof with Malina, his interpreter, obtained silence, a silence of death, and spoke to the people; no mild words of peace and conciliation, which was what he desired, but the cold anticipations of the general, designed for moral effect:

Now they could see for themselves, their temple destroyed, their gods reduced to dust, how could they think of resisting him?

Amicably, such and such terms; with continued resistance, not one stone left upon another in Mexico!

And these harsh words were translated by Malina into flute-like tones; the ocelot had the ear of the human ocean all to herself, and mewed out the utterances of the man of iron to the thousands of warriors, above whose heads the dust of war hovered in a cloud. She twisted her body charmingly and licked her pink lips, in feathers for the occasion, but with the gleam of her copper limbs shining through like a lavish fire, a willing and voluptuous echo of Cortes' destroying words.

They gave him an answer, some old cacique or other acted as spokesman and spoke very plainly, to the effect that in a short time they would have no more food, that most of them were wounded and patched up—and moreover the bridges on the causeways were broken, they needn't think they could get away!

It was true.

After the pause, drums, pipes, antelope-horn rattles and a hundred thousand howling, yelling Aztecs: the burial chorus started again and would not stop until the funeral was over. And what graves to end in!

Meanwhile Montezuma died. A blow to Cortes, for even if he was now quite out of favor he must have a party and might have been used again. But they could not keep life in him; he tore off his bandages, would not eat, preserved an obstinate silence, with downcast eyes, from the time he was stoned by his own people until his death. The chronicler notes that he refused to kiss the crucifix!

If Columbus was the most disappointed man in history, Montezuma rivaled him in a way; both of them had a great and genuine hope of seeing God, and one of them found a cannibal, the other Cortes.

The night after Montezuma's death Cortes commenced the retreat.

It was the famous night of sorrow, indelicately referred to by Diaz as the night when they were thrown out of Mexico. On this occasion he had an experience he had never known before, and of which he had never imagined the possibility—he was *afraid*. Yes, he mentions the fact with surprise and in remarkable terms, almost as though fear were some kind of horrible creature outside himself with which he here became acquainted. So terrible was the night.

With scattered features and incidents brought together in foreshortening the night appears thus—Popocatepetl in the leading part:

He stands flickering in his heaven, lost in his own glowing dreams, with his own long time, and in one of his instants, when he shoots up fire and lays bare the whole plateau beneath him in the gleam, a land of lava with black shadows, and a salt lake with heavy, sluggish waters, in the lake a city, seemingly caked together with blood and lime—in such an instant it is that they fight and make history down there, Eagle and Serpent, a duel in the air, the bird of prey has the reptile in its claws, and the snake writhes and tries to get at its breast with its poison-fang.

Cortes waited for the darkest hour of midnight, as far as it could be dark in Tenochtitlan with its hundreds of flaming altars, before he set out, with artillery, horses and all, his whole train and all his men, a special detachment to carry the great wooden bridge they had built in all secrecy to lay across the gap in the causeway.

It was this gap of sorrow that separated them from the dry land; here was the fighting, and here they suffered their losses, with the burning city at their back and the Mexicans after them on the causeway, the lake black with their canoes; for they had word of the departure only too soon, and set fire to everything that would burn in the city to show the enemy the way home, came after him with yells and roars and sharp spears, a whole world of splintered glass; and once more the Spaniards had to cut into them and keep them off rank by rank, while everlastingly fresh ranks and more canoes dashed up.

A frightful night. Some got across, then the bridge gave way; a living mush of men struggled in the water, drowned, were slaughtered; the gap was filled up with the guns and the sinking baggage, high enough for a few more to make their way across, last of the rearguard Alvarado, who *jumped* over; impossible, declares the sober Bernal Diaz, but to this day everybody says he did it; over he came.

Yes, down in the muddy bottom of the lake lay all the good guns. The greater part of all Cortes' gold, in chests and boxes, found there a safe deposit for eternity; a terrible pity, the sun and moon in heavy chased gold, as big as wheels, bars enough to build a little house, cast from all the art treasures of Tenochtitlan; precious stones to an untold amount. Only the melancholy songs of the Spanish homeland were capable of giving utterance to such a grief. Yes, they lost all. Yet one long chest was saved of the baggage, it *had* to come through—Cortes had put it in charge of his most trusted porters and given it an escort of his keenest blades; in it Malina was concealed, packed away in feathers like a jewel, a fortune in quetzal-feathers at any rate; we may guess her dreams were warm ones if she slept through the trip.

Malina survived the horrors of the night. Apart from her the Spaniards lost all their slaves, male and female; Montezuma's children, who were with the baggage, were slain. All but twenty of the horses perished. Diaz drops a tear over Alvarado's sorrel mare; she must have been worth it. We hear of one other woman being saved, the only Castilian woman who was ever with the expedition, according to Diaz, by name Maria de Estrada—street? platform?—and a remarkable woman she was, fought like a man on the causeway with a two-handed sword, and came through alive. What a woman! Imagine her experiences!

Seven hundred Spaniards perished that night, drowned or slain, some taken prisoner, nameless most of them, and yet every single one had once been swung up to the ceiling by his mother, a cherub in swaddling-clothes, growing up into a vagabond and soldier of fortune, to end here like chopped straw. But there were also grandees and caballeros among the fallen, Cortes' best friends and supporters, never, never to be forgotten!

The sacrifices: the poor, hapless ones who fell alive into the hands of the Aztecs and were slaughtered to the gods; white men, Christians, ah, their eyes mirrored the greatest horror ever seen, Tenochtitlan's night; they alone of all men knew what it was to go with open eyes, with all their wits about them, straight into Hell!

Their fellows on the causeway saw them being led naked up all the terraces of the temple, round and round, the whole way up, in a glare bright as daylight from burning altars, burning houses, while distant bursts of flame and lightning flashes from Popocatepetl flickered across the whole sky. Ay, up they had to go, the steep sacred way of the Mexicans, the symbol of the nation's wanderings, from the tropics up the ladder of the zones to the roof of the world, into a rarer air; the doomed white men were forced to pace it, with lash and stab, pinioned like sheep, and from the causeway and the shores of the lake their white bodies could be seen shining among black and red devils, the red priests in their robes of office, sacrificial jerkins, flowing hair—the young white-skinned sons of Spain, with their blue blood, *sangre azul*, showing through the skin like a map of fair rose-pink river-valleys, the skin of their exquisite mothers, milk of their milk—and when they appeared on the platform they were forced to dance before the altar of jasper, Huitzilopochtli's stone sacrifice; he himself was absent for the moment, but represented by his priests!

Face to face with them, the priests of Huitzilopochtli, they were brought, aloft on the top of the pyramid, as though in the air, with night and fire below, night and fire above their heads, the mountain brooding over the world like an evil red eye, and around them a pack of joyful tormentors, in garments as of clotted blood, vultures with befouled drooping wings, their hair matted with blood, long nails, most of them earless, clucking like birds and clinking their obsidian knives together. A clatter of cauldrons, forks and huge ladles down in the forecourt; flutes, antelope-horn rattles—the drum!

The great death-drum! Ay, to-night it sounded, from the top of Huitzilopochtli's temple, the doomsday drum, made of the skins of anacondas and audible for miles over the country as a deep bellowing, a sluggish, fearful pulse in the night, boom—boom! Down in the city the women, alone at home on this night of conflict, came out of doors and smeared blood on the mouth of the serpent totem on the wall of the house, when they heard the snake-drum, conjuring up the oldest, profoundest symbols of Mexico.

To the booming of this voice from the Abyss the doomed Spaniards went to their death. And all the images of death were before their eyes, the place of skulls below the temple lighted up by the fire, the scaffolding of bones, the elaborately built-up mounds of death's-heads, dried mummy heads stuck on stakes, an abyss as though paved with upturned faces, the grinning, naked human form . . . truly this was the Underworld itself!

The young Spanish noble . . . now they had hold of him, came close to him with the bestial warmth of their bodies, forced their way into his soul with their grins, the dogs; now they broke down his bearing, stretched him in a ridiculous posture, now they cut him open—ah well, that only hurt—but then they laid hold of his heart, then they laid hold of his heart!

Boom—boom!

And when his ears rang in the last lulling, when he began to be alone in a friendly darkness—why, then let the drum go on, let the rest be accomplished, hell for hell, let it bustle and boil over down in the priests' kitchens, let the vultures scream from the gods' aviaries, where the great birds fan together darkness and fiery gleam under their wings, let it snarl and hiss from the menageries, where puma and jaguar pad softly up and down and arch their backs, with yellow eyes watching for what their stinking keepers will bring, the ocelot pit like a snake-pen full of cats, marked like the boa and as noiseless, with the same narrow vertical pupil . . .

Splash, splash, sounded in the rattlesnake pit, as the entrails were flung to them, the share of the deadly gray serpent, and in the flickering light which crept in from a reflection in the sky, Popocatepetl's distant fires, a gliding life could be seen, scarcely to be distinguished from the dust underneath the fat, scaly reptiles; they came out of holes and corners, darting a dry tongue from their mouths, tasting the air, with scaly jaws and little enamel eyes, giving a faint rattle in the gloom, the castanets in their tail . . .

Boom—boom!

On the other side of the lake Cortes sat and listened to the ceaseless throbbing of the death-drum, saw the awful scene, recognized his friends in the distance. In the course of the night he had had heads flung at his feet by Aztecs infuriated to madness, the heads of his comrades; he saw them make that terrible progress, saw them die—and then Cortes wept, with a boy's hard, abandoned weeping that hurts the throat and strangles the breath, over the sufferings of his boys and brothers.

A creature stroked her head against him, rubbed her ear on him, Malina, trying to console him, to make up to him for all his loss; but Cortes flicked her away like a grain of dust that had got into his tears; she could not help him.

No, there was only one thing that could help him, as time would show, that which he swore as he shook his fist at the flaming temples of Mexico—that he would see them razed to the ground, and all their foul butchers rotting corpses in the earth! Was that so strange an oath?

And it came to pass as he had sworn. With murder and manslaughter he was hunted out of Mexico, with siege and starvation he returned.

Better would it have been if Popocatepetl had buried Mexico and the whole plateau under a layer of ashes than that *that* should be seen which was seen in the streets of Mexico when it was at the last gasp and the mothers took back into themselves that to which they had given life, and Huitzilopochtli's priests in hunger delirium, when the last rattlesnake had been devoured, stole glances at each other—no hope left even if they ate each other, nothing left to eat on them, plucked living corpses of vultures, staggering with the last of their strength to the carrion-heap and falling dead on their faces in it.

To such extremes does one misdeed drive another.

At dawn one more last sacrifice took place up on the platform with the smoking ruins of its towers, after Huitzilopochtli's image, with immense toil, fury and triumph, had been dragged up all the steps, hundreds of men pulling at it, like a swarm of impassioned ants round a caterpillar, and set up in his place again somewhat battered, with a chip knocked out of his forehead and all the precious stones and ornaments broken or shaken out, but still Huitzilopochtli the ancient. They trembled before him, for the insult he had suffered, the revenge he might take—but had they not already avenged him pretty well? Mexico purified, the great and rare offerings he had received—and now he was to receive the last and best, if that was good enough, the white strangers' own god!

Just before sunrise this extraordinary sacrifice took place; the tall life-size crucifix, which the Spaniards had set up in the square before the palace where they had been lodged and from which they had been turned out, was borne in solemn procession round all the steps of the temple the whole way up to the platform.

Here the two gods were confronted with one another. They were left in each other's company a good while, even the priests withdrawing from the platform to the next step below, and thousands of Mexicans filled the remaining terraces, still mad with the night's orgy of slaughter, silent, glaring like wild cattle.

Well, then the gods had a chance of looking at each other and making some remarks; they might have a good deal to talk about, their passions, their impressions of mankind for a thousand years, and so on. But the gods were dumb.

It was as though they spoke in the language that was spread out before the eyes of all in the dawning, the earth hidden by corpses, half the pueblo fallen in like bakers' ovens after a shower of stones, black smoking logs all that was left of cedarwood timbers, whose perfume was changed to the sour smell of burning; the temple drenched in blood from the top step to the bottom and covered with dead bodies, like a mountain of corpses; the lake stained red far out from the shore, a vast raw scent of blood hanging over the earth as high as the top of the temple.

Underneath the huge drum the drummer lay dead, burst by his own fury, after having danced the whole night long like a devil about his doomsday drum, howling, in a hurricane of his hair, naked, with limbs like glowing copper; now he was cooled down, lying crumpled up on his drumstick like a man of ashes.

Sunrise! Silence! Far and wide the land and mountains stare out into the clear, light air of the plateau, the ring of heaven and earth uniting in the distance. Popocatepetl smokes up into the morning sky, and to-day his smoke is not black but white.

Silence! The gods stand face to face. They do not budge. Huitzilopochtli broad, short in the neck, with a piece chipped out of one eye, nose gone, a good deal knocked about, but still a black; the white god stiff and mute on his cross, in an everlasting agony: Man, after his own handling.

Then they set fire to the crucifix, and as the sun's eye appeared over the horizon it burned, with a pale fire rising straight up into the air.

But Huitzilopochtli was soon to travel down all those steps again, and this time he would be left standing on his head among ruins and rubble, until one day a later generation pulled him out and put him in a museum with a label on him, a piece of monstrous sculpture, for the ecstatic delight of those who recognize their own genius in negro fetishes, to others only the hideous image of a nightmare from which mankind has awakened. Where his temple was, now stands the Cathedral of Mexico; if fear is no longer to be worked upon there are feelings to answer the purpose.

A gleaming white dome of snow fills the extinct crater of Popocatepetl.

Bertrand Russell

MARRIAGE AND MORALS

BERTRAND RUSSELL, *the 3rd Lord Russell, is probably the most versatile and controversial figure to win the Nobel Prize for Literature (1950). Born in 1872 in Monmouthshire, England, he was educated privately and at Cambridge, where he taught for two stretches (1895-1901, 1910-1916). His unorthodox views involved him in frequent difficulties. In 1916, he was deprived of his Cambridge position because of pacifist activities and in 1918, sentenced to jail for attacking the American army's reputation. An experimental nursery school he and his wife conducted in the twenties came under severe criticism (when an astonished visitor, greeted by a naked child, exclaimed, "My God!", he was answered, "There is no God. May I help you, please?") He lectured at Harvard in 1914, 1924, and 1927, but in 1939, an appointment to the City College of New York was withdrawn on the grounds that his views were immoral (the following essay from Marriage and Morals, 1929, is typical of them). He is known for his studies in logic and mathematics* (Principia Mathematica, *1910*); *his essays and books on philosophy* (The Problems of Philosophy, *1911*), *on politics* (Freedom versus Organization, *1934*), *on science* (The A.B.C. of Atoms, *1923*), *on social problems* The Conquest of Happiness, *1929*), *and on religion* (Why I Am Not a Christian, *1940*). *He has also written a volume of short stories,* Satan in the Suburbs. *In recent years, he has lectured and campaigned for international sanity.*

I propose to discuss marriage without reference to children, merely as a relation between men and women. Marriage differs, of course, from other sex relations by the fact that it is a legal institution. It is also in most communities a religious institution, but it is the legal aspect which is essential. The legal institution merely embodies a practice which exists not only among primitive men but among apes and various other animals. Animals practice what is virtually marriage, wherever the cooperation of the male is necessary to the rearing of the young. As a rule, animal marriages are monogamic, and according to some authorities this is the case in particular amongst the anthropoid apes. It seems, if these authorities are to be believed, that these fortunate animals are not faced with the problems that beset human communities, since the male, once married, ceases to be attracted to any other female, and the female, once married, ceases to be attractive to any other male. Among the anthropoid apes, therefore, although they do not have the assistance of religion, sin is unknown, since instinct suffices to produce virtue. There is some evidence that among the lowest races of savages a similar state of affairs exists. Bushmen are said to be strictly monogamous, and I understand that the Tasmanians (now extinct) were invariably faithful to their wives. Even in civilized mankind faint traces of a monogamic instinct can sometimes be perceived. Considering the influence of habit over behavior, it is perhaps surprising that the hold of monogamy on instinct is not stronger than it is. This, however, is an example of the mental peculiarity of human beings, from which spring both their vices and their intelligence, namely the power of imagination to break up habits and initiate new lines of conduct.

It seems probable that what first broke up primitive monogamy was the intrusion of the economic motive. This motive, wherever it has any influence upon sexual behavior, is invariably disastrous, since it substitutes relations of slavery or purchase for relations based upon instinct. In early agricultural and pastoral communities both wives and children were an economic asset to a man. The wives worked for him, and the children, after the age of five or six, began to be useful in the fields or in tending beasts. Consequently the most powerful men aimed at having as many wives as possible. Polygamy can seldom be the general practice of a community, since there is not as a rule a great excess of females; it is the prerogative of chiefs and rich men. Numerous wives and children form a valuable property, and will therefore enhance the already privileged position of their owners. Thus the primary function of a wife comes to be that of a lucrative domestic animal, and her sexual function becomes subordinated. At this level of civilization it is as a rule easy for a man to divorce his wife, though he must in that case restore to her family any dowry that she may have brought. It is, however, in general impossible for a wife to divorce her husband.

The attitude of most semi-civilized communities towards adultery is of a piece with this outlook. At a very low level of civilization adultery is sometimes tolerated. The Samoans, we are told, when they have to go upon a journey, fully expect their wives to console themselves for their absence.* At a slightly higher level, however, adultery in women is punished with death or at best with very severe penalties. Mungo Park's account of Mumbo Jumbo used to be well known when I was young, but I have been pained in recent years to find highbrow Americans alluding to Mumbo Jumbo as a god of the Congo. He was in fact neither a god nor connected with the Congo. He was a pretense demon invented by the men of the upper Niger to terrify women who had sinned. Mungo Park's account of him so inevitably suggests a Voltairean view as to the origins of religion that it has tended to be discreetly suppressed by modern anthropologists, who cannot bear the in-

* Margaret Mead, "Coming of Age in Samoa," 1928, p. 104 ff.

trusion of rational scoundrelism into the doings of savages. A man who had intercourse with another man's wife was, of course, also a criminal, but a man who had intercourse with an unmarried woman did not incur any blame unless he diminished her value in the marriage market.

With the coming of Christianity this outlook was changed. The part of religion in marriage was very greatly augmented, and infractions of the marriage law came to be blamed on grounds of taboo rather than of property. To have intercourse with another man's wife remained, of course, an offense against that man, but to have any intercourse outside marriage was an offense against God, and this, in the view of the Church, was a far graver matter. For the same reason divorce, which had previously been granted to men on easy terms, was declared inadmissible. Marriage became a sacrament and therefore lifelong.

Was this a gain or a loss to human happiness? It is very hard to say. Among peasants the life of married women has always been a very hard one, and on the whole it has been hardest among the least civilized peasants. Among most barbarous peoples a woman is old at twenty-five, and cannot hope at that age to retain any traces of beauty. The view of woman as a domestic animal was no doubt very pleasant for men, but for women it meant a life of nothing but toil and hardship. Christianity, while in some ways it made the position of women worse, especially in the well-to-do classes, did at least recognize their theological equality with men, and refused to regard them as absolutely the property of their husbands. A married woman had not, of course, the right to leave her husband for another man, but she could leave him for a life of religion. And on the whole progress towards a better status for women was easier, in the great bulk of the population, from the Christian than from the pre-Christian standpoint.

When we look round the world at the present day and ask ourselves what conditions seem on the whole to make for happiness in marriage and what for unhappiness, we are driven to a somewhat curious conclusion, that the more civilized people become the less capable they seem of lifelong happiness with one partner. Irish peasants, although until recent times marriages were decided by the parents, were said by those who ought to know them to be on the whole happy and virtuous in their conjugal life. In general, marriage is easiest where people are least differentiated. When a man differs little from other men, and a woman differs little from other women, there is no particular reason to regret not having married some one else. But people with multifarious tastes and pursuits and interests will tend to desire congeniality in their partners, and to feel dissatisfied when they find that they have secured less of it than they might have obtained. The Church, which tends to view marriage solely from the point of view of sex, sees no reason why one partner should not do just as well as another, and can therefore uphold the indissolubility of marriage without realizing the hardship that this often involves.

Another condition which makes for happiness in marriage is paucity of unowned women and absence of social occasions when husbands meet other women. If there is no possibility of sexual relations with any woman other than one's wife, most men will make the best of the situation and, except in abnormally bad cases, will find it quite tolerable. The same thing applies to wives, especially if they never imagine that marriage should bring much happiness. That is to say, a marriage is likely to be what is called happy if neither party ever expected to get much happiness out of it.

Fixity of social custom, for the same reason, tends to prevent what are called unhappy marriages. If the bonds of marriage are recognized as final and irrevocable, there is no stimulus to the imagination to wander outside and consider that a more ecstatic happiness might have been possible. In order to secure domestic peace where this state of mind exists, it is only necessary that neither the husband nor the wife should fall outrageously below the commonly recognized standard of decent behavior, whatever this may be.

Among civilized people in the modern world none of these conditions for what is called happiness exist, and accordingly one finds that very few marriages after the first few years are happy. Some of the causes of unhappiness are bound up with civilization, but others would disappear if men and women were more civilized than they are. Let us begin with the latter. Of these the most important is bad sexual education, which is a far commoner thing among the well-to-do than it can ever be among peasants. Peasant children early become accustomed to what are called the facts of life, which they can observe not only among human beings but among animals. They are thus saved from both ignorance and fastidiousness. The carefully educated children of the well-to-do, on the contrary, are shielded from all practical knowledge of sexual matters, and even the most modern parents, who teach children out of books, do not give them that sense of practical familiarity which the peasant child early acquires. The triumph of Christian teaching is when a man and woman marry without either having had previous sexual experience. In nine cases out of ten where this occurs, the results are unfortunate. Sexual behavior among human beings is not instinctive, so that the inexperienced bride and bridegroom, who are probably quite unaware of this fact, find themselves overwhelmed with shame and discomfort. It is little better when the woman alone is innocent but the man has acquired his knowledge from prostitutes. Most men do not realize that a process of wooing is necessary after marriage, and many well-brought-up women do not realize what harm they do to marriage by remaining reserved and physically aloof. All this could be put right by better sexual education, and is in fact very much better with the generation now young than it was with their parents and grandparents. There used to be a widespread belief among women that they were morally superior to men on the ground that they had less pleasure in sex. This attitude made frank companionship between husbands and wives impossible. It was, of course, in itself quite unjustifiable, since failure to enjoy sex, so far from being virtuous, is a mere physiological or psychological deficiency, like a failure to enjoy food, which also a hundred years ago was expected of elegant females.

Other modern causes of unhappiness in marriage are, however, not so easily disposed of. I think that uninhibited civilized people, whether men or women, are generally polygamous in their instincts. They may fall deeply in love and be for some years entirely absorbed in one person, but sooner or later sexual familiarity dulls the edge of passion, and then they begin to look elsewhere for a revival of the old thrill. It is, of course, possible to control this impulse in the interests of morality, but it is very difficult to prevent the impulse from existing. With the growth of women's freedom there has come a much greater opportunity for conjugal infidelity than existed in former times. The opportunity gives rise to the thought, the thought gives rise to the desire, and in the absence of religious scruples the desire gives rise to the act.

Women's emancipation has in various ways made marriage more difficult. In old days the wife had to adapt herself to the husband, but the husband did not have to adapt himself to the wife. Nowadays many wives, on grounds of woman's right to her own individuality and her own career, are unwilling to adapt themselves to their husbands beyond a point, while men who still hanker after the old tradition of masculine domination see no reason why they should do all the adapting. This trouble arises especially in connection with infidelity. In old days the husband was occasionally unfaithful, but as a rule his wife did not know of it. If she did, he confessed that he had sinned and made her believe that he was penitent. She, on the other hand, was usually virtuous. If she was not, and the fact came to her husband's knowledge, the marriage broke up. Where, as happens in many modern marriages, mutual faithfulness is not demanded, the instinct of jealousy nevertheless survives, and often proves fatal to the persistence of any deeply rooted intimacy even where no overt quarrels occur.

There is another difficulty in the way of modern marriage, which is felt especially by those who are most conscious of the value of love. Love can flourish only as long as it is free and spontaneous; it tends to be killed by the thought that it is a duty. To say that it is your duty to love so-and-so is the surest way to cause you to hate him or her. Marriage as a combination of love with legal bonds thus falls between two stools. Shelley says:

> I never was attached to that great sect
> Whose doctrine is, that each one should select
> Out of the crowd a mistress or a friend,
> And all the rest, though fair and wise, commend
> To cold oblivion, though it is in the code
> Of modern morals, and the beaten road
> Which those poor slaves with weary footsteps tread,
> Who travel to their home among the dead

By the broad highway of the world, and so
With one chained friend, perhaps a jealous foe,
The dreariest and the longest journey go.

There can be no doubt that to close one's mind on marriage against all the approaches of love from elsewhere is to diminish receptivity and sympathy and the opportunities of valuable human contacts. It is to do violence to something which, from the most idealistic standpoint, is in itself desirable. And like every kind of restrictive morality it tends to promote what one may call a policeman's outlook upon the whole of human life—the outlook, that is to say, which is always looking for an opportunity to forbid something.

For all these reasons, many of which are bound up with things undoubtedly good, marriage has become difficult, and if it is not to be a barrier to happiness it must be conceived in a somewhat new way. One solution often suggested, and actually tried on a large scale in America, is easy divorce. I hold, of course, as every humane person must, that divorce should be granted on more grounds than are admitted in the English law, but I do not recognize in easy divorce a solution of the troubles of marriage. Where a marriage is childless, divorce may be often the right solution, even when both parties are doing their best to behave decently; but where there are children the stability of marriage is to my mind a matter of considerable importance. I think that where a marriage is fruitful and both parties to it are reasonable and decent the expectation ought to be that it will be lifelong, but not that it will exclude other sex relations. A marriage which begins with passionate love and leads to children who are desired and loved ought to produce so deep a tie between a man and woman that they will feel something infinitely precious in their companionship, even after sexual passion has decayed, and even if either or both feels sexual passion for some one else. This mellowing of marriage has been prevented by jealousy, but jealousy, though it is an instinctive emotion, is one which can be controlled if it is recognized as bad, and not supposed to be the expression of a just moral indignation. A companionship which has lasted for many years and through many deeply felt events has a richness of content which cannot belong to the first days of love, however delightful these may be. And any person who appreciates what time can do to enhance values will not lightly throw away such companionship for the sake of new love.

It is therefore possible for a civilized man and woman to be happy in marriage, although if this is to be the case a number of conditions must be fulfilled. There must be a feeling of complete equality on both sides; there must be no interference with mutual freedom; there must be the most complete physical and mental intimacy; and there must be a certain similarity in regard to standards of values. (It is fatal, for example, if one values only money while the other values only good work.) Given all these conditions, I believe marriage to be the best and most important relation that can exist between two human beings. If it has not often been realized hitherto, that is chiefly because husband and wife have regarded themselves as each other's policeman. If marriage is to achieve its possibilities, husbands and wives must learn to understand that whatever the law may say, in their private lives they must be free.

Albert Schweitzer

THE RENUNCIATION OF THOUGHT

ALBERT SCHWEITZER, *clergyman, physician, philosopher, organist, musicologist, and writer, received the Nobel Prize for Peace in 1952, but just as appropriately he might have won it for his accomplishments in literature or his service to medicine. Born in the Alsace in 1875, he received his Ph.D. from the University of Strasbourg and soon afterwards became the head of the Theological College there. During the following period, he published an admirable biography, J. S. Bach (1905), and became a leading interpreter of his music. These achievements, with The Quest for the Historical Jesus (1906), brought him world renown. At the age of thirty, he turned his back on fame and resolved to devote himself to the service of mankind.*

He prepared by qualifying as a physician and in 1913, sailed for Lam-
barene, French Equatorial Africa, where he founded a missionary hos-
pital. He has spent his last fifty years conducting it and supporting
it from the proceeds of organ recitals in Europe and his many lecture
tours and publications. Schweitzer visited America in 1949 to deliver
an address at the Goethe celebration in Aspen, Colorado, in which
he emphasized his faith in the twin ideals of "purity and kindness."
The following essay, in the tradition of Emersonian non-conformity,
is from Out of My Life and Thought (1933). *Other noteworthy pub-*
lications are On the Edge of the Primeval Forest (1922), Self-Por-
trait (1920) *and* Indian Thought and Its Development (1936).

With the spirit of the age I am in complete disagreement,
because it is filled with disdain for thinking. That such is
its attitude is to some extent explicable by the fact that thought
has never yet reached the goal which it must set before itself.
Time after time it was convinced that it had clearly established a
world-view which was in accordance with knowledge and ethically
satisfactory. But time after time the truth came out that it had not
succeeded.

But today, in addition to that neglect of thought, there is also
prevalent a mistrust of it. The organized political, social, and
religious associations of our time are at work to induce individual
man not to arrive at his convictions by his own thinking but to
take as his own such convictions as they keep ready-made for him.
Any man who thinks for himself and at the same time is spiritually free is to the associations something inconvenient and even
uncanny. He does not offer sufficient guarantee that he will merge
himself in their organizations in the way they wish. All corpo-
rate bodies look today for their strength not so much to the
spiritual worth of the ideas they represent and to that of the people who belong to them, as to the attainment of the highest possible degree of unity and exclusiveness. It is here that they expect to find their strongest power for offense and defense.

Hence the spirit of the age rejoices, instead of lamenting, that
thinking seems to be unequal to its task, and gives it no credit for
what, in spite of imperfections, it has already accomplished. It

refuses to admit, what is nevertheless the fact, that all spiritual progress up to today has come about through the achievements of thought, or to reflect that thinking may still be able in the future to accomplish what it has not succeeded in accomplishing as yet. Of such considerations the spirit of the age takes no account. Its only concern is to discredit individual thinking in every possible way, dealing with such thought according to the saying: "Whosoever hath not, from him shall be taken away even that which he hath."

Thus, his whole life long, modern man is exposed to influences which are bent on robbing him of all confidence in his own thinking. The spirit of spiritual dependence to which he is called on to surrender is in everything that he hears or reads; it is in the people whom he meets every day; it is in the parties and associations which have claimed him as their own; it pervades all the circumstances of his life.

From every side and in the most varied ways it is dinned into him that the truth and convictions which he needs for life must be taken by him from the associations which have rights over him. The spirit of the age never lets him come to himself. Over and over again convictions are forced upon him in the same way as, by means of the electric advertisements which flare in the streets of every large town, any company which has sufficient capital to get itself securely established, exercises pressure on him at every step he takes to induce him to buy their boot polish or their soup tablets.

By the spirit of the age, then, the man of today is forced into skepticism about his own thinking, in order to make him receptive to truth which comes to him from authority. To all this constant influence he cannot make the resistance that is desirable because he is an overworked and distracted being without power to concentrate. Moreover, the manifold material trammels which are his lot work upon his mentality in such a way that he comes at last to believe himself unqualified even to make any claim to thoughts of his own.

His self-confidence is also diminished through the pressure exercised upon him by the huge and daily increasing mass of Knowledge. He is no longer in a position to take in all the new discoveries that are constantly announced; he has to accept them as fact although he does not understand them. This being his relation to scientific truth he is tempted to acquiesce in the idea that in matters of thought also his judgment cannot be trusted.

Thus do the circumstances of the age do their best to deliver us up to the spirit of the age.

The seed of skepticism has germinated. In fact, modern man has no longer any spiritual self-confidence at all. Behind a self-confident exterior he conceals a great inward lack of confidence. In spite of his great capacity in material matters he is an altogether stunted being, because he makes no use of his capacity for thinking. It will ever remain incomprehensible that our generation, which has shown itself so great by its achievements in discovery and invention, could fall so low spiritually as to give up thinking.

Renunciation of thinking is a declaration of spiritual bankruptcy. Where there is no longer a conviction that men can get to know the truth by their own thinking, skepticism begins. Those who work to make our age skeptical in this way, do so in the expectation that, as a result of renouncing all hope of self-discovered truth men will end by accepting as truth what is forced upon them with authority and by propaganda.

But their calculations are wrong. No one who opens the sluices to let a flood of skepticism pour itself over the land must expect to be able to bring it back within its proper bounds. Of those who let themselves get too disheartened to try any longer to discover truth by their own thinking, only a few find a substitute for it in truth taken from others. The mass of people remain skeptical. They lose all feeling for truth, and all sense of need for it as well, finding themselves quite comfortable in a life without thought, driven now here, now there, from one opinion to another.

But the acceptance of authoritative truth, even if that truth has both spiritual and ethical content, does not bring skepticism to an end; it merely covers it up. Man's unnatural condition of not believing that any truth is discoverable by himself, continues, and produces its natural results. The city of truth cannot be built on the swampy ground of skepticism. Our spiritual life is rotten throughout because it is permeated through and through with skepticism; in consequence, we live in a world which in every respect is full of falsehood. We are not far from shipwreck on the rock of wanting to have even truth organized.

Truth taken over by a skepticism which has become believing has not the spiritual qualities of that which originated in thinking. It has been externalized and rendered torpid. It does obtain influence over a man, but it is not capable of uniting itself with him to the very marrow of his being. Living truth is that alone which has its origin in thinking.

Just as a tree bears year after year the same fruit and yet fruit which is each year new, so must all permanently valuable ideas be continually born again in thought. But our age is bent on trying to make the barren tree of skepticism fruitful by tying fruits of truth on its branches.

It is only by confidence in our ability to reach truth by our own individual thinking, that we are capable of accepting truth from outside. Unfettered thought, provided it be deep, never degenerates into subjectivity. With its own ideas it stirs those within itself which enjoy any traditional credit for being true, and exerts itself to be able to possess them as knowledge.

Not less strong than the will to truth must be the will to sincerity. Only an age which can show the courage of sincerity can possess truth which works as a spiritual force within it.

Sincerity is the foundation of the spiritual life.

With its depreciation of thinking our generation has lost its feeling for sincerity and with it that for truth as well. It can therefore be helped only by its being brought once more on to the road of thinking.

Because I have this certainty I oppose the spirit of the age, and take upon myself with confidence the responsibility of taking my part in the rekindling of the fire of thought.

SCIENCE

Albert Einstein

THE FUNDAMENTS OF THEORETICAL PHYSICS

ALBERT EINSTEIN *was born in Ülm, Germany, in 1879. He studied at the University of Zurich, supporting himself as a tutor. While holding the post of examiner of patents in Bern for nine years, he completed his doctorate (1909) and developed the theory of relativity. His publications attracted so much attention among his colleagues that he was appointed professor of theoretical physics at Zurich. A few years later, he accepted the directorship of the Kaiser Wilhelm Physical Institute, a position which permitted him to pursue his researches. In 1921, still in his early forties, Einstein received the Nobel Prize for Physics. In 1933 when Hitler came to power, Einstein was a visiting professor at the University of California. When he returned to Europe but not to Germany, the Nazis deprived him of his citizenship and confiscated his property. He came back to America and joined the staff of the Institute of Advanced Studies at Princeton. He lived in Princeton until his death in 1955, offering his energy and time to causes for the promotion of world peace and international understanding.*

Science is the attempt to make the chaotic diversity of our sense-experience correspond to a logically uniform system of thought. In this system single experiences must be correlated with the theoretic structure in such a way that the resulting coordination is unique and convincing.

The sense-experiences are the given subject-matter. But the theory that shall interpret them is man-made. It is the result of an extremely laborious process of adaptation: hypothetical, never completely final, always subject to question and doubt.

The scientific way of forming concepts differs from that which we use in our daily life, not basically, but merely in the more precise definition of concepts and conclusions; more painstaking and systematic choice of experimental material; and greater logical economy. By this last we mean the effort to reduce all concepts and correlations to as few as possible logically independent basic concepts and axioms.

What we call physics comprises that group of natural sciences which base their concepts on measurements; and whose concepts and propositions lend themselves to mathematical formulation. Its realm is accordingly defined as that part of the sum total of our knowledge which is capable of being expressed in mathematical terms. With the progress of science, the realm of physics has so expanded that it seems to be limited only by the limitations of the method itself.

The larger part of physical research is devoted to the development of the various branches of physics, in each of which the object is the theoretical understanding of more or less restricted fields of experience, and in each of which the laws and concepts remain as closely as possible related to experience. It is this department of science, with its ever-growing specialization, which has revolutionized practical life in the last centuries, and given birth to the possibility that man may at last be freed from the burden of physical toil.

On the other hand, from the very beginning there has always been present the attempt to find a unifying theoretical basis for all these single sciences, consisting of a minimum of concepts and fundamental relationships, from which all the concepts and relationships of the single disciplines might be derived by logical process. This is what we mean by the search for a foundation of the whole of physics. The confident belief that this ultimate goal may be reached is the chief source of the passionate devotion which has always animated the researcher. It is in this sense that the following observations are devoted to the foundations of physics.

From what has been said it is clear that the word foundations in this connection does not mean something analogous in all respects to the foundations of a building. Logically considered, of course, the various single laws of physics rest upon this foundation. But whereas a building may be seriously damaged by a heavy storm or spring flood, yet its foundations remain intact, in science the logical foundation is always in greater peril from new experiences or new knowledge than are the branch disciplines with their closer experimental contacts. In the connection of the foundation with all the single parts lies its great significance, but likewise its greatest danger in face of any new factor. When we realize this, we are led to wonder why the so-called revolutionary epochs of the science of physics have not more often and more completely changed its foundation than has actually been the case.

The first attempt to lay a uniform theoretical foundation was the work of Newton. In his system everything is reduced to the following concepts: (1) Mass points with invariable mass; (2) action at a distance between any pair of mass points; (3) law of motion for the mass point. There was not, strictly speaking, any all-embracing foundation, because an explicit law was formulated only for the actions-at-a-distance of gravitation; while for other actions-at-a-distance nothing was established *a priori* except the law of equality of *actio* and *reactio*. Moreover, Newton himself fully realized that time and space were essential elements, as physically effective factors, of his system, if only by implication.

This Newtonian basis proved eminently fruitful and was regarded as final up to the end of the nineteenth century. It not only gave results for the movements of the heavenly bodies, down to the most minute details, but also furnished a theory of the mechanics of discrete and continuous masses, a simple explanation of the principle of the conservation of energy and a complete and brilliant theory of heat. The explanation of the facts of electrodynamics within the Newtonian system was more forced; least convincing of all, from the very beginning, was the theory of light.

It is not surprising that Newton would not listen to a wave theory of light; for such a theory was most unsuited to his theoretical foundation. The assumption that space was filled with a medium consisting of material points that propagated light waves without exhibiting any other mechanical properties must have seemed to him quite artificial. The strongest empirical arguments for the wave nature of light, fixed speeds of propagation, interference, diffraction, polarization, were either unknown or else not known in any well-ordered synthesis. He was justified in sticking to his corpuscular theory of light.

During the nineteenth century the dispute was settled in favor of the wave theory. Yet no serious doubt of the mechanical foundation of physics arose, in the first place because nobody knew where to find a foundation of another sort. Only slowly, under the irresistible pressure of facts, there developed a new foundation of physics, field-physics.

From Newton's time on, the theory of action-at-a-distance was constantly found artificial. Efforts were not lacking to explain gravitation by a kinetic theory; that is, on the basis of collision forces of hypothetical mass particles. But the attempts were superficial and bore no fruit. The strange part played by space (or the inertial system) within the mechanical foundation was also clearly recognized, and criticized with especial clarity by Ernst Mach.

The great change was brought about by Faraday, Maxwell and Hertz—as a matter of fact half-unconsciously and against their will. All three of them, throughout their lives, considered themselves adherents of the mechanical theory. Hertz had found the simplest form of the equations of the electromagnetic field, and declared that any theory leading to these equations was Maxwellian theory. Yet toward the end of his short life he wrote a paper in which he presented as the foundation of physics a mechanical theory freed from the force-concept.

For us, who took in Faraday's ideas so to speak with our mother's milk, it is hard to appreciate their greatness and audacity. Faraday must have grasped with unerring instinct the artificial nature of all attempts to refer electromagnetic phenomena to actions-at-a-distance between electric particles reacting on each other. How was each single iron filing among a lot scattered on a piece of paper to know of the single electric particles running round in a nearby conductor? All these electric particles together seemed to create in the surrounding space a condition which in turn produced a certain order in the filings. These spatial states, to-day called fields, if their geometrical structure and interdependent action were once rightly grasped, would, he was convinced, furnish the clue to the mysterious electromagnetic interactions. He conceived these fields as states of mechanical stress in a space-filling medium, similar to the states of stress in an elastically distended body. For at that time this was the only way one could conceive of states that were apparently continuously distributed in space. The peculiar type of mechanical interpretation of these fields remained in the background—a sort of placation of the scientific conscience in view of the mechanical tradition of Faraday's time. With the help of these new field concepts Faraday succeeded in forming a qualitative concept of the whole complex of electromagnetic effects discovered by him and his predecessors. The precise formulation of the time-space laws of those fields was the work of Maxwell. Imagine his feelings when the differential equations he had formulated proved to him that electromagnetic fields spread in the form of polarized waves and with the speed of light! To few men in the world has such an experience been vouchsafed. At that thrilling moment he surely never guessed that the riddling nature of light, apparently so completely solved, would continue to baffle succeeding generations. Meantime, it took physicists some decades to grasp the full significance of Maxwell's discovery, so bold was the leap that his genius forced upon the conceptions of his fellow-workers. Only after Hertz had demonstrated experimentally the existence of Maxwell's electromagnetic waves, did resistance to the new theory break down.

But if the electromagnetic field could exist as a wave independent of the material source, then the electrostatic interaction could no longer be explained as action-at-a-distance. And what was true for electrical action could not be denied for gravitation. Everywhere Newton's actions-at-a-distance gave way to fields spreading with finite velocity.

Of Newton's foundation there now remained only the material mass points subject to the law of motion. But J. J. Thomson pointed out that an electrically charged body in motion must, according to Maxwell's theory, possess a magnetic field whose energy acted precisely as does an increase of kinetic energy to the body. If, then, a part of kinetic energy consists of field energy, might that not then be true of the whole of the kinetic energy? Perhaps the basic property of matter, its inertia, could be explained within the field theory? The question led to the problem of an interpretation of matter in terms of field theory, the solution of which would furnish an explanation of the atomic structure of matter. It was soon realized that Maxwell's theory could not accomplish such a program. Since then many scientists have zealously sought to complete the field theory by some generalization that should comprise a theory of matter; but so far such efforts have not been crowned with success. In order to construct a theory, it is not enough to have a clear conception of the goal. One must also have a formal point of view which will sufficiently restrict the unlimited variety of possibilities. So far this has not been found; accordingly the field theory has not succeeded in furnishing a foundation for the whole of physics.

For several decades most physicists clung to the conviction that a mechanical substructure would be found for Maxwell's theory. But the unsatisfactory results of their efforts led to gradual acceptance of the new field concepts as irreducible fundamentals—in other words, physicists resigned themselves to giving up the idea of a mechanical foundation.

Thus physicists held to a field-theory program. But it could not be called a foundation, since nobody could tell whether a consistent field theory could ever explain on the one hand gravitation, on the other hand the elementary components of matter. In this state of affairs it was necessary to think of material particles as mass points subject to Newton's laws of motion. This was the procedure of Lorentz in creating his electron theory and the theory of the electromagnetic phenomena of moving bodies.

Such was the point at which fundamental conceptions had arrived at the turn of the century. Immense progress was made in the theoretical penetration and understanding of whole groups of new phenomena; but the establishment of a unified foundation for physics seemed remote indeed. And this state of things has even been aggravated by subsequent developments. The development during the present century is characterized by two theoretical systems essentially independent of each other: the theory of relativity and the quantum theory. The two systems do not directly contradict each other, but they seem little adapted to fusion into one unified theory. We must briefly discuss the basic idea of these two systems.

The theory of relativity arose out of efforts to improve, with reference to logical economy, the foundation of physics as it existed at the turn of the century. The so-called special or restricted relativity theory is based on the fact that Maxwell's equations (and thus the law of propagation of light in empty space) are converted into equations of the same form, when they undergo Lorentz transformation. This formal property of the Maxwell equations is supplemented by our fairly secure empirical knowledge that the laws of physics are the same with respect to all inertial systems. This leads to the result that the Lorentz transformation—applied to space and time coordinates—must govern the transition from one inertial system to any other. The content of the restricted relativity theory can accordingly be summarized in one sentence: all natural laws must be so conditioned that they are covariant with respect to Lorentz transformations. From this it follows that the simultaneity of two distant events is not an invariant concept and that the dimensions of rigid bodies and the speed of clocks depend upon their state of motion. A further consequence was a modification of Newton's law of motion in cases where the speed of a given body was not small compared with the speed of light. There followed also the principle of the equivalence of mass and energy, with the laws of conservation of mass and energy becoming one and the same. Once it was shown that simultaneity was relative and depended on the frame of reference, every possibility of retaining actions-at-a-distance within the foundation of physics disappeared, since that concept presupposed the absolute character of simultaneity (it must be possible to state the location of the two interacting mass points "at the same time").

The general theory of relativity owes its origin to the attempt to explain a fact known since Galileo's and Newton's time but hitherto eluding all theoretical interpretation: the inertia and the weight of a body, in themselves two entirely distinct things, are measured by one and the same constant, the mass. From this correspondence follows that it is impossible to discover by experiment whether a given system of coordinates is accelerated, or whether its motion is straight and uniform and the observed effects are due to a gravitational field (this is the equivalence principle of the general relativity theory). It shatters the concepts of the inertial system, as soon as gravitation enters in. It may be remarked here that the inertial system is a weak point of the Galilean-Newtonian mechanics. For there is presupposed a mysterious property of physical space, conditioning the kind of coordination-systems for which the law of inertia and the Newtonian law of motion hold good.

These difficulties can be avoided by the following postulate: natural laws are to be formulated in such a way that their form is identical for coordinate systems of any kind of states of motion. To accomplish this is the task of the general theory of relativity. On the other hand, we deduce from the restricted theory the existence of a Riemannian metric within the time-space continuum, which, according to the equivalence principle, describes both the gravitational field and the metric properties of space. Assuming that the field equations of gravitation are of the second differential order, the field law is clearly determined.

Aside from this result, the theory frees field physics from the disability it suffered from, in common with the Newtonian mechanics, of ascribing to space those independent physical properties which heretofore had been concealed by the use of an inertial system. But it can not be claimed that those parts of the general relativity theory which can to-day be regarded as final have furnished physics with a complete and satisfactory foundation. In the first place, the total field appears in it to be composed of two logically unconnected parts, the gravitational and the electromagnetic. And in the second place, this theory, like the earlier field theories, has not up till now supplied an explanation of the atomistic structure of matter. This failure has probably some connection with the fact that so far it has contributed nothing to the understanding of quantum phenomena. To take in these phenomena, physicists have been driven to the adoption of entirely new methods, the basic characteristics of which we shall now discuss.

In the year nineteen hundred, in the course of a purely theoretic investigation, Max Planck made a very remarkable discovery: the law of radiation of bodies as a function of temperature could not be derived solely from the laws of Maxwellian electrodynamics. To arrive at results consistent with the relevant experiments, radiation of a given frequency had to be treated as though it consisted of energy atoms of the individual energy h.v., where h is Planck's universal constant. During the years following it was shown that light was everywhere produced and absorbed in such energy quanta. In particular Niels Bohr was able largely to understand the structure of the atom, on the assumption that atoms can have only discrete energy values, and that the discontinuous transitions between them are connected with the emission or absorption of such an energy quantum. This threw some light on the fact that in their gaseous state elements and their compounds radiate and absorb only light of certain sharply defined frequencies. All this was quite inexplicable within the frame of the hitherto existing theories. It was clear that at least in the field of atomistic phenomena the character of everything that happens is determined by discrete states and by apparently discontinuous transitions between them, Planck's constant h playing a decisive role.

The next step was taken by De Broglie. He asked himself how the discrete states could be understood by the aid of the current concepts, and hit on a parallel with stationary waves, as for instance in the case of the proper frequencies of organ pipes and strings in acoustics. True, wave actions of the kind here required were unknown; but they could be constructed, and their mathematical laws formulated, employing Planck's constant h. De Broglie conceived an electron revolving about the atomic nucleus as being connected with such a hypothetical wave train, and made intelligible to some extent the discrete character of Bohr's "permitted" paths by the stationary character of the corresponding waves.

Now in mechanics the motion of material points is determined by the forces or fields of force acting upon them. Hence it was to be expected that those fields of force would also influence De Broglie's wave fields in an analogous way. Erwin Schrödinger showed how this influence was to be taken into account, re-interpreting by an ingenious method certain formulations of classical mechanics. He even succeeded in expanding the wave mechanical theory to a point where without the introduction of any additional hypotheses, it became applicable to any mechanical system consisting of an arbitrary number of mass points, that is to say possessing an arbitrary number of degrees of freedom. This was possible because a mechanical system consisting of n mass points is mathematically equivalent to a considerable degree, to one single mass point moving in a space of 3 n dimensions.

On the basis of this theory there was obtained a surprisingly good representation of an immense variety of facts which otherwise appeared entirely incomprehensible. But on one point, curiously enough, there was failure: it proved impossible to associate with these Schrödinger waves definite motions of the mass points—and that, after all, had been the original purpose of the whole construction.

The difficulty appeared insurmountable, until it was overcome by Born in a way as simple as it was unexpected. The De Broglie-Schrödinger wave fields were not to be interpreted as a mathematical description of how an event actually takes place in time and space, though, of course, they have reference to such an event. Rather they are a mathematical description of what we can actually know about the system. They serve only to make statistical statements and predictions of the results of all measurements which we can carry out upon the system.

Let me illustrate the general features of quantum mechanics by means of a simple example: we shall consider a mass point kept inside a restricted region G by forces of finite strength. If the kinetic energy of the mass point is below a certain limit, then the mass point, according to classical mechanics, can never leave the region G. But according to quantum mechanics, the mass point, after a period not immediately predictable, is able to leave the region G, in an unpredictable direction, and escape into surrounding space. This case, according to Gamow, is a simplified model of radioactive disintegration.

The quantum theoretical treatment of this case is as follows: at the time t_0 we have a Schrödinger wave system entirely inside G. But from the time t_0 onwards, the waves leave the interior of G in all directions, in such a way that the amplitude of the outgoing wave is small compared to the initial amplitude of the wave system inside G. The further these outside waves spread, the more the amplitude of the waves inside G diminishes, and correspondingly the intensity of the later waves issuing from G. Only after infinite time has passed is the wave supply inside G exhausted, while the outside wave has spread over an ever-increasing space.

But what has this wave process to do with the first object of our interest, the particle originally enclosed in G? To answer this question, we must imagine some arrangement which will permit us to carry out measurements on the particle. For instance, let us imagine somewhere in the surrounding space a screen so made that the particle sticks to it on coming into contact with it. Then from the intensity of the waves hitting the screen at some point, we draw conclusions as to the probability of the particle hitting the screen there at that time. As soon as the particle has hit any particular point of the screen, the whole wave field loses all its physical meaning; its only purpose was to make probability predictions as to the place and time of the particle hitting the screen (or, for instance, its momentum at the time when it hits the screen).

All other cases are analogous. The aim of the theory is to determine the probability of the results of measurement upon a system at a given time. On the other hand, it makes no attempt to give a mathematical representation of what is actually present or goes on in space and time. On this point the quantum theory of to-day differs fundamentally from all previous theories of physics, mechanistic as well as field theories. Instead of a model description of actual space-time events, it gives the probability distributions for possible measurements as functions of time.

It must be admitted that the new theoretical conception owes its origin not to any flight of fancy but to the compelling force of the facts of experience. All attempts to represent the particle and wave features displayed in the phenomena of light and matter, by direct course to a space-time model, have so far ended in failure. And Heisenberg has convincingly shown, from an empirical point of view, any decision as to a rigorously deterministic structure of nature is definitely ruled out, because of the atomistic structure of our experimental apparatus. Thus it is probably out of the question that any future knowledge can compel physics again to relinquish our present statistical theoretical foundation in favor of a deterministic one which would deal directly with physical reality.

Logically the problem seems to offer two possibilities, between which we are in principle given a choice. In the end the choice will be made according to which kind of description yields the formulation of the simplest foundation, logically speaking. At the present, we are quite without any deterministic theory directly describing the events themselves and in consonance with the facts.

For the time being, we have to admit that we do not possess any general theoretical basis for physics, which can be regarded as its logical foundation. The field theory, so far, has failed in the molecular sphere. It is agreed on all hands that the only principle which could serve as the basis of quantum theory would be one that constituted a translation of the field theory into the scheme of quantum statistics. Whether this will actually come about in a satisfactory manner, nobody can venture to say.

Some physicists, among them myself, can not believe that we must abandon, actually and forever, the idea of direct representation of physical reality in space and time; or that we must accept the view that events in nature are analogous to a game of chance. It is open to every man to choose the direction of his striving; and also every man may draw comfort from Lessing's fine saying, that the search for truth is more precious than its possession.

Niels Bohr

UNITY OF KNOWLEDGE

NIELS HENRIK DAVID BOHR *has long been regarded by his colleagues as their leading theoretical spokesman in the field of atomic physics and among scientists in general, he has an unchallenged reputation for lucidity and originality. Born and educated in Copenhagen, he undertook post-doctoral studies at Cambridge under Sir Joseph Thomson (Nobel Prize, 1906). In 1913, at the age of twenty-eight, he published three papers on the structure of the atom, which laid the groundwork for modern atomic developments. For this work, he* *received faculty status at the University of Manchester, where he studied under Sir Ernest Rutherford (Nobel Prize, 1908). In 1916, he was appointed professor of theoretical physics at the University of Copenhagen, and in 1920, established the Institute for Theoretical Physics there. Two years later, at the age of thirty-seven, he received the Nobel Prize. While at Princeton in 1939, he announced in collaboration with J. A. Wheeler the identity of Uranium 235. Trapped by the Nazis in Denmark during World War II, he was smuggled by fishing boat to Sweden in 1943, flown to England by the R.A.F., and eventually brought to the United States to aid in the completion of the atom bomb. Active despite his years, Bohr continues to direct the Institute he founded. Among the numerous honors he has received recently was the first $75,000 Atoms for Peace Award in 1957. The following essay was originally an address delivered at a conference in 1954 in connection with the Bicentennial of Columbia University.*

Before trying to answer the question to what extent we may speak of unity of knowledge, we may ask for the meaning of the word knowledge itself. It is not my intention to enter into an academic philosophical discourse for which I would hardly possess the required scholarship. Every scientist, however, is constantly confronted with the problem of objective description of experience, by which we mean unambiguous communication. Our basic tool is, of course, plain language which serves the needs of practical life and social intercourse. We shall not be concerned here with the origins of such language, but with its scope in scientific communication, and especially with the problem of how objectivity may be retained during the growth of experience beyond the events of daily life.

The main point to realize is that all knowledge presents itself within a conceptual framework adapted to account for previous experience and that any such frame may prove too narrow to comprehend new experiences. Scientific research in many domains of knowledge has indeed time and again proved the necessity of abandoning or remolding points of view which, because of their fruitfulness and apparently unrestricted applicability, were regarded as indispensable for rational explanation. Although such developments have been initiated by special studies, they entail a general lesson of importance for the problem of unity of knowledge. In fact, the widening of the conceptual framework not only has served to restore order within the respective branches of knowledge, but has also disclosed analogies in our position with respect to analysis and synthesis of experience in apparently separated domains of knowledge, suggesting the possibility of an ever more embracing objective description.

When speaking of a conceptual framework, we refer merely to the unambiguous logical representation of relations between experiences. This attitude is also apparent in the historical development in which formal logic is no longer sharply distinguished from studies of semantics or even philological syntax. A special role is played by mathematics which has contributed so decisively to the development of logical thinking, and which by its well-defined abstractions offers invaluable help in expressing harmonious relationships. Still, in our discussion, we shall not consider pure mathematics as a separate branch of knowledge, but rather as a refinement of general language, supplementing it with appropriate tools to represent relations for which ordinary verbal expression is imprecise or cumbersome. In this connection, it may be stressed that, just by avoiding the reference to the conscious subject which infiltrates daily language, the use of mathematical symbols secures the unambiguity of definition required for objective description.

The development of the so-called exact sciences, characterized by the establishing of numerical relationships between measurements, has indeed been decisively furthered by abstract mathematical methods originating from detached pursuit of generalizing logical constructions. This situation is especially illustrated in physics which was originally understood as all knowledge concerning that nature of which we ourselves are part, but gradually came to mean the study of the elementary laws governing the properties of inanimate matter. The necessity, even within this comparatively simple theme, of paying constant attention to the problem of objective description has deeply influenced the attitude of philosophical schools through the ages. In our day, the exploration of new fields of experience has disclosed unsuspected presuppositions for the unambiguous application of some of our most elementary concepts and thereby given us an epistemological lesson with bearings on problems far beyond the domain of physical science. It may therefore be convenient to start our discussion with a brief account of this development.

It would carry us too far to recall in detail how, with the elimination of mythical cosmological ideas and arguments referring to the purpose for our own actions, a consistent scheme of mechanics was built up on the basis of Galileo's pioneering work and reached such completion through Newton's mastery. Above all, the principles of Newtonian mechanics meant a far-reaching clarification of the problem of cause and effect by permitting, from the state of a physical system defined at a given instant by measurable quantities, the prediction of its state at any subsequent time. It is well known how a deterministic or causal account of this kind led to the mechanical conception of nature and came to stand as an ideal of scientific explanation in all domains of knowledge, irrespective of the way knowledge is obtained. In this connection, therefore, it is important that the study of wider fields of physical experience has revealed the necessity of a closer consideration of the observational problem.

Within its large field of application, classical mechanics presents an objective description in the sense that it is based on a well-defined use of pictures and ideas referring to the events of daily life. Still, however rational the idealizations used in Newtonian mechanics might appear, they actually went far beyond the range of experience to which our elementary concepts are adapted. Thus, the adequate use of the very notions of absolute space and time is inherently connected with the practically instantaneous propagation of light, which allows us to locate the bodies around us independently of their velocities and to arrange events in a unique time sequence. However, the attempt to develop a consistent account of electromagnetic and optical phenomena revealed that observers moving relative to each other with large velocities will coordinate events differently. Not only may such observers take a different view of shapes and positions of rigid bodies, but events at separate points of space which to one observer appear as simultaneous may be judged by another as occurring at different times.

Far from giving rise to confusion and complication, the exploration of the extent to which the account of physical phenomena depends on the standpoint of the observer proved an invaluable guide in tracing general physical laws common to all observers. Retaining the idea of determinism, but relying only on relations between unambiguous measurements referring ultimately to coincidences of events, Einstein succeeded in remolding and generalizing the whole edifice of classical physics and in lending to our world picture a unity surpassing all previous expectations. In the general theory of relativity, the description is based on a curved four-dimensional spacetime metric which automatically accounts for gravitational effects and the singular role of the speed of light signals representing an upper limit for any consistent use of the physical concept of velocity. The introduction of such unfamiliar but well-defined mathematical abstractions in no way implies ambiguity but rather offers an instructive illustration of how a widening of the conceptual framework affords the appropriate means of eliminating subjective elements and enlarging the scope of objective description.

New, unsuspected aspects of the observational problem were disclosed by the exploration of the atomic constitution of matter. As is well known, the idea of a limited divisibility of substances, introduced to explain the persistence of their characteristic properties in spite of the variety of natural phenomena, goes back to antiquity. Still, almost to our day, such views were regarded as essentially hypothetical in the sense that they seemed inaccessible to direct confirmation by observation because of the coarseness of our sense organs and tools, themselves composed of innumerable atoms. Nevertheless, with the great progress in chemistry and physics in the last centuries, atomic ideas proved increasingly fruitful. In particular, the direct application of classical mechanics to the interaction of atoms and molecules during their incessant motions led to a general understanding of the principles of thermodynamics.

In this century, the study of newly discovered properties of matter such as natural radioactivity has convincingly confirmed the foundations of atomic theory. In particular, through the development of amplification devices, it has been possible to study phenomena essentially dependent on single atoms, and even to obtain extensive knowledge of the structure of atomic systems. The first step was the recognition of the electron as a common constituent of all substances, and an essential completion of our ideas of atomic constitution was obtained by Rutherford's discovery of the atomic nucleus which contains within an extremely small volume almost the whole mass of the atom. The invariability of the properties of the elements in ordinary physical and chemical processes is directly explained by the circumstance that in such processes, although the electron binding may be largely influenced, the nucleus remains unaltered. With his demonstration of the transmutability of atomic nuclei by more powerful agencies, Rutherford, however, opened a quite new field of research, often referred to as modern alchemy, which, as is well known, was eventually to lead to the possibility of releasing immense amounts of energy stored in atomic nuclei.

Although many fundamental properties of matter were explained by the simple picture of the atom, it was evident from the beginning that classical ideas of mechanics and electromagnetism did not suffice to account for the essential stability of atomic structures, as exhibited by the specific properties of the elements. However, a clue to the elucidation of this problem was afforded by the discovery of the universal quantum of action to which Planck was led in the first year of our century by his penetrating analysis of the laws of thermal radiation. This discovery revealed in atomic processes a feature of wholeness quite foreign to the mechanical conception of nature, and made it evident that the classical physical theories are idealizations valid only in the description of phenomena in the analysis of which all actions are sufficiently large to permit the neglect of the quantum. While this condition is amply fulfilled in phenomena on the ordinary scale, we meet in atomic phenomena regularities of quite a new kind, defying deterministic pictorial description.

A rational generalization of classical physics, allowing for the existence of the quantum but retaining the unambiguous interpretation of the experimental evidence defining the inertial mass and electric charge of the electron and the nucleus, presented a very difficult task. By concerted efforts of a whole generation of theoretical physicists, a consistent and, within a wide scope, exhaustive description of atomic phenomena was, however, gradually developed. This description makes use of a mathematical formalism in which the variables in the classical physical theories are replaced by symbols subject to a noncommutable algorism involving Planck's constant. Owing to the very character of such mathematical abstractions, the formalism does not allow pictorial interpretation on accustomed lines, but aims directly at establishing relations between observations obtained under well-defined conditions. Corresponding to the circumstance that different individual quantum processes may take place in a given experimental arrangement, these relations are of an inherently statistic character.

By means of the quantum mechanical formalism, a detailed account of an immense amount of experimental evidence regarding the physical and chemical properties of matter has been achieved. Moreover, by adapting the formalism to the exigencies of relativistic invariance, it has been possible, within wide limits, to order the rapidly growing new knowledge concerning the properties of elementary particles and the constitution of atomic nuclei. Notwithstanding the astounding power of quantum mechanics, the radical departure from accustomed physical explanation, and especially the renunciation of the very idea of determinism, has given rise to doubts in the minds of many physicists and philosophers as to whether we are here dealing with a temporary expedient or are confronted with an irrevocable step as regards objective description. The clarification of this problem has actually demanded a radical revision of the fundamentals to the description and comprehension of physical experience.

In this context, we must recognize above all that, even when the phenomena transcend the scope of classical physical theories, the account of the experimental arrangement and the recording of observations must be given in plain language, suitably supplemented by technical physical terminology. This is a clear logical demand, since the very word "experiment" refers to a situation where we can tell others what we have done and what we have learned. However, the fundamental difference with respect to the analysis of phenomena in classical and in quantum physics is that in the former the interaction between the objects and the measuring instruments may be neglected or compensated for, while in the latter this interaction forms an integral part of the phenomena. The essential wholeness of a proper quantum phenomenon finds indeed logical expression in the circumstance that any attempt at its well-defined subdivision would require a change in the experimental arrangement incompatible with the appearance of the phenomenon itself.

In particular, the impossibility of a separate control of the interaction between the atomic objects and the instruments indispensable for the definition of the experimental conditions prevents the unrestricted combination of space-time coordination and dynamical conservation laws on which the deterministic description in classical physics rests. In fact, any unambiguous use of the concepts of space and time refers to an experimental arrangement involving a transfer of momentum and energy, uncontrollable in principle, to fixed scales and synchronized clocks which are required for the definition of the reference frame. Conversely, the account of phenomena which are characterized by the laws of conservation of momentum and energy involves in principle a renunciation of detailed space-time coordination. These circumstances find quantitative expression in Heisenberg's indeterminacy relations which specify the reciprocal latitude for the fixation of kinematical and dynamical variables in the definition of the state of a physical system. In accordance with the character of the quantum mechanical formalism, such relations cannot, however, be interpreted in terms of attributes of objects referring to classical pictures, but we are here dealing with the mutually exclusive conditions for the unambiguous use of the very concepts of space and time on the one hand, and of dynamical conservation laws on the other.

In this context, one sometimes speaks of "disturbance of phenomena by observation" or "creation of physical attributes to atomic objects by measurements." Such phrases, however, are apt to cause confusion, since words like phenomena and observation, just as attributes and measurements, are here used in a way incompatible with common language and practical definition. On the lines of objective description, it is indeed more appropriate to use the word phenomenon to refer only to observations obtained under circumstances whose description includes an account of the whole experimental arrangement. In such terminology, the observational problem in quantum physics is deprived of any special intricacy and we are, moreover, directly reminded that every atomic phenomenon is closed in the sense that its observation is based on registrations obtained by means of suitable amplification devices with irreversible functioning such as, for example, permanent marks on a photographic plate, caused by the penetration of electrons into the emulsion. In this connection, it is important to realize that the quantum-mechanical formalism permits well-defined applications referring only to such closed phenomena. Also in this respect it represents a rational generalization of classical physics in which every stage of the course of events is described by measurable quantities.

The freedom of experimentation, presupposed in classical physics, is of course retained and corresponds to the free choice of experimental arrangements for which the mathematical structure of the quantum mechanical formalism offers the appropriate latitude. The circumstance that, in general, one and the same experimental arrangement may yield different recordings is sometimes picturesquely described as a "choice of nature" between such possibilities. Needless to say, such a phrase implies no allusion to a personification of nature, but simply points to the impossibility of ascertaining on accustomed lines directives for the course of a closed indivisible phenomenon. Here, logical approach cannot go beyond the deduction of the relative probabilities for the appearance of the individual phenomena under given experimental conditions. In this respect, quantum mechanics presents a consistent generalization of deterministic mechanical description which it embraces as an asymptotic limit in the case of physical phenomena on a scale sufficiently large to allow the neglect of the quantum of action.

A most conspicuous characteristic of atomic physics is the novel relationship between phenomena observed under experimental conditions demanding different elementary concepts for their description. Indeed, however contrasting such experiences might appear when attempting to picture a course of atomic processes on classical lines, they have to be considered as complementary in the sense that they represent equally essential knowledge about atomic systems and together exhaust this knowledge. The notion of complementarity does in no way involve a departure from our position as detached observers of nature, but must be regarded as the logical expression of our situation as regards objective description in this field of experience. The recognition that the interaction between the measuring tools and the physical systems under investigation constitutes an integral part of quantum phenomena has not only revealed an unsuspected limitation of the mechanical conception of nature, as characterized by attribution of separate properties to physical systems, but has forced us, in the ordering of experience, to pay proper attention to the conditions of observation.

Returning to the much debated question of what has to be demanded of a physical explanation, one must keep in mind that classical mechanics had already implied the renunciation of a cause for uniform motion and furthermore that relativity theory has taught us how arguments of invariance and equivalence must be treated as categories of rational explanation. Similarly, in the complementary description of quantum physics, we have to do with a further self-consistent generalization which permits the inclusion of regularities decisive for the account of fundamental properties of matter, but which transcends the scope of deterministic description. The history of physical science thus demonstrates how the exploration of ever wider fields of experience, in revealing unsuspected limitations of accustomed ideas, indicates new ways of restoring logical order. As we shall now proceed to show, the epistemological lesson contained in the development of atomic physics reminds us of similar situations with respect to the description and comprehension of experience far beyond the borders of physical science, and allows us to trace common features promoting the search for unity of knowledge.

The first problem with which we are confronted when leaving the proper domain of physics is the question of the place of living organisms in the description of natural phenomena. Originally, no sharp distinction between animate and inanimate matter was made, and it is well known that Aristotle, in stressing the wholeness of the individual organisms, opposed the views of the atomists, and even in the discussion of the foundations of mechanics retained ideas like purpose and potency. However, as a result of the great discoveries in anatomy and physiology at the time of the Renaissance, and especially of the advent of classical mechanics in the deterministic description of which any reference to purpose is eliminated, a completely mechanistic conception of nature suggested itself, and a large number of organic functions could in fact be accounted for by the same physical and chemical properties of matter which found far-reaching explanation on simple atomic ideas. It is true that the structure and functioning of organisms involve an ordering of atomic processes which has sometimes seemed difficult to reconcile with the laws of thermodynamics, implying a steady approach towards disorder among the atoms constituting an isolated physical system. If, however, sufficient account is taken of the circumstance that the free energy necessary to maintain and develop organic systems is continually supplied from their surroundings by nutrition and respiration, it becomes clear that there is in such respect no question of any violation of general physical laws.

In the last decades, great advances have been achieved in our knowledge of the structure and functioning of organisms, and in particular it has become evident that quantum regularities in many respects here play a fundamental role. Not only are such regularities basic of the remarkable stability of the highly complex molecular structures which form the essential constituents of the cells responsible for the hereditary properties of the species, but research on mutations produced by exposing organisms to penetrating radiation offers a striking application of the statistical laws of quantum physics. Also, the sensitivity of perceptive organs, so important for the integrity of the organisms, has been found to approach the level of individual quantum processes, and amplification mechanisms play an important part especially in the transmission of nervous messages. The whole development has again, although in a novel manner, brought the mechanistic approach to biological problems to the foreground, but at the same time the question has become acute as to whether a comparison between the organisms and highly complex and refined systems, such as modern industrial constructions or electronic calculation machines, offers the proper basis for an objective description of the self-regulating entities which living organisms present.

Returning to the general epistemological lesson which atomic physics has given us, we must in the first place realize that the closed processes studied in quantum physics are not directly analogous to biological functions for the maintenance of which a continual exchange of matter and energy between the organism and the environments is required. Moreover, any experimental arrangement which would permit control of such functions to the extent demanded for their well-defined description in physical terms would be prohibitive to the free display of life. This very circumstance, however, suggests an attitude to the problem of organic life providing a more appropriate balance between a mechanistic and finalistic approach. In fact, just as the quantum of action appears in the account of atomic phenomena as an element for which an explanation is neither possible nor required, the notion of life is elementary in biological science where, in the existence and evolution of living organisms, we are concerned with manifestations of possibilities in that nature to which we belong rather than with the outcome of experiments which we can ourselves perform. Actually, we must recognize that the requirements of objective description, in tendency at least, are fulfilled by the characteristic complementary way in which arguments based on the full resources of physical and chemical science, and concepts directly referring to the integrity of the organism transcending the scope of these sciences, are practically used in biological research. The main point is that only by renouncing an explanation of life in the ordinary sense do we gain a possibility of taking into account its characteristics.

Of course, in biology just as in physics, we retain our position as detached observers, and the question is only that of the different conditions for the logical comprehension of experience. This applies also to the study of the innate and conditioned behavior of animals and man to which psychological concepts readily lend themselves. Even in an allegedly behavioristic approach, it is hardly possible to avoid such concepts, and the very idea of consciousness presents itself when we deal with behavior of so high a degree of complexity that its description virtually involves introspection on the part of the individual organism. We have here to do with mutually exclusive applications of the words instinct and reason, illustrated by the degree to which instinctive behavior is suppressed in human societies. Although we meet in trying to account for the state of our mind ever greater difficulties as regards observational detachment, it is still possible to uphold the requirements of objective description to a great extent even in human psychology. In this connection, it is interesting to note that, while in the early stages of physical science one could directly rely on such features of the events of daily life which permitted a simple causal account, an essentially complementary description of the content of our mind has been used since the origin of languages. In fact, the rich terminology adapted to such communication does not point to an unbroken course of events, but rather to mutually exclusive experiences characterized by different separations between the content on which attention is focused and the background indicated by the word ourselves.

An especially striking example is offered by the relationship between situations in which we ponder on the motives for our actions and in which we experience a feeling of volition. In normal life, such shifting of the separation is more or less intuitively recognized, but symptoms characterized as "confusion of the egos," which may lead to dissolution of the personality, are well known in psychiatry. The use of apparently contrasting attributes referring to equally important aspects of the human mind presents indeed a remarkable analogy to the situation in atomic physics, where complementary phenomena for their definition demand different elementary concepts. Above all, the circumstance that the very word "conscious" refers to experiences capable of being retained in the memory suggests a comparison between conscious experiences and physical observations. In such an analogy, the impossibility of providing an unambiguous content to the idea of subconsciousness corresponds to the impossibility of pictorial interpretation of the quantum-mechanical formalism. Incidentally, psychoanalytical treatment of neuroses may be said to restore balance in the content of the memory of the patient by bringing him new conscious experience, rather than by helping him to fathom the abysses of his subconsciousness.

From a biological point of view, we can only interpret the characteristics of psychical phenomena by concluding that every conscious experience corresponds to a residual impression in the organism, amounting to an irreversible recording in the nervous system of the outcome of processes which are not open to introspection and hardly adapted to exhaustive definition by mechanistic approach. Certainly, such recordings in which the interplay of numerous nerve cells is involved are essentially different from the permanent structures in any single cells of the organism which are connected with genetic reproduction. From a finalistic point of view, however, we may stress not only the usefulness of permanent recordings in their influence on our reactions to subsequent stimuli, but equally the importance that later generations are not encumbered by the actual experiences of individuals but rely only on the reproduction of such properties of the organism as have proved serviceable for the collection and utilization of knowledge. In any attempt to pursue the enquiry we must, of course, be prepared to meet increasing difficulties at every step, and it is suggestive that the simple concepts of physical science lose their immediate applicability to an ever higher degree the more we approach the features of living organisms related to the characteristics of our mind.

To illustrate the argument, we may briefly refer to the old problem of free will. From what has already been said it is evident that the word volition is indispensable to an exhaustive description of psychical phenomena, but the problem is how far we can speak about freedom to act according to our possibilities. As long as unrestricted deterministic views are taken, the idea of such freedom is of course excluded. However, the general lesson of atomic physics, and in particular of the limited scope of mechanistic description of biological phenomena, suggests that the ability of organisms to adjust themselves to environment includes the power of selecting the most appropriate way to this purpose. Because it is impossible to judge such questions on a purely physical basis, it is most important to recognize that psychological experience may offer more pertinent information on the problems. The decisive point is that, if we attempt to predict what another person will decide to do in a given situation, not only must we strive to know his whole background, including the story of his life in all respects which may have contributed to form his character, but we must realize that what we are ultimately aiming at is to put ourselves in his place. Of course, it is impossible to say whether a person wants to do something because he believes he can, or whether he can because he will, but it is hardly disputable that we have the feeling of, so-to-speak, being able to make the best out of the circumstance. From the point of view of objective description, nothing can here be added or taken away, and in this sense we may both practically and logically speak of freedom of will in a way which leaves the proper latitude for the use of words like responsibility and hope, which themselves are as little definable separately as other words indispensable to human communication.

Such considerations point to the epistemological implications of the lesson regarding our observational position, which the development of physical science has impressed upon us. In return for the renunciation of accustomed demands on explanation, it offers a logical means of comprehending wider fields of experience, necessitating proper attention to the placing of the object-subject separation. Since, in philosophical literature, reference is sometimes made to different levels of objectivity or subjectivity or even of reality, it may be stressed that the notion of an ultimate subject as well as conceptions like realism and idealism find no place in objective description as we have defined it; but this circumstance of course does not imply any limitation of the scope of the enquiry with which we are concerned.

Having touched upon some of the problems in science which relate to the unity of knowledge, I shall turn to the further question, whether there is a poetical or spiritual or cultural truth distinct from scientific truth. With all the reluctance of a scientist to enter into such fields, I shall venture, with an attitude similar to that indicated in the preceding, to comment on this question. Taking up the argument of the relation between our means of expression and the field of experience with which we are concerned, we are indeed directly confronted with the relationship of science and art. The enrichment which art can give us originates in its power to remind us of harmonies beyond the grasp of systematic analysis. Literary, pictorial and musical art may be said to form a sequence of modes of expression, where the ever more extensive renunciation of definition, characteristic of scientific communication, leaves fantasy a freer display. In particular, in poetry this purpose is achieved by the juxtaposition of words related to shifting observational situations, thereby emotionally uniting manifold aspects of human knowledge.

Notwithstanding the inspiration required in all work of art, it may not be irreverent to remark that even at the climax of his work the artist relies on the common human foundation on which we stand. In particular, we must realize that a word like improvisation, which comes so readily to the tongue when speaking of artistic achievements, points to a feature essential to all communication. Not only are we in ordinary conversation more or less unaware of the verbal expressions we are going to choose in communicating what is on our minds, but even in written papers, where we have the possibility of reconsidering every word, the question whether to let it stand or change it demands for its answer a final decision essentially equivalent to an improvisation. Incidentally, in the balance between seriousness and humor, characteristic of all truly artistic achievements, we are reminded of complementary aspects conspicuous in children's play and no less appreciated in mature life. Indeed, if we always endeavor to speak quite seriously, we run the risk of very soon appearing ridiculously tedious to our listeners and ourselves, but if we try to joke all the time, we soon find ourselves, and our listeners too, in the desperate mood of the jesters in Shakespeare's dramas.

In a comparison between science and art, we must of course not forget that in the former we have to do with systematic concerted efforts to augment experience and develop appropriate concepts for its comprehension, resembling the carrying and fitting of stones to a building, while in the latter we are presented with more intuitive individual endeavors to evoke sentiments which recall the wholeness of our situation. We are here at a point where the question of unity of knowledge evidently contains ambiguity, like the word "truth" itself. Indeed, with respect to spiritual and cultural values we are also reminded of epistemological problems related to the proper balance between our desire for an all-embracing way of looking at life in its multifarious aspects and our power of expressing ourselves in a logically consistent manner.

Here, essentially different starting points are taken by science, aiming at the development of general methods for ordering common human experience, and religions, originating in endeavors to further harmony of outlook and behavior within communities. Of course, in any religion, all knowledge shared by the members of the community was included in the general framework, a primary content of which were the values and ideals emphasized in cult and faith. Therefore, the inherent relation between content and frame hardly demanded attention until the subsequent progress of science entailed a novel cosmological or epistemological lesson. The course of history presents many illustrations in such respects, and we may refer especially to the veritable schism between science and religion which accompanied the development of the mechanical conception of nature at the time of the European Renaissance. On the one hand, many phenomena, hitherto regarded as manifestations of divine providence, appeared as consequences of general immutable laws of nature. On the other hand, the physical methods and viewpoints were far remote from the emphasis on human values and ideals essential to religion. Common to the schools of so-called empirical and critical philosophy, there prevailed therefore an attitude of more or less vague distinction between objective knowledge and subjective belief.

In emphasizing the necessity in unambiguous communication of paying proper attention to the placing of the object-subject separation, modern development of science has, however, created a new basis for the use of such words as knowledge and belief. Above all, the recognition of inherent limitations in the notion of causality has offered a frame in which the idea of universal predestination is replaced by the concept of natural evolution. With respect to the organization of human societies, we may particularly stress that description of the position of the individual within his community presents typically complementary aspects related to the shifting border between the appreciation of values and the background on which they are judged. Surely, every stable human society demands fair play specified in judicial rules, but at the same time, life without attachment to family and friends would obviously be deprived of some of its most precious values. Still, though the closest possible combination of justice and charity presents a common goal in all cultures, it must be recognized that any occasion which calls for the strict application of law has no room for the display of charity and that, conversely, benevolence and compassion may conflict with all ideas of justice. This point, in many religions mythically illustrated by the fight between deities personifying such ideals, is stressed in old Oriental philosophy in the admonition never to forget as we search for harmony in human life that on the scene of existence we are ourselves actors as well as spectators.

In comparing different cultures resting on traditions fostered by historical events, we meet with the difficulty of appreciating the culture of one nation on the background of traditions of another. In this respect, the relation between national cultures has sometimes been described as complementary, although this word cannot here be taken in the strict sense in which it is used in atomic physics or in psychological analysis, where we are dealing with invariable characteristics of our situation. In fact, not only has contact between nations often resulted in the fusion of cultures retaining valuable elements of national traditions, but anthropological research is steadily becoming a most important source for illuminating common features of cultural developments. Indeed, the problem of unity of knowledge can hardly be separated from the striving for universal understanding as a means of elevating human culture.

In concluding, I feel that I ought to apologize for speaking on such general topics with so much reference to the special field of knowledge represented by physical science. I have tried, however, to indicate a general attitude suggested by the serious lesson we have in our day received in this field and which to me appears of importance for the problem of unity of knowledge. This attitude may be summarized by the endeavor to achieve a harmonious comprehension of ever wider aspects of our situation, recognizing that no experience is definable without a logical frame and that any apparent disharmony can be removed only by an appropriate widening of the conceptual framework.

Charles Scott Sherrington

BRAIN COLLABORATES WITH PSYCHE

CHARLES SCOTT SHERRINGTON, *who devoted his life to the study and description of the nervous system, also wrote a book of verse and numerous essays on general topics. Born in London in 1857, he attended Cambridge and in 1884, a year before he received his medical degree, he published his first paper on the nervous system. He continued his development on the Continent, studying cholera in Italy and Spain and advanced pathology in Berlin. He started his career as a teacher of physiology at St. Thomas's Hospital in London and in his thirties, was appointed professor-superintendent of the Brown Institute for Advanced Research. During his tenure there he visited Strasbourg to study under the famous nerve specialist Goltz, and from 1895, taught at the University of Liverpool until he was offered a chair at Oxford eighteen years later. Sherrington was seventy-five when he shared the 1932 Nobel Prize in Medicine and Physiology with Edgar Douglas Adrian "for discoveries regarding the function of the neurons," but he lived for twenty more years to enjoy his deserved fame. The following essay is an extract from* Man on His Nature (1941).

Leaning upon the physicist the physiologist has finer means now than ever before for asking the ways and doings of the brain. Electrical technique enables him to detect happenings in the brain which formerly he could not, and in that very part of the brain which evidence bespeaks as having correlation with the mind. One approach to the correlation might be minute enquiry into the character of the energy processes detectable in the living brain, especially the "mental" part of it. Changes of temperature might serve the purpose, but they are slight and little accessible to examination. Again, chemical study though as successful as any in getting at the inner processes of life is at a disadvantage in the brain. Chemical search cannot usually be made without disorganization of the very substance it would examine. Chemistry cannot at present in its examination of the brain pay regard there to cellular arrangement, though that must be a datum for the ways of the brain's doings.

Chemistry does show that the roof-brain is especially sensitive to changes in the oxygen-tension in its fluids, or, less technically, to the pressure of its oxygen supply. In the pigeon suffering from beri-beri, along with dramatic relief of its symptoms by vitamin B_1, runs dramatic improvement of the impaired respiratory process in the brain (Peters). The roof-brain is more sensitive to shortage of oxygen than is the brain elsewhere. Such shortage impairs mentally as well as physiologically. There is disturbance of thought and derangement of ideas. Barcroft, in the High Andes, observed disaptitude for arithmetic. Glucose, the typical physiological sugar, is urgently important to the brain. It is the brain's usual fuel. The brain draws it from the blood. It does not, as do some organs, take it into storage. It takes it to use it at once. Judged by its chemical turn-over the brain is not a homogeneous organ any more than it is as judged by its microscopical structure. In the roof-brain or cortex the need for oxygen is greater than in nearly every other part. Narcotics diminish the oxidation of sugar by the brain. The greater the narcotic power the more the interference with the brain's oxidation. When the quantity of sugar supplied to the brain by the blood-stream is less the oxidative turn-over is less owing to the lack of oxidative food. Without vitamin B the brain cannot make proper use of glucose as a food. With shortage of sugar the working processes of the brain suffer. Thought and behavior alter. If the conditions be prolonged, unconsciousness ensues, and if prolonged further the brain-cells are permanently damaged. But if not so prolonged when the normal supply of sugar is restored the brain-cells recover and thought and behavior again become normal. In this light, mind is a function of the chemistry of the roof-brain.

It is however by electrical means that the activity of nervous organs can be most intimately followed. Electrical potentials indicate nerve activity closely and quickly. The nerve-impulse—the process by which universally, and perhaps exclusively, nerve-cells communicate one with another—seems in essence electrical. Traveling impulses of less than a thousandth of a thousandth of a volt and lasting, as they pass any spot, one/10,000th of a second only, are photographed or seen or listened to, and in their almost undistorted time-relations. They are fleeting and self-mending electrical leaks which move along the skin of the nerve-thread. Intensity of action does not increase an impulse but sets up successive impulses more quickly. The upkeep of the membrane ready for transmitting impulses is an activity as is the impulse itself. When therefore we speak of a nerve or of the brain as being at rest in the sense that nervous impulses are not traveling it, the expression "at rest" stands simply for another and a steadier activity. The disturbance which we call "action" can be thought of as rhythmic, and rhythmic at different rates. The activity we identify with rest is a balanced activity, a dynamic equilibrium, which can maintain itself. Its upset, which is "action," is not an equilibrium, it cannot be maintained long. It spends a reserve which will have to be made good. It brings in its train "fatigue."

It may be objected that it is not nerve-impulses which are likely to tell us what we want to know of the brain. They are a concern of nerve-fibers. Nerve-fibers are merely the wires to and from the telephone-exchange. We want the activities of the exchange itself. Activity of the brain involves great numbers, not to say, vast numbers, of nerve-cells co-operating. Yet the means of securing that co-operation is by impulses via the nerve-fibers connecting cells. A large and an essential part of even the highest brain activity must therefore consist of nerve-impulses.

We turn to the actual cells of the brain. They, if we pursue the simile of the telephone system, are not the mere wires but are the actual exchange; they do the retransmitting. They too have now come under examination by electrical methods. Their changes of potential are of two kinds; the more usual fall and an opposed rise of potential. Since in these situations the neural process is known to be of two kinds, one activation, the other arrest of activation, these changes of opposed electrical sign suggest a significant fit into the physiological picture. And there are too, the rhythmic electrical waves which can be picked up by pad-electrodes placed on the head. They come probably from the surface-sheet of the brain cells. The rhythm of the beat is not too quick to be easily distinguishable by us were it perceptible to our consciousness at all. But our consciousness knows nothing about it. Through all the ages no suspicion of it has dawned upon us. Not even when now told of it do we feel it. The seat of the rhythm is in the visual region of the brain; vision sees nothing of it. Yet with a shift of mind the beat is altered; to open the closed eyes immediately disturbs it. It is possible to upset the rhythm by trying, without opening the eyes, to see something. A flash of light on the eye and a whole series of waves can be picked up from the visual part of the brain.

Physiology has got so far therefore as examining the activity in the "mental" part of the brain when activity there is in normal progress. The desideratum to carry observation into the telephone-exchange itself with that exchange normally at work seems thus at last fulfilled. But has it brought us to the "mind"? It has brought us to the brain as a telephone-exchange. All the exchange consists of is switches. What we wanted really on the brain was, it would seem, the subscribers using the exchange. The subscribers with their thoughts, their desires, their anticipations, their motives, their anxieties, their rejoicings. If it is mind we are searching the brain for, then we are supposing the brain to be much more than a telephone-exchange. We are supposing it a telephone-exchange along with the subscribers as well. Does our admirably delicate electrical exploration vouchsafe us any word about them? Its finger is ultra-sensitive, but energy is all that it can feel. And is the mind energy?

The "subject" whose eye opens and whose brain-waves then alter, experiences as the most significant fact of the moment the mental change that he now sees something whereas before he did not. Do the concurrent electrical potentials contribute anything at all to the conception of, or to the understanding of, this visual experience?

It is now some seventy years since the words of a great biological leader of his time to his hearers were "the thoughts to which I am now giving utterance and your thoughts regarding them are the expression of molecular changes in that matter of life which is the source of our other vital phenomena" (Huxley). The terminology is a little "dated," but is the main position thus set forth altered today? The concomitance in time and place between the "molecular changes" and "the thoughts" is still all we have correlating the two. Regarded as a paradox it has become more intriguing; regarded as a gap in knowledge more urgent.

It has its practical consequences. One is that in the training and in the exercise of medicine a remoteness abides between the field of neurology and that of mental health, psychiatry. It is sometimes blamed to prejudice on the part of the one side or the other. It is both more grave and less grave than that. It has a reasonable basis. It is rooted in the energy-mind problem. Physiology has not enough to offer about the brain in relation to the mind to lend the psychiatrist much help. It has occupied itself largely with what are called the lower levels of nervous action. Results of general value have emerged. The nature of the nerve-impulse, the properties of cell-contacts as one-way gates compelling one-way traffic on nerve-paths, the occurrence not only of action but of active suppression of action, the knowledge that intensity of action means not larger impulses but more frequent impulses, that impulse-effects can sum, or cancel, that there are places where impulses spontaneously arise. Much of this knowledge certainly applies to the brain, and to that part of it which interests us here, the roof of the forebrain. Every nerve-cell of the millions in it is clearly at a glance a nerve-cell. But nerve-cells as a class are elsewhere not specially concerned with mind. It is partly conjecture whether the properties of all these nerve-cells, their fibers, their cell-contacts (synapses), their cell-bodies, have rigidly those characters observed in the more accessible nerve-cells of the spinal cord and elsewhere. That the properties will not differ fundamentally from those elsewhere seems safe to suppose.

Were for instance the one-way traffic along nervous paths which obtains in the spinal cord not to hold in the case of paths in the roof-brain, that would allow new possibilities of interaction which our present interpretation does not bargain for. But the visible concatenation of the cells as studied by the microscope does not hint that if one-way traffic obtains in the spinal cord it is departed from in the roof-brain.

In one respect the highly specialized nerve-cells most studied, those of the spinal cord, fail as a type of nerve-cells in general. Their specialization for reflex action has reduced to vanishing point the feature of self-excitation. The rhythmic volleying of cell-groups in the roof-brain may be such self-stimulation. But self-firing in itself gives no presumption for correlation between the roof-brain and mind. The roof-brain cells, whether because the latest and so less stereotyped in their ways than others of hoary ancestral tradition, are more plastic and open to modification than the old. They can attach old motor acts to fresh unwonted calls on them. They can acquire new habits. Then, as counterpart to that, if we pass over to "mind" they compose the organ which *par excellence* can learn.

Nature is a great teacher. But for teaching there must be learners. A certain proportion of what we call living nature can learn. What is commonly called the survival of the fittest turns partly on the capacity of certain forms of life to learn. Not that what is learnt is inherited. But the ability to learn favors survival and is heritable. A vast number, perhaps the numerical majority, of animal forms cannot be shown unequivocally to possess mind. But none the less the student of their behavior finds that while they "seek" and prolong contact with some items of their surround, e.g. food, they "avoid" or break off contact with other items, which, as the observer notes, would harm them. Thus, with the reflex action of the brain-less frog, a morsel of acidified paper wet with acid is pushed away (defense) by the mindless limb or the limb is withdrawn from it (escape). This class of reflexes which imply defense or escape are known as "protective." They are physical behavior which in higher forms of life where mind is recognizable have mental accompaniment, and their mental accompaniment is "pain." The act and the pain then make one integral reaction—but they are still separable to experimental observation. Widely apart in evolutionary age they lie apart from each other in the nervous system, the one is spinal the other cerebral. In the spinal dog the limbs are insentient; yet, if one foot tread on a thorn, it is at once held up out of further harm while the other three legs run away. The protective reflex is there, but the little wound causes no pain, because it has no nexus with the mind. Again, in appendicitis, the muscles are characteristically tightened over the inflamed part; thus protecting it and keeping it quiet. This is a reflex contraction, so automatic that the patient cannot even relax it. It is quite separable from the pain, for ether inhalation will annul the pain by paralyzing the brain long before it annuls the contraction.

The protective reflexes are innate. They afford a measure of protection to their individual beset by a world of danger and damage. They instance the psalmist's "wisdom of the body." Their service we may suppose has given them survival value. Where they are yoked with mind we know from our own experience that their sensual accompaniment is rich in affect, an acute psychical urge, in short "pain." This urge reinforces and amplifies the measure of protection and relief the pure reflex act affords. Being mental it develops the situation into a mental situation involving perception and affect and imbuing it with "time" and "space," the attributes of mind. This mental reaction, like the pure reflex it accompanies, is protective but comprising "time" as it does it is not indefinitely of *any* moment as is the reflex. Its "pain" brands it into the time-system of the finite mind as unpleasant and not to be repeated. It is a "lesson." As we say, "the burnt child shuns the fire." The experiments of Thorndike and of Pavlov have shown how important this is in the methodology of training. It has a positive counterpart, training by reward, a seeking to repeat remembered satisfaction. The principle enters into our own education, formal education as well as natural and social.

Here our contact with it turns merely on two points. One is the practically universal distribution through animal life of a special set of receptor organs whose sole scope is that of making the animal react to infliction of physical injury, and making it react either by "defense" or "escape." This shows us that extraneous injury to life is taken by Nature as part of the normal routine of life. This special set of so-called "noci-ceptor" organs, which evokes protective movements, seems more widely broadcast in the animal series than is recognizable mind itself. It is found in animal forms where there is no evidence of mind. In animal forms however which partake of mind its noci-ceptor organs pertain to sentience, and provoke "pain." Physical pain is thus the psychical adjunct of a protective reflex. The only modality of sense which the noci-ceptor organ evokes is pain. Other of our sense-organs evoke their modes of sensation—sight, hearing, touch, cold, warmth, smell, bitter, sweet, and so on—without "pain," but these injury-organs provoke pain and nothing but pain. They are pain-organs and are called so.

Their specific stimulus is, in the narrow sense, not specific at all, but in the biological sense it is specific enough. It is anything which does injury to the part it reaches. The little pain-organ so to say watches over the part at and immediately around where it is situate. Pain therefore is in the evolution of mind treated and provided for as part of the normal economy of animate nature; further it is the more developed the higher its organism in the scale of mind. It does not require much study of the pain-organs and their arrangement to show that the infliction of injury which they envisage and react to is in vast preponderance injury inflicted by other species of life. The infliction of injury by one species of life upon another is therefore treated by Nature as part of Nature's normal scheme.

Evolution has thus supplied the body with a special sense of its own injuries, a sense so drastically affecting the mind as to capture the mind's attention even to exclusion for the time being of all else. The development of this pain-sense has the interest that it illustrates the evolutionary process dealing with the mental side of the organism as effectively as with the material side. For all the evidence we have evolution draws no pragmatic distinction between the two. A mental event, pain, superadded to a reflex, the protective reflex, seems here to reinforce and amplify the physical act. The local reflex itself affords its limited protection and relief, e.g. by holding the part taut and quiet. But the "pain" through the mind can enjoin keeping the whole body motionless though tense. In ourselves, social and sophisticated, it may provoke the train of action of "calling in" the doctor. In short, under the rubric "pain" we meet mind moving matter to help mind in mind's distress. Mind invoking the body to do something and, in spite of the eternal psycho-physical difficulty, effectively. "Pain" seems to pay no heed to that old dilemma. My raging tooth drives me to the dentist as if it operated my motion thither.

The roof-brain is the nervous organ which *par excellence* can learn by experience. One structural feature of it is so pronounced that, as a dry fact, it is impressive. Its cell-population is enormous. The numbers in our own brain-roof run to ten thousand millions (Judson Herrick). To microscope this nerve-mass is to be struck by a seemingly reckless profusion of nerve-cells. It is the reason of the greater size of the higher types of brain. In the dog it is larger than the whole of the rest of the nervous system taken together. In ourselves the relation is hugely increased further. It is out of all proportion to our bodily bulk. As old Laurent Joubert said in his picturesque way* the brain of a man is larger than the brains of two oxen together. In the bygone geological world some of life's ancient shapes attained bodies 100 feet in length; but they had a forebrain not larger than a nut. Our forebrain is so large as to bulge out the contour of the head. Our brain is a monster brain. It gives the ball-like top-end of us. Æsthetic or not it is an over-grown nerve-ganglion protected by a bony case. Our sophistication and prejudice may regard it as a thing of beauty. It symbolizes our prerogative, human mind, and in common belief contains it.

Of three aspects of mind broadly distinguishable, the affective, conative, and cognitive, one inference perhaps to be drawn from the human brain is that growth of cognitive processes makes wholesale demand on numbers of nerve-cells. We can understand how this might be if a principle such as the "association" of old-time psychology be largely engaged in it. An automatic card-index on an enormous scale with copious cross-references may be asked for. This part of the brain is evidently cumulative in time. And so is knowledge. May it not be that there is a correlation between the two? Again, where intellectual activity is required it is as

* *Traité du Ris*, Paris, 1579.

though a pressure-reservoir were kept at hand. This great many-celled spongework in the human roof-brain is something like a continuum from end to end furnished with perhaps a million discharging mouths. It might well provide reinforcement, and reinforce vicariously as occasion requires here or there. The cerebellum was once thought a reservoir-organ for reinforcing the motor powers of the cerebrum. Apart from that restricted strip whence electricity can evoke bodily movement, by far the greater part of the roof-brain is, as the phrase goes, "silent," that is in response to electricity yields nothing detectable at all. There is the psychological theory that a general factor, *g*, enters into mental ability. Of this Spearman its author tells us that a permissible picture of it is as a "power" which can be supplied to the mental factory from a general power-station and distributed to any required particular engine. Lashley would perhaps identify *g* with a "mass-action" of the cortex of the brain.

The neural basis of affect we can suppose need not entail much neural superstructure. It might use chemical reinforcement. This lets us stress the roof-organ of the forebrain as especially cognitive, with below it the old kernel-organ of the forebrain especially related to "affect"; and we remember that every cognition has, potentially at least, an emotive value; emotive, and, along with that, conative effort as a further factor. How do they hang together? What is the significance of their so doing? Not in man alone but infra-humanly in due degrees, no doubt less cognitive. What is the tie which conjoins these several aspects of mind so inseparably? What is it else than "urge-to-live"? Human cognition may like the winged horse take at times its flights toward the stars and forget earth. None the less it is harnessed to life's car, whose charioteer is "urge-to-live" sublimed to "zest-to-live." It and its fellow-steeds, endeavor, will, emotion, passion or whatever else we call them, pull under the same lash.

The student of the mind, for instance the practical psychiatrist at the mental hospital, must find the physiology of the brain still remote and vague for his desiderata on his subject. He may have hoped from it some knowledge which would serve to found the norm from which psycho-pathology could take its points of de-

parture in this direction or in that. There is for instance the condition "anxiety." None is I suppose more far-reaching as a warper
of the mind. But where does neurophysiology contribute anything
to the knowledge of the norm from which anxiety causes departure, and what has cerebral physiology to offer on the whole subject of "anxiety"? The psychiatrist has perforce to go on his way
seeking things more germane to what he needs. The mind is a
something with such manifold variety, such fleeting changes, such
countless nuances, such wealth of combinations, such heights
and depths of mood, such sweeps of passion, such vistas of imagination, that the bald submission of some electrical potentials
recognizable in nerve-centers as correlative to all these may seem
to the special student of mind almost derisory. It is, further, more
than mere lack of corresponding complexity which frustrates the
comparison.

The mental is not examinable as a form of energy. That in
brief is the gap which parts psychiatry and physiology. No mere
running round the cycle of the "forms of energy" takes us across
that chasm. Perhaps that is what William MacDougall* was
meaning when he exclaimed, "medicine has nothing to learn
from psychology nor psychology from medicine."

The question of the relation between the working of the brain
and the working of the mind is, we hear often, one improper to
put. It is "by nature insoluble," "ignorabimus," "the data at the
present time are insufficient," or it is not of practical importance.
The cogency of these grounds depends, I would think, partly on
the purpose for which the question may be asked. To put the
question may serve as we have said "pour préciser les idées." And
to do that may have urgency. Witness the training of the psychiatrist and the physiologist. Only *after* the question has been discussed can they go on their respective ways, as perforce they
ultimately must, disappointed it may be, but wiser, if sadder, practi-
tioners and men.

In such an impasse it seems permissible for the man in the
street, such as myself, to outline to himself briefly, although he
can do so but naïvely, the position. I would feel he is almost
called upon to do so. The busy everyday world ignores the diffi-

* *Brit. Med. J.* April 1939.

culty. That however does not remove the enigma. It was easy for the old classical *a priori* materialism to run roughshod over mind. It used the term matter without any scientific delimitation of the concept. It was a doctrine which knew far less and spread itself far more than does the scientific study of matter, or energy, today. What is the reply when to the student of energy, in other words to the follower of Natural Science, there comes today someone who asks, "Mind presents itself as thoughts, feelings, and so on. They are the outcome of the brain. The brain is matter, energy. Matter and energy can only be matter and energy. Therefore thoughts, feelings and so on are matter and energy. Therefore mind is matter and energy?" I trust I do no violence to the argument; I have no wish to do so. The reply by the follower of Natural Science of today, if I as a man in the street may guess it, will not be, even in trend, at all like that which Lucretius gave in a famous and vehement passage, about specially small and well-rounded atoms. Such materialism was merely a frame of mind. The materialist standpoint today is a scientific position. Its answer today is of a different order. As I surmise it, it would say: Thoughts, feelings, and so on are not amenable to the energy (matter) concept. They lie outside it. Therefore they lie outside Natural Science. If as you say thoughts are an outcome of the brain we as students using the energy-concept know nothing of it; as followers of natural science we know nothing of any relation between thoughts and the brain, except as a gross correlation in time and space.

In some ways this is embarrassing for biology. Biology cannot go far in its subject without being met by mind. Biology as its name says is the study of life. And biology is a branch of natural science. Natural science has studied life to the extent of explaining away life as any radically separate category of phenomena. The categories of living and lifeless as regards science disappear; there is no radical scientific difference between living and dead. Time was when to think and to breathe were on an equality as attributes of life. Now, living, so far as breathing, moving, assimilating, growing, reproducing, etc. amount to life, has by natural science been accounted for—some might say, "explained." There is nothing in them which does not fall within the province of science. They are chemistry and physics. But though living is analyzable and describable by natural science, that associate of living, thought, escapes and remains refractory to natural science. In fact natural science repudiates it as something outside its ken. A radical distinction has therefore arisen between life and mind. The former is an affair of chemistry and physics; the latter escapes chemistry and physics. And yet the occurrence of mind—recognizable finite mind—is confined to a certain particular field of chemistry and physics, namely, that of highly integrated animal lives. "Thinking," in this its limited field of occurrence, appears as a phase of living. If, as is practical, we continue to subsume mind under life, we have to distinguish it as an activity of life selectively and uniquely apart from the rest. The psycho-physical difficulty places us in the position of empirics as to much. By ways which may be judged roundabout, we find ourselves at length pragmatically alongside of general commonsense opinion. That may be taken either as sanity or superficiality or perhaps both.

The sixteenth-century physician Jean Fernel would have smiled at this difficulty which presents itself to us. For him there is no difference between thought and the rest of living. The cause of the brain's thinking was for him the life-spirit in it. That spirit has the brain for habitation, its temporary dwelling. He would tell us that what his boat is for the time being to the mariner, such the brain is for the time being to this spirit. That the brain should obey and do what the spirit would he finds no more remarkable than that the boat obeys the handling of him who sails it. But we recall a railway-coach attached to its locomotive solely by good-will between guard and driver and it did not arrive.

For Fernel there was duality but that duality created a situation of no difficulty. Its members, matter and spirit, combined in perfectly satisfying co-operation. Matter was the servant. Spirit, mind, was the master. Perhaps that was from the Phædo, where we remember the soul rules, the body obeys. Today the duality is there; and combination is there, but the footing on which the combination rests, so obvious to Fernel, is for our enquiry still to seek. Perhaps the "servant and master" phrase had in view an assertion of free-will. But where in nature shall we find "servant and master"? Where our knowledge halts our description will resort to metaphor. Long will man's fancy deal with the tie between body and mind by metaphor and often half forget the while that metaphor it is. Regarding this problem will a day come when metaphors can be dispensed with?

Werner Karl Heisenberg

SCIENCE AS A MEANS OF INTERNATIONAL UNDERSTANDING

WERNER KARL HEISENBERG, *a pioneer in nuclear physics and quantum mechanics, was born in Duisberg, Germany, the son of an illustrious Byzantine scholar. After receiving his doctorate from the University of Munich in 1924, he became an assistant to Max Born (Physics Prize, 1954) at Göttingen and studied under Niels Bohr (Physics, 1922) at Copenhagen. He returned to Germany as professor of theoretical physics at the University of Leipzig, and then during the second World War, became director of the Max Planck Institute at Berlin and professor at the University. At present he is director of the Max Planck Institute for Physics at Göttingen. He is best known to the world as the recipient of the Nobel Prize in 1933 and the father of the "uncertainty principle," which marked a revolution in scientific thought comparable only with Einstein's theory of relativity. According to this principle, there are limits to the accuracy with which certain atomic occurrences can be known, limitations not imposed entirely by imperfection of the senses of measuring instruments, but inherent in the very nature of atomic phenomena. Recently, his "unified field" theory stirred great attention among scientists. The following essay, based upon an address at Göttingen University in 1946, appears in his book,* Philosophical Problems in Nuclear Science.

It has often been said that science should be a bridge between peoples and should help to better international understanding. It has also repeatedly been stressed, with full justification, that science is international and that it directs man's thoughts to matters which are understood by all peoples and in whose solution scientists of the most diverse languages, races or religions can participate equally. At this particular time it is important that we should not make things too easy for ourselves. We must also discuss the opposite thesis, which is still fresh in our ears, that science is national and that the ideas of the various races are fundamentally different. It was held that science had to serve one's own people in the first instance and help to secure one's own political power: that science forms the basis of all technical developments, and hence of all progress, as well as of all military power. It was also held that the task of the pure sciences as well as of philosophy was to support our Weltanschauung and our beliefs. These in turn were regarded as the foundations of political power among our own people. I should like to discuss which of these two views is correct and what are the relative merits of the arguments that can be produced in their favor.

I.   To gain clarity on this question we shall have to discover, in the first instance, how science is carried on, how an individual is brought into contact with scientific problems and how these problems excite his interest. Since I know only my own science well, you will not misunderstand me if I first speak about atomic physics and if I recall my own experiences as a student.

When I left school in 1920 in order to attend at the University of Munich, the position of our youth as citizens was very similar to what it is to-day. Our defeat in the first world war had produced a deep mistrust of all the ideals which had been used during the war and which had lost us that war. They seemed hollow now and we wanted to find out for ourselves what was of value in this world and what was not: we did not want to rely on our parents or our teachers. Apart from many other values we re-discovered science in this process. After having studied a few popular books I began to take an interest in the branch of science concerned with atoms, and wanted to form an opinion of the peculiar statements which were being made about space and time in the theory of relativity. In this way I came to attend the lectures of my later teacher, Sommerfeld, who fanned this interest and from whom I learnt, in the course of the term, how a new and deeper understanding of atoms had developed as a result of the researches of Röntgen, Planck, Rutherford, and Bohr. I came to know that the Dane, Niels Bohr, and the Englishman, Lord Rutherford, imagined an atom to be a planetary system in miniature and that it was likely that all the chemical properties of the elements would, in future, be predictable with the help of Bohr's theory, by making use of the planetary orbits of the electrons. At that time, however, this had not been achieved. This last point naturally interested me most and every new work of Bohr was discussed at the Munich Seminar with vigor and passion. You can well imagine what it meant for me when Sommerfeld invited me, in the summer of 1921, to accompany him to Göttingen to hear a series of lectures given by Niels Bohr about his atomic theory. It was held in this very "Collegienhaus." This cycle of lectures in Göttingen, which in future was always to be referred to as the "Bohr Festival," has in many ways determined my future attitude to science and especially to atomic physics.

First of all, we could sense in Bohr's lectures the power of the ideas of a man who had seriously grappled with these problems and who understood them better than anyone else in the whole world. Secondly, there were some points on which I had previously formed an opinion different from that expounded by Bohr. These questions were fought out during long walks to the Rohn and to the Hainberg.

These conversations left a deep impression on me. First I learnt that when trying to understand atomic structure it was obviously quite immaterial whether one was German, Danish or English. I also learnt something perhaps even more important, namely that in science a decision can always be reached as to what is right and what is wrong. It was not a question of belief, or Weltanschauung, or hypothesis; but a certain statement could either be simply right and another statement simply wrong. Neither origin nor race decides this question: it is decided by nature, or if you prefer, by God, in any case not by man.

Very much enriched by these experiences, I returned to Munich and continued, under Sommerfeld's direction, with my own experiments on atomic structures. When I had completed my Doctor's examination I went to Copenhagen, in the autumn of 1924, with the aid of a so-called Rockefeller Grant, in order to work with Bohr. There I came into a circle of young people of the most diverse nationalities—English, American, Swedish, Norwegian, Dutch and Japanese—all of whom wanted to work on the same problem, Bohr's atomic theory. They nearly always joined together like a big family for excursions, games, social gatherings and sports. In this circle of physicists I had the opportunity of really getting to know people from other nations and their ways of thought. The learning and speaking of other languages which this necessitated was the best way of becoming really familiar with other ways of life, foreign literatures and foreign art. I could see more and more clearly how little mattered the diversity of nations and races when there was common effort centered on a difficult scientific problem. The differences of thought which were so clearly shown in art seemed to me more of an enrichment of one's own possibilities than a disturbing factor.

With this background I arrived in Cambridge in the summer of 1925, and spoke about my work to a small circle of theoreticians in a College, in the study of the Russian physicist Kapitza. Among those present, there was an unusually gifted student hardly twenty-three years old who took my problems and constructed, within a few months, a comprehensive theory of the atomic shell. His name was Dirac and he was a man of outstanding mathematical ability. His methods of thought were vastly different from mine, his mathematical methods more elegant and more unusual than those to which we were used at Göttingen. However, in the end, he arrived at the same results as Born, Jordan and I, at least on all points of importance. This confirmation and the fact that the results were so beautifully complementary served as further proof of the "objectivity" of science and its independence of language, race or belief.

As well as Copenhagen and Cambridge, Göttingen remained a center for this international family of atomic physicists. The work was directed by Franck. Born and Pohl and many of the scientists about whom you read in the newspapers in connection with the atom bomb, such as Oppenheimer and Blackett, as well as Fermi studied in Göttingen at that time.

I have quoted these personal reminiscences only in order to give an example of the internationalism of the community of science. It has, of course, been the same for centuries in many other sciences and this family of atomic physicists was in no way out of the ordinary. I could quote many international groups of "savants" from the history of science who were linked through the frontiers of nations by common work.

Perhaps I might mention one other group of scientists who, in the seventeenth century, founded mathematical science in Europe. It is especially appropriate to do so because the memory of Leibnitz is being celebrated this year as well as the foundation of the Scientific Academies. I should like to quote a few sentences of Dilthey's description of that epoch:

> A bond, unhampered by any limitations of language or nationality, linked the few individuals who devoted their lives to this new science. They formed a new aristocracy and were conscious of it, just as before in the days of the Renaissance, humanists and artists had felt themselves to be such an aristocracy. The Latin and, later on, the French language rendered the easiest mutual understanding possible and they became the instrument of a scientific world literature. Already around the middle of the seventeenth century, Paris had become the center of collaboration between philosophers and scientists. There Gassendi, Marsenne and Hobbes exchanged ideas and even the proud recluse Descartes joined their circle for a time. His presence made an unforgettable impression on Hobbes and later Leibnitz; for it was there that both became devoted to the ideas of mathematical science. Later, London became another center. . . .*

We can see then that science has been carried on in this way throughout history and that the "Republic of Sages" has always played an important part in the life of Europe. It has always been considered self-evident that adherence to such an international circle would not prevent the individual scientist from devotedly serving his own people and feeling himself one of them. On the contrary, such a broadening of one's horizon frequently enhances esteem for the best aspects of the life of one's own country. One learns to love it and feels indebted to it.

* Dilthey: Gesammelte Werke Bd. III, S 15, 16

II.   Having said all this I must now also deal with the question of why all this scientific collaboration, all these real human relationships, seemingly do so little in preventing animosity and war.

First of all it must be stressed that science represents only a small part of public life and that only very few people in each country are really connected with science. Politics, however, are shaped by stronger forces. They have to take into account the actions of large masses of people, their economic position and the struggle for power of a few privileged groups favored by tradition. These forces have, so far, always overpowered the small number of people who were ready to discuss disputed questions in a scientific way—that is, objectively, dispassionately and in the spirit of mutual understanding. The political influence of science has always been very small, and this is understandable enough. It does, however, frequently place the scientist in a position which is in some ways more difficult than that of any other group of men. For science has, in its practical applications, a very great influence on the life of the people. Prosperity and political power depend on the state of science and the scientist cannot ignore these practical consequences even if his own interest in science is of a less practical nature. Thus, the action of an individual scientist often carries far more weight than he would wish and he frequently has to decide, according to his own conscience, whether a cause is good or bad. When the differences between nations can no longer be reconciled he is therefore often faced with the painful decision either of cutting himself off from his own people or from those friends who are linked with him by their common work. The position in the various sciences is here somewhat different. The medical practitioner, who helps people irrespective of their nationality, can more easily reconcile his actions to the demands of the state and of his own conscience than the physicist, whose discoveries may lead to the manufacture of weapons of destruction. But, by and large, there always remains this tension; there are on the one hand the demands of the state, which wants to enlist science particularly for the benefit of its own people and hence the strengthening of its own political power. On the other hand there is the duty owed by the scientist to his work which links him to people of other nations.

The relations between the scientist and the state have changed in a characteristic way during the past decades. During the first world war the scientists were so closely tied to their states that Academies frequently expelled scientists of other countries or signed resolutions in favor of their own cause and against the cause of the other nations. This hardly happened at all during the second world war. The link between the scientists was frequently much stronger, even to the extent, in many countries, of difficulties arising between them and their own governments. Scientists claimed the right to judge the policies of their governments independently and without ideological bias. The State, on its side, viewed the international relations of scientists with deep mistrust so that eventually scientists were sometimes even treated like prisoners in their own country and their international relations considered almost immoral. Conversely it has now become almost a matter of course that scientists will help their colleagues wherever possible, even though they belong to the enemy country. This development may lead to a fortunate strengthening of international, as against national, relations, but care will have to be taken that it does not become the origin of a dangerous wave of mistrust and enmity of large masses of people against the profession of science itself.

There have been such difficulties in previous centuries when men of science stood up for the principle of tolerance and independence from dogma against the current political power. We need only think of a Galileo or a Giordano Bruno. That these difficulties have assumed even greater importance to-day may be because the practical effects of science can directly decide the fate of millions of people.

This brings me to a frightening aspect of our present-day existence which has to be clearly recognized so that the correct action can be taken. I am not only thinking of the new sources of energy which physics has mastered during the last year and which could lead to unimaginable destruction. New possibilities of interfering with nature are threatening us in many other fields, though it is true that chemical means of destroying life have hardly been used in this last war. In biology, too, we have gained such insight into the processes of heredity and into the structure and chemistry of large albumen molecules that it has become a practical possibility to produce infectious diseases artificially, and perhaps worse, even the biological development of man may be influenced in the direction of some predetermined selective breeding. Finally, the mental and spiritual state of people could·be influenced and, if this were carried out from a scientific point of view, it could lead to terrible mental deformations of great masses of people. One has the impression that science approaches on a broad front a region in which life and death of humanity at large can become dependent on the actions of a few, very small groups of people. Up to now these things have been discussed in a journalistic and sensational way in the newspapers and most people have not realized the terrible danger which threatens them as a result of further inevitable scientific developments. It is certainly the task of science to rouse humanity to these dangers and to show them how important it is that all mankind, independent of national and ideological views, should unite to meet the peril. Of course, this is more easily said than done, but it is certainly a task which we can no longer escape.

For the individual scientist there remains, however, the necessity of deciding according to his own conscience and free from all ties, whether a cause is good or even which of two causes is less bad. We cannot escape the fact that large masses of people, and with them those who hold the power of government, often act senselessly and with blind prejudice. By giving them the scientific knowledge the scientist can easily be maneuvered into a position which Schiller describes in these verses:

"Woe to those who bestow the light of heaven on him who is for ever blind, it sheds no light for him, it can but char and blacken lands and cities."

Can science really contribute to understanding between the peoples when it is faced with such a situation? It has the power to release great forces, greater than have ever before been in the control of man, but these forces will lead into chaos unless they are sensibly used.

III. This leads me to the real inherent task of science. The development which I have just described and which has apparently turned against himself those forces which man controls and which can lead to the most terrible destruction, this development must certainly be closely connected with some spiritual processes of our time, and it is necessary to speak briefly about these.

Let us look back a few centuries. At the end of the Middle Ages man discovered, apart from the Christian reality centered round the divine revelation, yet another reality of material experience. That was "objective" reality which we experience through our senses or by experiment. But in this advance into a new field certain methods of thought remained unchanged. Nature consisted of things in space which changed in time according to cause and effect. Outside of this there was the world of spirit, that is, the reality of one's own mind which reflected the external world like a more or less perfect mirror. Much as the reality determined by the sciences differed from the Christian reality, it nevertheless represented also a divine world order with man's action based on a firm foundation, and in which there could be little doubt about the purpose of life. The world was infinite in space and time, it had in a way replaced God or had at least become, by its infinity, a symbol of the divine.

But this view of nature has also become undermined during our century. Fundamental attitudes of thought lost their absolute importance as concrete action moved more and more into the center of our world. Even time and space became a subject of experience and lost their symbolic content. In science we realize more and more that our understanding of nature cannot begin with some definite cognition, that it cannot be built on such a rock-like foundation, but that all cognition is, so to speak, suspended over an unfathomable depth.

This development of science corresponds probably to the increasingly relative assessment of all values in the life of man, an assessment which has been noticeable for some decades and which can easily end up in a generally skeptical attitude capped by the desperate question "for what purpose." Thus develops the attitude of unbelief which we call "nihilism." From this point of view life appears to be purposeless or, at best, an adventure which we have to endure while having had no say in it. We find this attitude in many parts of the world to-day and its most unpleasant form is illusionary nihilism, as v. Weizsäcker recently called it. It is a nihilism disguised by illusion and self-deception.

The characteristic trait of every nihilist attitude is the lack of a solid belief which can give direction and strength to all the reactions of an individual. Nihilism shows itself in the life of an individual by his lack of an unerring instinct for right and wrong, for what is an illusion and what is a reality. In the life of nations it leads to a change of direction in which the immense forces, which have been gathered for the achievement of a certain aim, have the very opposite result and this can cause great destruction. People are often so blinded by hatred that they cynically watch this change and dispose of it with a shrug of the shoulder.

I said a little earlier that this development in the outlook of men may have some relation to the development of scientific thought. We must therefore ask whether science too has lost its solid beliefs. I am very anxious to make it quite clear that there can be no question of this. The very opposite is true. The present situation of science is probably the strongest argument we possess for a more optimistic attitude to the great problems of the world.

For in *those* branches of science in which we have found that our knowledge is "suspended in mid-air" in *just those* branches have we achieved a crystal clear understanding of the relevant phenomena. This knowledge is so transparent and carries such force of conviction that scientists of the most diverse peoples and races have accepted it as the undoubted basis of all further thought and cognition. Of course, we also make mistakes in science and it may take some time before these are found and corrected. But we can rest assured that there will be a final decision as to what is right and what is wrong. This decision will not depend on the belief, race or origin of the scientists, but it will be taken by a higher power and will then apply to all men for all time. While we cannot avoid in political life a constant change of values, a struggle of one set of illusions and misleading ideas against another set of illusions and equally misleading ideas, there will always be a "right or wrong" in science. There is a higher power, not influenced by our wishes, which finally decides and judges. The core of science is formed, to my mind, by the pure sciences, which are not concerned with practical applications. They are the branches in which pure thought attempts to discover the hidden harmonies of nature. Mankind today may find this innermost circle in which science and art can hardly be separated, in which the personification of pure truth is no longer disguised by human ideologies and desires.

You may, of course, object that the great mass of people has no access to this truth and that it can therefore exert little influence on the attitude of people. But at no time did the great mass of people have direct access to the center and it may be that people today will be satisfied to know that though the gate is not open to everyone there *can* be no deceit beyond the gate. We have no power there—the decisions are taken by a higher power. People have used different words at different times for this "center." They called it "spirit" or "God," or they spoke in similes, or in terms of sound or picture. There are many ways to this center, even today, and science is only one of them. Perhaps we have no longer a generally recognized language in which we can make ourselves intelligible. That may be the reason why so many people cannot see it, but it is there today as it has always been, and any world order must be based on it. Such a world order must be guided by men who have not lost sight of it.

Science can contribute to the understanding between peoples. It can do so not because it can render succor to the sick, nor because of the terror which some political power may wield with its aid, but only by turning our attention to that "center" which can establish order in the world at large, perhaps simply to the fact that the world is beautiful. It may appear presumptuous to attribute such importance to science but may I remind you that though we have cause to envy previous epochs in many aspects of life, our age is second to none in scientific achievement, in the pure cognition of nature.

Whatever may happen, interest in knowledge itself will remain a potent force in mankind for the next few decades. Even though this interest may for sometime be overshadowed by the practical consequences of science and by the struggle for power it must eventually triumph and link together people of all nations and races. In all parts of the world people will be happy when they have gained new knowledge and they will be grateful to the man who first discovered it.

Thomas Hunt Morgan

THE SOCIAL EVOLUTION OF MAN

THOMAS HUNT MORGAN, *recipient of the 1933 Prize in Physiology and Medicine, was born in Lexington, Kentucky, in 1866. After undergraduate study at the University of Kentucky, he took a Ph.D. from Johns Hopkins (1890). He left a teaching post at Bryn Mawr to join the faculty of Columbia University, and in 1928, became the director of the Biology Laboratory at CalTech. Until his death in 1945, he devoted himself to the study of genetics. Using the fruit fly, which has since become a standard research tool of geneticists, Morgan was able to demonstrate the physical basis of heredity. His extensive study of the laws and mechanism of heredity brought him the Nobel Prize. Before he died in 1945, he wrote many books which have become classics in the increasingly important field of genetics:* Heredity and Sex (1913), The Theory of the Gene (1926) *and* Genetics (1934). *The following essay is from* The Scientific Basis of Evolution.

While biologists have come to reject the theory of the inheritance of acquired characters by means of the germ-cells, nevertheless they recognize the fact that the human race has succeeded in another way in transmitting certain traits acquired in one generation to the next. There are, then, in man two processes of inheritance: one through the physical continuity of the germ-cells; and the other through the transmission of the experiences of one generation to the next by means of example and by spoken and written language. It is his ability to communicate with his fellows and train his offspring that has probably been the chief agency in the rapid social evolution of man. In the animal kingdom we find many cases in which the young are protected and cared for by their parents. Such beginnings furnish the background out of which has evolved the more complex relation of parents and offspring in the human race, where a prolonged period of childhood furnishes exceptional opportunities for the transmission of tradition and experience.

In no other group of animals is there evidence that the experiences of one generation are handed on to the next, except to a very limited degree in the higher vertebrates. Any advancement must depend on a physical change in the germinal materials, and this may be a very slow process. But in man the power to alter the behavior of the race is possible because each individual begins his life with relatively few inherited instincts, and even these may be rapidly altered by the training he undergoes from birth to maturity. It is the plasticity of man's brain that makes him unique amongst living creatures.

There is abundant evidence that the physical traits of man are inherited in the same way as those of other animals. Of course, there is every *a priori* reason to expect this, since man propagates in the same way as other animals. In hardly a single respect does he depart from the characteristics of the group of mammals to which he belongs.

In human inheritance we meet with examples of nearly all of the kinds of inheritance shown by other animals and by plants. The inheritance of albinism is an example of a completely recessive character. Albinos are reported from all parts of the world. Their sudden appearance may sometimes be due to mutation, but generally the mutation has occurred in the past. The meeting of two individuals carrying each one recessive gene for albinism, gives three normals to one albino. Of the three normals, two carry one gene for albinism. Should an albino marry a normal, all the offspring will be normal, but each will carry one gene for albinism. If these offspring marry normal individuals, the gene will be further spread in the population. In time, two individuals, each carrying one gene for albinism, may meet, and, as we have just seen, will produce three normals to one albino. An individual albino is at a slight disadvantage compared with normal individuals because, in the absence of pigment in the iris, too much light falls on the retina. Dark glasses correct to some extent this defect. Only once in the human race has albinism been established on any large scale. In the forests of Darien there is a human group containing a large number of albinos. Whether this is the same albinism that occurs sporadically elsewhere is not certain. It appears to be another form of the more familiar type.

Blue eyes is another example of a recessive human character. In certain parts of the world this eye-color is a racial characteristic. It is highly probable that the primitive or original races of man had dark eyes. The blue color of the iris is due to the absence of pigment in the outer layer of the iris, so that the inner layer is exposed. It contains a whitish substance which by reflected light appears blue. Probably in those parts of the world where there is much brilliant sunlight, the dark eye is a protection to the retina. At any rate, the blue eye-color first established itself in the more northern parts of Europe. In all other respects blue-eyed individuals appear to be as capable as dark-eyed individuals. We find them competing in the same group without any obvious advantage to either. But there may be more subtle differences that have not yet been identified. It is known that a gene often produces many far-reaching and sometimes subtle effects other than the one we pick out as the most obvious. But he would be a bold man or a fanatic who at present would attempt to ascribe the peculiarities of behavior of blue-eyed and brown-eyed races to a difference in the genes for these two eye-colors.

Only a few strictly dominant mutational changes are known in man. The most striking involves the shortening of the fingers and toes. It is called brachydactyly. A short-fingered man marrying a normal woman produces children half of whom are short-fingered, half normal. The normals never transmit the character. No pure dominants are known, and no cases of two short-fingered individuals marrying. It seems not impossible that the pure dominant is lethal, i.e., if such a combination is formed, the embryo dies before or at the time of birth. There are at least two localities where short-fingered individuals occur, but there is no evidence that the character is spreading.

Another interesting type of Mendelian heredity is called sex-linked inheritance. At first this puzzled even Mendelian students, as it presented the apperance of an exception to Mendel's laws. But with the application of the laws of chromosomal behavior, and especially with the discovery of inequality in the sex chromosomes, sex-linked inheritance turned out to be a confirmation of the chromosome theory and hence can be explained on the same basis as straight Mendelian inheritance.

A few clear-cut cases of sex-linked inheritance are known in man. Color-blindness is the most familiar. Color-blindness is not in itself a defect that is serious, except when the discrimination between red and green is important, as in ship or in railroad signalling. It is not known to be associated with any other mental peculiarity. The next example is, however, a very serious defect. Hæmophilia, or failure of the blood to coagulate when exposed to air, owing to deficiency of an enzyme, may cause the death of an individual. Any internal lesions that lead to bleeding may be fatal. The character is transmitted in the same way as all other cases of sex-linked inheritance. The most celebrated cases are those of the late Czarevich of Russia, and the Prince of the Asturias, the son of the former King of Spain.

There are several cases in man where there is evidence that certain kinds of immunity to protein substances, and to other external agents, are inherited, and many more where there is a suspicion that this is true. In this respect the situation is much the same as in other organisms, where the evidence is more satisfactory.

The most convincing evidence of the far-reaching importance of physical inheritance in man is furnished by the resemblance of identical twins. Twins of this kind come from one and the same fertilized egg, and have exactly the same genetic composition. They are always of the same sex—two boys or two girls. As everyone knows, they are so much alike that an intimate familiarity with them is often necessary to tell them apart. Moreover, this likeness continues throughout life, even when they have been reared under different conditions. There can remain little doubt that down to the minutest details our physical characters are due to inheritance.

How far the psychic behavior of identical twins is due to their heredity and how much to their environment is a more difficult problem. There are many stories of the psychic similarities of identical twins, but this evidence when based on hearsay is of little value. Moreover, most identical twins have lived together in the same surroundings. In only a few cases have they been separated in babyhood, and in only a few have their reactions been carefully studied. The evidence here is not entirely satisfactory. In the first fully examined case, that of Muller, the mental tests of the twins were closely similar, but the emotional reactions less so. In three cases recently studied by Newman this was not so evident. Until more cases can be studied and better tests have been devised for measuring such resemblances and differences, many questions must remain in doubt. But there can be no question that we have here placed in our hands an important opportunity for a study of the influence of heredity on psychological traits.

The inheritance of derangements of the mental faculties of man is a very difficult problem, partly because there are few, if any, parallels in other animals that can be experimentally tested, partly because the diagnosis in man is often uncertain, and partly because the environment is a complicating agency. Anyone familiar with the medical literature must be appalled at the widespread occurrence of these traits in the human race when compared with wild species. It is often said that the protection afforded to weaklings and defectives in communal life helps, or is responsible for, this excess of defectives; they would quickly perish if their existence depended on their own responsibility. While there is no certain evidence to show that man produces new mutational defective types more often than other animals, nevertheless, in so far as mental defects or aberrations are concerned, it is to be remembered that modern life is extremely complex and artificial, so that a slight difference or deficiency at the beginning of the individual's life may become greatly magnified as more and more demands are made on him.

At the other extreme is human intelligence, man's most valuable asset. Is intelligence inherited? There is a widespread belief that it is, and I should be far from wishing to gainsay it. The main difficulty is one of definition. It is commonly assumed that there is one, and only one, criterion of intelligence—that we are speaking always of the same thing when we use the word. In reality our ideas are vague on the subject. The so-called intelligence test that may give a rough estimate of a certain type of reaction, is assumed to be a measure of a phenomenon called intelligence; but it can do little more, in my opinion, than give a numerical value for a certain situation depending on the physiological and mental conditions of the patient at the moment. It also serves to give some clue to his previous experience in the same or related fields, and may furnish an average result of his innate awareness or quickness of reaction. But this averaging of many heterogeneous things has in the past often led to very erroneous conclusions. So far as heredity is concerned, it is a procedure that the majority of geneticists avoid if possible. Accurate work in heredity can only be attained when the diagnosis of the elements of a situation are known. I have no wish to avoid the issue as to whether "intelligence" is inherited. Let me say, then, that superficial experience seems to indicate that in general better brains may be inherited, as are other bodily characteristics; not perhaps in a 3:1 ratio, but as a combination of a few or even many elements. The difficulty, of course, is—aside from our inability to define what is meant by intelligence—that we do not know here how much is due to nature and how much to nurture.

In contrast to his germinal inheritance, mankind passes on from each generation to the next some of the experiences of the race. Beginning probably by simple reactions and imitation, the conservation of traditions must have been, at first, communicated by sounds, then by speech, then by writing and printing, until today there is a mountain of literature in which is imbedded nearly all human experience. While accessibility to the world's literature leaves each one free to take from it what he needs, this has at times been forbidden and even now conventions, prohibitions, bigotry and ignorance restrict the free use of this accumulated wealth. Racial taboos and prejudices are also orally transmitted, and at times may influence the behavior of the generality of mankind to a greater extent than all the wisdom of the ages.

Owing to the twofold method of human inheritance it is haz-ardous to predict the future course of man's evolution. At most we can try to study, as impartially as possible, the conflicting inter-ests in the situation; for when the two factors come into conflict, as they frequently do, it is not easy to form an estimate of what the future has in store. For example: genetics has taught us how congenital malformations can be most quickly eliminated from the germinal material, or at least reduced. On the other hand, it is obvious that wise human conventions will not permit any such extremely drastic treatment as this procedure might suggest to the fanatically-minded uplifter. The doctrine that all men are born free and equal carries with it the assumption that they be allowed to breed as they will.

Scientific ethics, based on a knowledge of the harm that may be done to future generations by reckless propagation, is not yet strong enough to persuade those carrying injurious traits to desist from propagation. The difficulty is even greater in the case of psychic disorders. There are a few kinds of insanity, such as Huntington's chorea, where the pedigrees of certain families make it practically certain that the background of the disease is inher-ited. This does not mean necessarily that the brain itself is ini-tially defective, but that its derangement may be brought about by abnormal functioning of other organs of the body.

In many cases of insanity, the diagnosis is still too uncertain to warrant interference, especially when a particular environment is a contributory factor. It has often been suggested that the pressure of civilization itself is too heavy a strain in many cases for certain individuals. If so, the cure may be rather in returning such persons to a simpler life, where they may be useful, than to attempt to breed a more resistant race.

The contrast between the two methods under consideration finds excellent examples in communicable diseases that have been at times veritable scourges to humanity—cholera, smallpox, dys-entery, scarlet fever, yellow fever, measles, malaria, grippe, and a long list of other terrors. In some of these cases it might, of course, be possible to produce a resistant strain, but it would be extrava-gant at the present time to recommend such a procedure. The great scourges that have swept away countless numbers of human beings—the black death, cholera, yellow fever—may have left behind them the more resistant individuals, and, if this resistance was in part transmitted, it may seem that, as a result of the dreadful holocaust, a local racial immunity has been gained. But no one would recommend such a procedure today, because, in the first place, it is extremely doubtful whether much, if anything permanent, would result from the occasional elimination of the more susceptible. The escape of a large part of the population may be due more often to chance or to location than to resistance. Therefore, unless the elimination was continued for several or many generations the gain would soon be lost. In the second place, there is a suspicion that the gain in resistance sometimes observed after a pestilence has swept over a country, is due to a milder or less virulent type of germ that replaces the original one, and if so, the resistance is more apparent than real. We artificially protect ourselves in the case of smallpox by taking on a mild form of the disease, and in a steadily increasing number of other diseases the same procedure is carried out.

It is apparent, then, that here the genetic method is far less efficient than the curative or preventive procedure. The progress of the human race in its battle with disease is one of the greatest triumphs of evolution. It is, if you like, a social evolution, but it is evolution none the less.

Before we determine how far to make use of the methods that genetics has placed in our hands in regulating the characteristics of the human race, it would be necessary to determine first what standard to adopt—whether, for example, to work toward a homogeneous, average, mediocre, stable group, or whether to work for as great a variety of types as possible. Unless there is agreement on this point, it would be quite futile to set out on such an errand. Who, then, shall determine what standard to set up? What ideal to build towards? A compromise is followed by some of the advocates of the eugenics movement to the extent of sterilizing the imbecile and insane, those with known or supposed inherited defects. The argument that these defectives and their descendants are a menace to society, in the sense that their supposed greater breeding capacity would in time lead to the replacement of the more capable members, cannot, I think, be taken too seriously; but that this defective class would be a perpetual burden to the social group that supports it in asylums and penitentiaries cannot be doubted. There is not much that is novel, however, in the recommendation that these defectives be segregated and prevented from breeding. Confinement has long been in practice. It is here only a question of perpetual confinement or returning them sterilized to the community. A more intelligent understanding of the conditions, both genetic and social, that produce these unfortunate types is much to be desired. While segregation may be recommended on strictly genetic grounds for certain types, on the other hand imprisonment may be at times dictated by the social or political exigencies of a governing group. While this may promote the stability of a particular system it may not be an advantage for the evolution or advancement of another type of individual. Where democracy is the system in vogue, it is often implied that each individual has the same capacity to fulfill every social requirement as has any other individual. A very little knowledge of the composition of the human species dispels such a conclusion as an illusion.

Now, it would seem to be much easier to make rules for a population that was nearly homogeneous than for a population composed of many types of individuals. But from the point of view of evolution it is by no means certain that a stable, comfortable, commonplace group would be as desirable as one in which the greatest possible variability existed. There are at least two arguments that may seem to favor a mixed human population as better serving the purposes of evolution. The first is the genetic advantage; the chance of new combinations would be greater, and amongst these the opportunity for improvement might be expected. The second is social. The betterment of the conditions of life often depends on single, unique individuals—inventors or leaders arising at a time when circumstances offer an opportunity for new discoveries or progress. The far-reaching benefits of such discoveries may be enormously important for human advancement. We usually think of these in terms of material improvements with the accompanying monetary values, but this is only one side of the question. Even more important for human welfare may be the intellectual and ethical and scientific discoveries that our postulated gifted individuals might contribute to human welfare. They might, for example, help us to find out how the evolution of mankind may so continue that the germ-plasm contribution and the social contribution could both be utilized most advantageously in promoting substantial progress.

What has been said so far relates to the improvement of mankind as it exists today. Evolution in the past, however, has meant the appearance of novelties in the germinal material. Now, if the kind of evolution depending solely on the intelligent control of human conditions is not destined to suppress forever the biological evolution through germinal changes, our chief consideration here is to discuss whether biological evolution, if I may so call it, has come to an end with man's advent on this planet, or whether we can make a plausible plea for further evolution of this kind. Despite the apparent conflicts between the two principles that I have just discussed, I think the question is still open. At least there is nothing to prevent our considering it, and least of all is there any necessity for throwing up our hands in despair. Let us look, then, at the question from the biological end.

The plasticity of man's physical, and especially of his psychic nature would seem to allow further development in many different directions. It has been said that man's brain is so highly differentiated that specialization can go no further. On the contrary, it is the very plasticity of the human brain that would seem to make endless additions possible. There is only one danger, viz., that he may stop propagating as a result of social considerations, based on selfishness, fear, ambition, and self-indulgence.

There is very little real reason to suppose that civilized man is becoming physiologically sterile. The process is, in a sense, self-regulatory in so far as sterility depends on hereditary factors; for the later generations will come from the more prolific stocks, good or bad.

Nor is the picture very different if we consider the whole population, rather than some particular caste within it. It is true that, in certain of the older civilizations of Europe, the birth rate has been declining for some time, until in extreme cases increase in numbers has stopped. The causes for this are pretty well understood: deferred marriage and intentional limitation of offspring.

Aside from purely selfish motives the restriction seems due to the expense of raising children, and a laudable desire to conserve the health and welfare of the mother, and to give those children that are born the benefit of the best that civilization has to offer. But the danger is that restriction may be pushed too far. The desire to make possible these benefits should be weighed against the possibility that too few offspring increases the chance that the line will run out. If this should be disregarded, nature will step in and hand over the future of the human race to those branches of it where selfishness or an exaggerated idea of the importance of social rank does not submerge the instinct to perpetuate themselves.

These questions have also a still wider bearing when evolution is considered an end in itself. The increase in population has in the past found an outlet in various ways—by improvement of the industrial and agricultural output, or peaceful penetration into countries where the pressure of population is less; or by successful warfare; or by changing the standard of living through a more equal distribution of the necessities of life. Sometimes one, sometimes another of these methods has been followed. In addition, some enthusiastic optimists believe that through the inventiveness of mankind—as in his production of artificial food by chemical means from the raw chemical elements—there are enormous possibilities for the increase in number of the human species.

Without attempting to judge the merits of these different methods to meet population growth, an important question for the evolutionist is whether an increase in numbers alone gives any advantage in the chances of the occurrence of new types that will replace existing ones.

If mutations appear only sporadically, and, so far as we can see, without respect to the condition of life in which a given species exists, the first guess would be, I think, that the greater the number of individuals the greater the chance of something new turning up. But, on further thought, it will be seen that the answer is not so simple; for while it might take a longer time for a smaller population to produce favorable mutations, this might be more than compensated for by the better chances of survival when the conditions of life are more favorable for all individuals. If an intelligent appreciation of the importance of sustaining better types after they had appeared should be in force, a smaller group might have an advantage.

The converse picture is that of a society grown so large that only the barest livelihood is possible for most of its members. Here we can fancy that all the energy and thought of each individual are concentrated on keeping alive. It seems unlikely that much concern would be given to the difficult problem of discovering and fostering new types. If intelligent understanding of the problem is the means by which man is going to direct his future evolution, success seems more likely in a highly organized society limited in numbers.

It may be said that only extreme cases have been selected; that human society at present is composed of many different strata or castes, that leisure is granted to or gained by only a few, and that from this group the intelligent direction of the future will come. This may be partly true, but it is the leisure class at present that shows little concern with problems of this sort, and if its members are not sufficiently interested to look after the future of their own breeding, how can they be expected to become actively interested in altruistic plans for others?

The popular idea of the role of natural selection suggests a somewhat different line of argument. One of Darwin's basic assumptions was over-production, but as I have pointed out, over-production may mean no more than that more eggs are produced than there are individuals reaching maturity. If only the same population is maintained—that is, if the same number reach maturity—the elimination is in the embryos or young and only indirectly affects the adults. Consequently selection may bear little relation to the number of eggs laid or of young born. But if not more than fifty per cent of adult human beings are the parents of the next generation, then we really meet with a more difficult situation, for we do not know for certain, in human society, the relative importance to a social group of those who do not propagate. The queen bee is the only member of her community that leaves offspring, yet the other members are as essential to the colony as is the queen. It is possible to exaggerate the importance of over-production in a social group with its consequent elimination of the unfit, if this be one of the essentials of Darwin's theory. In man the discovery of a new environment or of a new method of utilizing existing conditions may at times play a far more significant role than competition. In other words: a new variation may be of great value, not because it beats all its competitors in a crowded environment, but because it has something new to offer, making new possibilities for the welfare of the group.

It is conceivable that when man undertakes to direct the evolution of his race he may blunder badly. It might even be asked why he should meddle, since nature unassisted has brought about the evolution of man. Why not trust natural processes to do all that is possible under the circumstances? This may or may not be good advice. But let it not be forgotten that man by his ideals as well as by his blundering and selfishness and lack of social consideration, is now determining his future by active interference for good or evil with the course of nature. He may not be able to map out his future, but he has shown at times an astonishing power to interfere with what is taking place.

Erwin Schrödinger

THE FUTURE OF UNDERSTANDING

ERWIN SCHRÖDINGER, *born in Austria in 1887, has been professor of physics at the University of Berlin, a fellow of Magdalen College, Oxford, professor at the University of Graz and the Dublin Institute for Advanced Studies. In 1933, he shared the Nobel Prize for Physics with Paul Dirac. He came into international prominence through his studies of the quantum theory. He has applied his scientific knowledge to a wide range of general topics, and has the facility, too rare with the scientific specialist, of writing clearly and simply enough to share his knowledge and views with the layman. Among his more general books are* Nature and the Greeks *and* Science and Humanism.

We may, I believe, regard it as extremely improbable that our understanding of the world represents any definite or final stage, a maximum or optimum in any respect. By this I do *not* mean merely that the continuation of our research in the various sciences, our philosophical studies and religious endeavor, is likely to enhance and improve our present outlook. What we are likely to gain in this way in the next, say, two and a half millennia —estimating it by what we have gained since Protagoras, Democritus and Antisthenes—is insignificant compared with what I am here alluding to. There is no reason whatever for believing that our brain is the supreme *ne plus ultra* of an organ of thought in which God's world is reflected. It is more likely than not that a species could acquire a similar contraption whose corresponding imagery compared with ours as ours with that of the dog, or his in turn with that of a snail.

If this be so, then—though it is not relevant in principle—it interests us, as it were for personal reasons, whether anything of the sort could be reached on our globe by our own offspring or the offspring of some of us. The globe is all right. It is a fine young leasehold, to run under acceptable conditions of living still for at least the time it took us (about 1000 million years) to develop into what we are from the earliest beginnings. But are we all right? If one accepts the present theory of evolution—and we have no better—it might seem that we have been very nearly cut off from future evolution. Is there still physical evolution to be expected in man, I mean to say relevant changes in our physique that become gradually fixed as inherited features, just as our present bodily self is fixed by inheritance—genotypical changes, to use the technical term of the biologist? This question is difficult to answer. We may be approaching the bottom of a blind alley, we may even have reached it. This would not be an exceptional event and it would not mean that our species would have to become extinct very soon. From the geological records we know that some species or even large groups seem to have reached the end of their evolutionary possibilities a very long time ago, yet they have not died out, but remained unchanged, or without appreciable change, for many millions of years. The tortoises, for instance, and the crocodiles are in this sense very old groups, relics of a far remote past; we are also told that the whole large group of *insects* are more or less in the same boat—and they comprise a greater number of separate species than all the rest of the animal kingdom taken together. But they have changed very little in millions of years, while the rest of the living surface of the earth has during this time undergone change beyond recognition. What barred further evolution in the insects was probably this, that they had adopted the plan—you will not misunderstand this figurative expression —that they had adopted the plan of wearing their skeleton outside instead of inside, as we do. Such an outside armor, while affording protection in addition to mechanical stability, *cannot grow* as the bones of a mammal do between birth and maturity. This circumstance is bound to render gradual adaptive changes in the life history of the individual very difficult.

In the case of man several arguments seem to militate against further evolution. The spontaneous inheritable changes (now called *mutations*) from which, according to Darwin's theory, the "profitable" ones are automatically selected, are as a rule only small evolutionary steps, affording, if any, only a slight advantage. That is why in Darwin's deductions an important part is attributed to the usually enormous abundance of offspring, of which only a very small fraction can possibly survive. For only thus does a small amelioration in the chance of survival seem to have a reasonable likelihood of being realized. This whole mechanism appears to be blocked in civilized man—in some respects even reversed. We are, generally speaking, not willing to see our fellow-creatures suffer and perish, and so we have gradually introduced legal and social institutions which on the one hand protect life, condemn systematic infanticide, try to help every sick or frail human being to survive, while on the other hand they *have to* replace the natural elimination of the less fit by keeping the offspring within the limits of the available livelihood. This is achieved partly in a direct way, by birth control, partly by preventing a considerable proportion of females from mating. Occasionally—as this generation knows all too well—the insanity of war and all the disaster and blunder that follow in its wake contribute their share to the balance. Millions of adults and children of both sexes are killed by starvation, exposure, epidemics. While in the far remote past the warfare between small tribes or clans is supposed to have had a positive selectional value, it seems doubtful whether it ever had in historical times, and doubtless that war at present has none. It means an indiscriminate killing, just as the advances in medicine and surgery result in an indiscriminate saving of lives. While justly and diametrically opposite in our esteem yet both, war and medical art, seem to be of no selectional value whatever.

These considerations suggest that as a developing species we have come to a standstill and have little prospect of further biological advance. Even if this were so, it need not bother us. We might survive without any biological change for millions of years, like the crocodiles and many insects. Still, from a certain philosophical point of view the idea is depressing, and I should like to try and make out a case for the contrary. To do so I must enter on a certain aspect of the theory of evolution which I find supported in Professor Julian Huxley's well-known book *Evolution: The Modern Synthesis*, an aspect which, according to him, is not always sufficiently appreciated by recent evolutionists.

Popular expositions of Darwin's theory are apt to lead you to a gloomy and discouraging view, on account of the apparent passivity of the organism in the process of evolution. Mutations occur spontaneously in the gene—the "hereditary substance." We have reason to believe that they are mainly due to what the physicist calls a thermodynamic fluctuation—in other words to pure chance. The individual has not the slightest influence on the hereditary treasure it receives from its parents, nor on the one it leaves to its offspring. Mutations that occur are acted on by "natural selection of the fittest." This again seems to mean pure chance, since it means that a favorable mutation increases the prospect for the individual of survival and of begetting offspring, to which it transmits the mutation in question. Apart from this, its activity during its lifetime seems to be biologically irrelevant. For, nothing of it has any influence on the offspring. *Acquired properties are not inherited.* Any skill or training attained is lost, it leaves no trace, it dies with the individual, it is not transmitted. An intelligent being in this situation would find that nature, as it were, refuses his collaboration—she does all herself, dooms the individual to inactivity, indeed to nihilism.

As you know, Darwin's theory was not the first systematic theory of evolution. It was preceded by the theory of Lamarck, which rests entirely on the assumption that any new features an individual has acquired by specific surroundings or behavior during its lifetime before procreation can be, and usually are, passed on to its progeny, if not entirely, at least in traces. Thus if an animal by living on rocky or sandy soil produced protecting calluses on the soles of its feet, this callosity would gradually become hereditary so that later generations would receive it as a free gift without the hardship of acquiring it. In the same way the strength or skill or even substantial adaptation produced in any organ by its being continually used for certain ends, would not be lost, but passed on, at least partly, to the offspring. This view does afford a very simple understanding of the amazingly elaborate and specific adaptation to environment which is so characteristic of all living creatures. It is also beautiful, elating, encouraging and invigorating. It is infinitely more attractive than the gloomy aspect of passivity apparently offered by Darwinism. An intelligent being which considers itself a link in the long chain of evolution may, under Lamarck's theory, be confident that its striving efforts to improve its abilities, both bodily and mental, are not lost in the biological sense but form a small but integrating part of the striving of the species towards higher and ever higher perfection.

Unhappily Lamarckism is untenable. The fundamental assumption on which it rests, viz. that acquired properties can be inherited, is wrong. To the best of our knowledge they are not. The single steps of evolution are those spontaneous and fortuitous mutations which have nothing to do with the behavior of the individual during its lifetime. And so we appear to be thrown back on the gloomy aspect of Darwinism that I have depicted above.

I now wish to show you that this is not quite so. Without changing anything in the basic assumptions of Darwinism, we can see that the behavior of the individual, the way it makes use of its innate faculties, plays a relevant part, nay, plays the most relevant part, in evolution. There is a very true kernel in Lamarck's view, namely that there is an irrescindable causal connection between the functioning, the actually being put to profitable use, of a character—an organ, any property or ability or bodily feature—and its being developed in the course of generations, and gradually improved for the purposes for which it is profitably used. This connection, I say, between being used and being improved was a very correct cognition of Lamarck's, and it subsists in our present Darwinistic outlook, but it is easily overlooked on viewing Darwinism superficially. The course of events is almost the same *as if* Lamarckism were right, only the "mechanism" by which things happen is more complicated than Lamarck thought. The point is not quite easy to explain or to grasp, and so it may be useful to summarize the result in advance. To avoid vagueness, let us think of an *organ*, though the feature in question might be any property, habit, device, behavior, or even any small addition to, or modification of, such a feature. Lamarck thought that the organ (a) is used, (b) is thus improved and (c) the improvement is transmitted to the offspring. This is wrong. We have to think that the organ (a) undergoes chance variations, (b) *the profitably used ones* are accumulated or at least accentuated by selection, (c) this continues from generation to generation, the selected mutations constituting a lasting improvement. The most striking *simulation* of Lamarckism occurs—according to Julian Huxley—when the initial variations that inaugurate the process are not true mutations, not yet of the inheritable type. Yet, if profitable, they may be accentuated by what he calls *organic selection*, and, so to speak, pave the way for true mutations to be immediately seized upon when they happen to turn up in the "desirable" direction.

Let us now go into some details. The most important point is to see that a new character or modification of a character, acquired by variation, by mutation, or by mutation plus some little selection, may easily arouse the organism in relation to its environment to an activity that tends to increase the usefulness of that character and hence the "grip" of selection on it. By possessing the new or changed character the individual may be caused to *change* its environment—either by actually *transforming* it, or by *migration*—or it may be caused to change its behavior towards its environment, all this in a fashion so as strongly to reinforce the usefulness of the new character and thus to speed up its further selective improvement in the same direction.

This assertion may strike you as daring, since it seems to require purpose on the side of the individual, and even a high degree of intelligence. But I wish to make the point that my statement, while it includes, of course, the intelligent, purposeful behavior of the higher animals, is by no means restricted to them. Let us give a few simple examples:

Not all the individuals of a population have exactly the same environment. Some of the flowers of a wild species happen to grow in the shadow, some in sunny spots, some in the higher ranges of a lofty mountain-slope, some in the lower parts or in the valley. A mutation—say hairy foliage—which is beneficial at higher altitude, will be favored by selection in the higher ranges but will be "lost" in the valley. The effect is the same as if the hairy mutants had migrated towards an environment that will favor further mutations that occur in the same direction.

Another example: their ability to fly enables birds to build their nests high up in the trees where their young ones are less accessible to some of their enemies. Primarily those who took to it had a selectional advantage. The second step is that this kind of abode was bound to select the proficient fliers among the young ones. Thus a certain ability to fly produces a change of environment, or behavior towards the environment, which favors an accumulation of the same ability.

The most remarkable feature among living beings is that they are divided into species which are, many of them, so incredibly specialized on quite particular, often tricky performances, on which they rely especially for survival. A zoological garden is almost a curiosity show, and would be much more so could it include an insight into the life history of insects. Non-specialization is the exception. The rule is specialization in peculiar studied tricks which "nobody would think of if nature had not made them." It is difficult to believe that they all have resulted from Darwinian "accumulation by chance." Whether one wants it or not, one is taken by the impression of forces or tendencies away from "the plain and simple" in certain directions towards the complicated. The "plain and simple'" seems to represent an unstable state of affairs. A departure from it provokes forces—so it seems—towards a further departure *in the same direction.* That would be difficult to understand if the development of a particular device, mechanism, organ, useful behavior, were produced by a long pearl-string of chance events, independent of each other, as one is used to think in terms of Darwin's original conception. Actually, I believe, only the first small start "in a certain direction" has this structure. It itself produces circumstances which "hammer the plastic material"—by selection—more and more systematically in the direction of the advantage gained at the outset. In metaphorical speech one might say: the species has found out in which direction its chance in life lies, and pursues this path.

We must try to understand in a general way and to formulate in a non-animistic fashion how a chance mutation, which gives the individual a certain advantage and favors its survival in a given environment, should tend to do more than that, namely to increase the opportunities for its being profitably made use of, so as to concentrate on itself, as it were, the selective influence of the environment.

To reveal this mechanism let the environment be schematically described as an ensemble of favorable and unfavorable circumstances. Among the first are food, drink, shelter, sunlight and many others, among the latter are the dangers from other living beings (enemies), poisons and the roughness of the elements. For brevity we shall refer to the first kind as "needs" and to the second as "foes." Not every need can be obtained, not every foe avoided. But a *living* species must have acquired a behavior *that strikes a compromise* in avoiding the deadliest foes and satisfying the most urgent needs from the sources of easiest access, so that it *does* survive. A favorable mutation makes certain sources more easily accessible or reduces the danger from certain foes or both. It thereby increases the chance of survival of the individuals endowed with it, but in addition *it shifts the most favorable compromise,* because it changes the relative *weights* of those needs or foes on which it bears. Individuals which, by chance or intelligence, change their behavior will accordingly be more favored, and thus selected. This change of behavior is not transmitted to the next generation *by the gene*, not by direct inheritance, but this does not mean that it is not transmitted. The simplest, most primitive example is afforded by our species of flowers (with a habitat along an extended mountain slope) that develops a hairy mutant. The hairy mutants, favored mainly in the top ranges, disperse their seeds in the top ranges, so that the next generation of "hairies" taken as a whole has "climbed up the slope," as it were, "to make better use of their favorable mutation."

In all this one must bear in mind that as a rule the whole situation is extremely dynamic, the struggle is a very stiff one. In a fairly prolific population that, at the time, survives without appreciably increasing, the "foes" *usually* overpower the "needs"— individual survival is an exception. Moreover foes and needs are frequently coupled, so that a pressing need can only be met by braving a certain foe. (For instance, the antelope has to come to the river for drink, but the lion knows the place just as well as he.) The total pattern of foes and needs is intricately interwoven. Thus a slight reduction of a certain danger by a given mutation may make a considerable difference for *those* mutants who brave that danger and thereby avoid others. This may result in a noticeable selection not only of the genetic feature in question but also with regard to the (intended or haphazard) skill in using it. That kind of behavior is transmitted to the offspring by example—by *learning*, in a generalized sense of the word. The shift of behavior, in turn, enhances the selective value of any further mutation in the same direction.

The effect of such a display may have great similarity to the mechanism as pictured by Lamarck. Though neither an acquired behavior nor any physical change that it entails is directly transmitted to the offspring, yet behavior has an important say in the process. But the causal connection is not what Lamarck thought it to be, rather just the other way round. Not the behavior changes the physique of the parents and, by physical inheritance, that of the offspring. It is the physical change in the parents that modifies—directly or indirectly, by selection—their behavior; and this change of behavior is, by example or teaching or even more primitively, transmitted to the progeny, along with the physical change carried by the gene. Nay, even if the physical change is not yet an inheritable one, the transmission of the induced behavior "by teaching" can be a highly efficient evolutionary factor, because it throws the door open to receive future *inheritable* mutations with a prepared readiness to make the best use of them and thus to subject them to intense selection.

One might object that what we have here described may happen occasionally, but cannot continue indefinitely to form the essential mechanism of adaptive evolution. For, the change of behavior is not itself transmitted by physical inheritance, by the hereditary substance, the chromosomes. It is therefore at first certainly not fixed genetically and it is difficult to see how it should ever come to be incorporated in the hereditary treasure. This is an important problem in itself. For we do know that habits are inherited, as, for instance, habits of nest-building in the birds, the various habits of cleanliness we observe in our dogs and cats, to mention a few obvious examples. If this could not be understood along orthodox Darwinian lines, Darwinism would have to be abandoned. The question becomes of singular significance in its application to man, since we wish to infer that the striving and laboring of a man during his lifetime constitute an integrating contribution to the development of the species, in the quite strict biological sense as well. I believe the situation to be, briefly, as follows.

According to our assumptions the behavior changes parallel to the physique, first as a consequence of a chance change of the latter, but very soon directing the further selectional mechanism into definite channels, because, according as behavior has availed itself of the first rudimentary benefits, only further mutations in the same direction have any selective value. But as—let me say— the new organ develops, behavior becomes more and more bound up with its mere possession. Behavior and physique mix into one. You simply cannot possess clever hands without using them for obtaining your aims, they would be in your way (as they often are to an amateur on the stage, because he has only fictitious aims). You cannot have efficient wings without attempting to fly. You cannot have a modulated organ of speech without trying to imitate the noises you hear around you. To distinguish between the possession of an organ and the urge to use it and to increase its skill by practice, to regard them as two different characteristics of the organism in question, would be an artificial distinction, made possible by an abstract language but having no counterpart in nature. We must, of course, not think that "behavior" after all gradually intrudes into the chromosome structure (or what not) and acquires "loci" there. It is the new organs themselves (and they do become genetically fixed) that carry along with them the habit and the way of using them. Selection would be powerless in "producing" a new organ, if selection were not aided all along by the organism's making appropriate use of it. And this is very essential. For in this way the two things go quite parallel and are ultimately, or indeed at every stage, fixed genetically as one thing: *a used organ*—as if Lamarck were right.

It is illuminating to compare this natural process with the making of an instrument by man. At first sight there appears to be a marked contrast. If *we* manufacture a delicate mechanism, we should in most cases spoil it, if we were impatient and tried to use it again and again long before it was finished. Nature, one is inclined to say, proceeds differently. She cannot produce a new organism and its organs otherwise than whilst they are continually used, probed, examined, with regard to their efficiency. *But actually this parallel is wrong.* The making of a single instrument by man corresponds to ontogenesis, that is, to the growing up of a single individual from the seed to maturity. Here too interference is not welcome. The young ones must be protected, they must not be put to work before they have acquired the full strength and skill of their species. The true parallel of the evolutionary development of organisms could be illustrated, e.g., by a historical exhibition of bicycles, showing how this machine gradually changed from year to year, from decade to decade; or in the same way by railway engines, motorcars, airplanes, typewriters, etc. Here, just as in the natural process, it is obviously essential that the machine in question should be continually used *and thus improved*; not literally improved by use, but by the experience gained and the alterations suggested. The bicycle, by the way, illustrates the case, mentioned before, of an *old* organism, which has reached the attainable perfection and has therefore pretty well ceased to undergo further changes. Still it is not about to become extinct!

Let us now return to the beginning of these talks. We started from the question: Is further biological development in man likely? Our discussion has, I believe, brought to the fore two relevant points.

The first is the biological importance of behavior. By conforming to innate faculties as well as to the environment, and by adapting itself to changes in either of these factors, behavior, though not itself inherited, may yet speed up the process of evolution by orders of magnitude. While in plants and in the lower ranges of the animal kingdom adequate behavior is brought about by the slow process of selection, in other words by trial and error, man's high intelligence enables him to enact it by choice. This incalculable advantage may easily outweigh his handicap of slow and comparatively scarce propagation, which is further reduced by the biologically dangerous consideration not to let our offspring exceed the volume for which livelihood can be secured.

The second point (concerning the question whether biological development is still to be expected in man) is intimately connected with the first. In a way we get the full answer, viz. *This will depend on us and our doing.* We must not wait for things to come, believing that they are decided by irrescindable destiny. If we want it, we must do something about it. If not, not. Just as the political and social development and the sequence of historical events in general are not thrust upon us by the spinning of the Fates, but largely depend on our own doing, so our biological future, being nothing else but history on the large scale, must not be taken to be an unalterable destiny that is decided in advance by any law of Nature. To us at any rate, who are the acting subjects in the play, it is not, even though to a superior being, watching us as we watch the birds and the ants, it might appear to be. The reason why man tends to regard history, in the narrower and in the wider sense, as a predestined happening, controlled by rules and laws that he cannot change, is very obvious.

It is because every single individual feels that he by himself has very little say in the matter, unless he can put his opinions over to many others and persuade them to regulate their behavior accordingly.

As regards the concrete behavior, necessary to secure our biological future, I will only mention one general point that I consider of primary importance. We are, I believe, at the moment in grave danger of missing the "path to perfection." From all that has been said, *selection* is an indispensable requisite for biological development. If it is entirely ruled out, development stops, nay, it may be reversed. To put it in the words of Julian Huxley: ". . . the preponderance of degenerative (loss) mutation will result in degeneration of an organ when it becomes useless and selection is accordingly no longer acting on it to keep it up to the mark." Now, I believe that the increasing mechanization and "stupidization" of most manufacturing processes involve the serious danger of a general degeneration of our organ of intelligence. The more the chances in life of the clever and of the unresponsive worker are equalled out by the repression of handicraft and the spreading of tedious and boring work on the assembly line, the more will a good brain, clever hands and a sharp eye become superfluous. Indeed the unintelligent man, who naturally finds it easier to submit to the boring toil, will be favored: he is likely to find it easier to thrive, to settle down and to beget offspring. The result may easily amount even to a negative selection as regards talents and gifts.

The hardship of modern industrial life has led to certain institutions calculated to mitigate it, such as protection of the workers against exploitation and unemployment, and many other welfare and security measures. They are duly regarded as beneficial and they have become indispensable. Still, we cannot shut our eyes to the fact that, by alleviating the responsibility of the individual to look after himself and by leveling the chances of every man, they also tend to rule out the competition of talents and thus to put an efficient brake on biological evolution. I realize that this particular point is highly controversial. One may make a strong case, that the care of our present welfare must override the worry about our evolutionary future. But fortunately, so I believe, they go together according to my main argument. Next to want, boredom has become the worst scourge in our lives. Instead of letting the ingenious machinery we have invented produce an increasing amount of superfluous luxury, we must planfully develop it so that it takes off human beings all the unintelligent, mechanical, "machine-like" handling. The machine must take over the toil for which man is too good, not man the work for which the machine is too expensive, as quite often happens. This will not tend to make production cheaper, but those who are engaged in it happier. There is small hope of putting this through as long as the competition between big firms and concerns all over the world prevails. But this kind of competition is as uninteresting as it is biologically worthless. Our aim should be to reinstate in its place the interesting and intelligent competition of the single human beings.

I. I. Rabi

SCIENTIST AND HUMANIST

ISADOR ISAAC RABI's long and distinguished academic career was crowned in 1944 when he received the Nobel Prize in Physics for discovering radiations emitted by atoms and a method for measuring them. Born in Austria in 1898 and brought here as an infant, Rabi began his training as a scientist at Cornell (B. Chem., 1919) and continued it at Columbia (Ph.D., 1927). His post-graduate studies were conducted under the outstanding physicists of our time, at the Universities of Munich, Copenhagen, Hamburg, Leipzig, and Zürich. Upon his return, he was appointed to a tutorship at the City College of New York from 1924 to 1927, and in 1929 joined the staff at neighboring Columbia University as a lecturer. Since then, except for the period from 1940 to 1945, when he engaged in wartime radar research at M.I.T., he has been associated with the physics department of Columbia University. Combining his ability in theoretical physics with a grasp of delicate *experimental techniques, Rabi, with his students, has performed a series of important experiments dealing with the magnetic properties of molecules, atoms, and atomic nuclei. When better facilities were needed for research in nuclear physics and atomic energy, he strongly supported the plan to establish the Brookhaven National Laboratory at Upton, Long Island. He has contributed articles on his specialities to all the leading professional journals, and in recent years, has addressed himself to the intelligent layman on the problems of science and scientists.*

For more than half a century, from the period of the Darwinian controversy till the end of the 1930s, science remained almost unchallenged as the source of enlightenment, understanding, and hope for a better, healthier, and safer world. The benefits brought by science were and are still visible everywhere one looks. Human ills are being overcome; food supplies are becoming more abundant; travel and communication are quick and easy; and the comforts of life, especially for the common man, are vastly increased. In the person of Albert Einstein science enjoyed a world-wide respect almost akin to reverence and hardly equaled since the time of Isaac Newton.

In the last decade or so we have begun to detect signs of significant change. The knowledge and techniques developed through science for the illumination of the mind and the elevation of the spirit, for the prolongation and the amelioration of life, have been used for the destruction of life and the degradation of the human spirit. Technological warfare, biological warfare, psychological warfare, brainwashing, all make use of science with frightening results.

I do not suggest that warfare and its attendant horror is a result of modern science. Ancient Greece, at the zenith of that remarkable civilization, in a land united by a common culture and a common religion, destroyed itself in a bitter and useless war more thoroughly than Europe has done in the present century even with the aid of electronics, aviation, and high explosives. What I mean is that our epoch in history, which has produced one of the greatest achievements of the human race, may be passing into a twilight that does not precede the dawn.

Science, the triumph of the intellect and the rational faculties, has resulted in the hydrogen bomb. The glib conclusion is that science and the intellect are therefore false guides. We must seek elsewhere, some people say, for hope and salvation; but, say the same people, while doing so we must keep ahead of the Russians in technology and in the armaments race. Keep the fearsome fruits but reject the spirit of science. Such is the growing mood of some people at the present time. It is a mood of anti-intellectualism which can only hasten the destruction which these people fear. Anti-intellectualism has always been endemic in every society, perhaps in the heart of every human being. In times of stress this attitude is stimulated and people tend to become impatient and yield to prejudice and emotion just when coolness, subtlety, and reason are most needed.

We are told, and most of us believe, that we are living in a period of crisis unequaled in history. To be cheerful and proud of our accomplishment and optimistic of the future is almost akin to subversion. To be considered objective and realistic, one must view with alarm. Yet we are not living in a period of hard times and unemployment! We have, I cannot say enjoyed but, rather, bemoaned, a period of prosperity and world-wide influence for good unequaled in history. Nevertheless, despite all, we seem to be acquiring a complacency of despair. In this mood, unable to adjust to new values we hark back to a past which now looks so bright in retrospect, and we raise the banner of "Back to the Humanities."

What is meant by the slogan "Back to the Humanities"? What are people really looking for? What knowledge, what guidance, what hope for salvation, what inspiration, or what relief from anxiety does a practical-minded people like ours expect from a knowledge of the humanities? They do not wish to re-establish the study of the Greek and Roman classics in their original tongues, or to re-create the Greek city-state in Metropolitan Boston.

I venture to suggest that what they mean is something quite different from what is meant by the humanities. The progress of civilization in the modern age, especially in our own century, has brought with it an immense increase of knowledge of every kind, from archæology to zoology. More is known of the history of antiquity than was known to Herodotus. We have penetrated farther into the heavens and into the innermost secrets of the structure of matter than anyone could have dreamt of in previous generations. We have run through the satisfactions of representational art to the puzzling outlines of abstract art. The increase in physical comfort and in communication has brought with it a whole set of new problems. The great increase in population necessarily means further crowding and additional social and cultural adjustment. Under these circumstances, it is natural for people to look for guidance toward a balanced adjustment.

What people are really looking for is wisdom. To our great store of knowledge we need the added quality of wisdom.

Wisdom is inseparable from knowledge: it is knowledge plus a quality which is within the human being. Without it knowledge is dry, almost unfit for human consumption, and dangerous in application. The absence of wisdom is clearly noticeable: the learned fool and the educated bore have been with us since the beginnings of recorded history. Wisdom adds flavor, order, and measure to knowledge. Wisdom makes itself most manifest in the application of knowledge to human needs.

Every generation of mankind has to remake its culture, its values, and its goals. Changing circumstances make older habits and customs valueless or obsolete. New knowledge exposes the limitations and the contingent nature of older philosophies and of previously accepted guides to action. Wisdom does not come in formulas, proverbs, or wise saws, but out of the living actuality. The past is important for understanding the present, but it is not the present. It is in a real sense created in the present, and changes from the point of view of every generation.

When change is slow, the new is gradually assimilated, and only after a number of generations is it noticeable that the world is really different. In our century enormous changes in the circumstances of our lives and in our knowledge have occurred rapidly —in every decade. It is therefore not at all surprising that our intellectual, our social, and our political processes have failed to keep abreast of contemporary problems. It is not surprising that we become confused in the choice of our goals and the paths which we must take to reach them.

Clearly a study of the Greek and Roman classics in their original tongues or even in a good translation is a most rewarding venture in itself. This literature has never been surpassed in any age. And in reading this literature one is struck by how applicable the situations are to the present day. The fact that we can still be moved strongly by this literature is an illustration not merely of the constancy of structure of the human nervous system but also of the fact that great art and profound insights have a character which is independent of any age.

The humanities preserve and create values; even more they express the symbolic, poetic, and prophetic qualities of the human spirit. Without the humanities we would not be conscious of our history; we would lose many of our aspirations and the graces of expression that move men's hearts. Withal the humanities discern but a part of the life of man—true, a vital part but only a part.

It has often been claimed that the chief justification for the study of the humanities is that it teaches us values. In fact some people go even further and claim that the humanities, in which literature, parts of philosophy, and the history and appreciation of the fine arts are included, are the *only* sources of values other than the more spiritual values of religion.

This claim cannot pass without challenge. It cannot be said that it is absurd, but rather that it is a symptom of our failure in the present age to achieve a unity and balance of knowledge which is imbued with wisdom. It is a symptom of both ignorance and a certain anti-rational attitude which has been the curse of our century. It betrays a lack of self-confidence and faith in the greatness of the human spirit in contemporary man. It is the expression of a form of self-hatred which is rationally unjustifiable although deeply rooted.

Man is made of dust and to dust returneth; he lives in a universe of which he is also a part. He is free only in a symbolic sense: his nature is conditioned by the dust out of which he is made. To learn to understand himself he must learn to understand the universe in which he lives. There is more than enough in this enterprise to engage the boldest, the most imaginative, and the keenest minds and spirits of every generation. The universe is not given to us in the form of a map or guide. It is made by human minds and imaginations out of slight hints which come from acute observation and from the profound strategems of experiments.

How can we hope to obtain wisdom, the wisdom which is meaningful in our own time? We certainly cannot attain it as long as the two great branches of human knowledge, the sciences and the humanities, remain separate and even warring disciplines.

Why is science, even more than the humanities, as a living component of our society so misunderstood? A glance at a current dictionary definition may give us a clue.

Science: "A branch of knowledge dealing with facts or truths systematically arranged and showing the operation of general law."

This definition brings to my mind a solitaire player or head bookkeeper for a mail-order concern. It is a partial truth which is also a caricature. It is out of harmony with the picture of Archimedes jumping out of his bath crying Eureka! or Galileo in misery and degradation during his trial and recantation, or Einstein creating the universe out of one or two deductions from observation and a profound æsthetic feeling for symmetry. Nor does this definition account for the violence of the opposition to scientific discovery which still exists in the same quarters in our own age.

It is often argued that physical science is inherently simple, whereas the study of man is inherently complicated. Yet a great deal is known of man's nature. Wise laws for government and personal conduct were known in remotest antiquity. The literature of antiquity shows a profound understanding of human natures and emotions. Not man but the external world was bewildering. The world of nature instead of seeming simple was infinitely complex and possessed of spirits and demons. Nature had to be worshiped and propitiated by offerings, ceremonies, and prayers. Fundamentally nature was unpredictable, antagonistic to human aspiration, full of significance and purpose, and generally evil. Knowledge of nature was suspect because of the power which it brought, a power which was somehow allied with evil. There were of course always men who had insights far beyond these seemingly naive notions, but they did not prevail over what seemed to be the evidence of the senses and of practical experience.

It was therefore not until late in the history of mankind, not until a few seconds ago so to speak, that it was recognized that nature is understandable and that a knowledge of nature is good and can be used with benefit: that it does not involve witchcraft or a compact with the devil. What is more, any person of intelligence can understand the ideas involved and with sufficient skill learn the necessary techniques, intellectual and manual.

This idea which is now so commonplace represents an almost complete break with the past. To revere and trust the rational faculty of the mind—to allow no taboo to interfere in its operation, to have nothing immune from its examination—is a new value which has been introduced into the world. The progress of science has been the chief agent in demonstrating its importance and riveting it into the consciousness of mankind. This value does not yet have universal acceptance in this country or in any other country. But in spite of all obstacles it will become one of the most treasured possessions of all mankind because we can no longer live without it. We have gone too far along the direction which it implies ever to turn back without unimaginable disaster.

The last world war was started in an attempt to turn back to dark reaction against the rational faculty and to introduce a new demonology into the world. It failed as will every other such attempt. Once the mind is free it will be destroyed rather than be put back in chains.

To my mind the value content of science or literary scholarship lies not in the subject matter alone: it lies chiefly in the spirit and living tradition in which these disciplines are pursued. The spirit is almost always conditioned by the subject. Science and the humanities are not the same thing; the subject matter is different and the spirit and tradition are different. Our problem in our search for wisdom is to blend these two traditions in the minds of individual men and women.

Many colleges and universities are trying to do just this, but there is one serious defect in the method. We pour a little of this and a little of that into the student's mind in proportions which result from mediation between the departments and from the particular predilections of the deans and the president. We then hope that these ingredients will combine through some mysterious alchemy and the result will be a man educated, well-rounded, and wise. Most often, however, these ingredients remain well separated in the compartmentalized mind, or they may form an indigestible precipitate which is not only useless but positively harmful, until time the healer washes it all away.

Wisdom is by its nature an interdisciplinary quality and not the product of a collection of specialists. Although the colleges do indeed try to mold the student toward a certain ideal of the educated man of the twentieth century, it is too often a broad education administered by specialists. The approximate counterpart to this ideal of the educated man, embodied in a real living person, is a rare being on any college faculty. Indeed, in most colleges and universities the student is the only really active connecting link between the different departments. In a certain paradoxical sense the students are the only broadly educated body in the university community, at least in principle.

The affairs of this country—indeed of almost every country—whether in government, education, industry, or business, are controlled by people of broad experience. However, this broad experience rarely includes the field of science. How can our leaders make wise decisions now in the middle of the twentieth century without a deep understanding of scientific thought and feeling for scientific traditions? The answer is clear in the sad course that events have taken.

This anguished thought has impelled many scientists, often to their own personal peril, to concern themselves with matters which in the past were the exclusive domain of statesmen and military leaders. They have tried to advise, importune, and even cajole our leaders to include the scientific factor in our fateful policy decisions. They have been successful, but only in special instances.

I am not making a plea for the scientist statesman comparable to the philosopher king. The scientist rarely has this kind of ambition. The study of nature in its profundity, beauty, and subtlety is too attractive for him to wish to forsake his own creative and rewarding activity. The scientist away from his science is like an exile who longs for the sights and sounds of his native land. What the scientist really desires is for his science to be understood, to become an integral part of our general culture, to be given proper weight in the cultural and practical affairs of the world.

The greatest difficulty which stands in the way of a meeting of the minds of the scientist and the non-scientist is the difficulty of communication, a difficulty which stems from some of the defects of education to which I have alluded. The mature scientist, if he has any taste in these directions, can listen with pleasure to the philosopher, the historian, the literary man, or even to the art critic. There is little difficulty from that side because the scientist has been educated in our general culture and lives in it on a day-to-day basis. He reads newspapers, magazines, books, listens to music, debates politics, and participates in the general activities of an educated citizen.

Unfortunately this channel of communication is often a one-way street. The non-scientists cannot listen to the scientist with pleasure and understanding. Despite its universal outlook and its unifying principle, its splendid tradition, science seems to be no longer communicable to the great majority of educated laymen. They simply do not possess the background of the science of today and the intellectual tool necessary for them to understand what effects science will have on them and on the world. Instead of understanding, they have only a naïve awe mixed with fear and scorn. To his colleagues in the university the scientist tends to seem more and more like a man from another planet, a creature scattering antibiotics with one hand and atomic bombs with the other.

The problems to which I have addressed myself are not particularly American. The same condition exists in England, France, and indeed in all other countries. From my observation we are perhaps better off than most. Our American colleges and universities, since they are fairly recent and are rapidly expanding, have not settled into complacency. They are quite ready to experiment to achieve desired ends. Our experimental methods have taught us how to impart the most diverse forms of knowledge. Although wisdom is more elusive, once the objective is clear that the ultimate end of education is knowledge imbedded in wisdom we shall find ways to move toward that ideal. The ideal of the well-rounded man is a meaningless ideal unless this sphericity means a fusion of knowledge to achieve balanced judgment and understanding, which are qualities of wisdom.

The problems are, of course, depressingly difficult. In the secondary schools—with their overcrowding, their teachers overworked and inadequately trained, the school boards, and, not least, the powerful clique of professional educators, who form a society within our society—all that is unique and characteristic of science and mathematics is being crowded out of the curriculum and replaced by a fairy tale known as general science. The colleges and universities are in much better shape, although the great population increase is about to hit them with masses of inadequately prepared students. Most people would be quite content with a holding operation in which we could maintain the quality that is already possessed.

However, it seems to me that something could be done even now with the faculty members of the colleges and the universities. Wisdom can achieve a hybrid vigor by crossing the scientist and the humanist through a more extensive and intensive interaction within the faculty. Why should not the professor of physics be expected to refresh himself periodically by taking a course in æsthetics or comparative literature or in the Greek drama? Why shouldn't the professor of medieval philosophy or the professor of ancient history take a course in modern physics and become acquainted with the profound thoughts underlying relativity and quantum mechanics? It would let in some fresh air, or at least different air, to blow away some of the cobwebs which grow in the unventilated ivory towers.

Somewhere a beginning has to be made to achieve a more architectural quality in our culture, a quality of proportion and of organic unity, and it is reasonable to start with the members of the faculties of our institutions of higher learning. Here are all the strands of the tapestry which is to represent our culture, living in close proximity but separate, adding up to nothing more than the sum of the parts. The scientists must learn to teach science in the spirit of wisdom and in the light of the history of human thought and human effort, rather than as the geography of a universe uninhabited by mankind. Our colleagues in the non-scientific faculties must understand that if their teachings ignore the great scientific tradition and its accomplishments, their words, however eloquent and elegant, will lose meaning for this generation and be barren of fruit.

Only with a united effort of science and the humanities can we hope to succeed in discovering a community of thought which can lead us out of the darkness and the confusion which oppress all mankind.

Percy Williams Bridgman

SCIENCE AND COMMON SENSE

PERCY WILLIAMS BRIDGMAN *received the Nobel Prize in Physics in 1946 for inventing apparatus to obtain very high pressures and for the discoveries he made by means of this apparatus in the field of high-pressure physics. His book on the subject has become a standard work on the effect that high pressure has on water, on electrical resistance, on thermonuclear phenomena, on the viscosity of fluids, and on the elastic properties of solid bodies. Born in Cambridge, Mass. in 1882, he has spent his entire career at Harvard, where he received his degrees (Ph.D., 1908), began his teaching career in 1919 and continued it until his recent retirement as Hollis Professor of mathematics and natural philosophy. He has received numerous honorary degrees and belongs to all the significant scientific societies. His interest in the role of the individual in society is revealed in such books as* The Intelligent Individual and Society *(1938) and* Reflections of a Physicist *(1950), while his* The Logic of Modern Physics *(1927) has long been prescribed reading for students of general semantics. The following essay first appeared in* The Scientific Monthly *of June, 1954.*

I shall have to begin by recalling some matters that have been said so many times that I can expect only to bore you, but this is a risk that I can see no way to avoid if I am to make my main point. You all know that, since the turn of the century, discoveries have been made in physics, culminating in the unlocking of nuclear energy in the atomic bomb, which have entirely revolutionized our outlook, not only our outlook with regard to the construction of the world around us, but our philosophical ideas as well with regard to our relationship to the world. It is the latter to which I would like to direct your attention.

The new discoveries that have forced the revolution were in the realms of relativity and quantum phenomena. We shall see later that the quantum phenomena were more revolutionary in their implications than the relativity phenomena, but historically it is probable that the relativity phenomena played the more important role at first. The new relativity phenomena were highly paradoxical and included such effects as meter sticks whose length changed when they were set in motion, clocks that ran slow when moving, and weights that became heavier when moving. In fact, these effects were so paradoxical and contrary to common sense that some physicists and most men in the street refused to accept them and even sought to throw them out of court by ridicule.

But the facts refused to be thrown out of court, and the paradoxes were resolved by Einstein's theory of restricted relativity. This theory embraced, in the first place, the mathematical machinery by which all the experimental facts were correlated into a single mathematical structure. But no less notable as an intellectual achievement and equally essential to the removal of paradox was Einstein's handling of the physical concepts that entered the mathematical edifice. It is this latter that is our concern.

There are two aspects of Einstein's handling of the physical concepts. There is, in the first place, a realization that the paradoxes involved primarily questions of meaning and that the common-sense meanings of such terms as *length* and *time* were not sharp enough to serve in the situations presented by the new facts. In the second place, there was the method by which the necessary increased sharpness was imparted to the meanings. This method was to specify the operations that were involved in concrete instances in applying the term whose meaning was in question. For example, what do we mean when we say that two events are simultaneous? Einstein insisted that we do not know what we mean unless we can give some concrete procedure by which we may determine whether or not any two specific events are simultaneous. Analysis of the concrete procedures that we might use brings out the fact, not noticed before, that what we do to determine whether or not two events are simultaneous depends to a certain extent on the events themselves and is different and more complicated if the two events take place at different places than if they take place here. Furthermore, this analysis disclosed that what an observer does to determine whether two distant events are simultaneous is different from what another observer does who is in motion with respect to him. Simultaneity of two distant events is, therefore, not an absolute property of the events, the same for all observers, but is relative to the observers.

It is the same with length. What do we mean when we ask what the length of a moving object is? Applying the operational criterion of meaning, the meaning is to be sought in what we do when we measure the length of the moving object. When we analyze what we might do, we discover that there are several different possible procedures, equally acceptable to common sense. Thus, if we are asked to measure the length of a moving street-car, we might take an instantaneous photograph of it and measure the length of the photograph, or we might board the car, meter stick in hand, and proceed to measure it as we would any ordinary stationary object. If we get the same answer by the two procedures, we shall doubtless be satisfied and think that our catechizer was unnecessarily fussy in insisting that we tell exactly what we do to measure the length.

But here is where the new experimental facts come in that were not suspected before relativity theory. For it turns out that when we make our measurements with extreme precision, or when the streetcar is moving with very great velocity, the results of the two methods are not the same, so that the precise method must be specified if we want to talk exactly about the length of the moving car. In other words, it is ambiguous to talk about the "length" of a moving object until we have specified exactly how the length is to be measured; and when we have specified the exact procedure, the results we get are generally different, depending on what the exact procedure is. In particular, by one of the two procedures just indicated, the length of the moving car would be the same as when it is stationary; and, by the other, it would be less. We see at once that we cannot treat this situation by the methods of common sense and say that it is absurd that the length should change when the car moves, because it *must* change according to at least one of our possible definitions. Realization of this at once removes the atmosphere of paradox from the statement that the length changes when the object is set in motion.

The precise way that we define length when the body moves is a matter of choice, and we will make our choice in the way most convenient for us in the light of all the experimental facts. It would take us much too deeply into relativity theory to attempt to see why the method that Einstein chose for defining the length of a moving object is, all things considered, the most convenient for the physicist. Suffice it to say that the method chosen was not the method that leaves the length unchanged by the motion, although such a method is possible and, for certain restricted purposes, might be considered more convenient.

Relativity theory has thus shown the importance of precision of meanings. It has disclosed that some of the apparently simple terms of common sense are actually complex when we attempt to apply them in situations beyond the bounds of ordinary experience. In these new situations, we are forced to make a choice between procedures that are equivalent in the ordinary range. The account we give of the new situation depends on the procedure that we choose—that is, on the meaning we give our terms. In discovering that in fact we do need to make distinctions of which we have never thought and which to a naive first impression appear a matter of indifference, we are discovering that in fact the world is not constructed according to the preconceptions of common sense.

The sort of phenomena with which quantum theory is concerned teach the same lesson as relativity theory, namely, that the world is not constructed according to the principles of common sense. However, the way in which common sense fails is somewhat different in the case of quantum phenomena. The unfamiliar world of relativity theory was the world of high velocities; the new world of quantum theory is the world of the very small.

Quantum theory began modestly enough with the discovery that some of the most familiar facts of daily life cannot be understood on the basis of the common-sense views of matter prevalent at the end of the last century. For example, it was impossible to understand why we cannot see a kettle full of boiling water in the dark. Common sense, when translated into mathematics, said that we should see it, but every burned child knows that we cannot. The paradox has now been removed from this and other related effects, so that we now understand, in a way that would have been incredible twenty-five years ago, most of the phenomena displayed by ordinary matter. This understanding has been provided by quantum theory. The theory is highly mathematical and it is wellnigh impossible to give an adequate outline of it in nontechnical language, but the one simple crude idea back of it all is that when we deal with very small things, such as atoms or electrons, the ordinary common-sense conception of *things* is no longer valid. The renunciation of common sense thus demanded by quantum theory is more drastic than that demanded by relativity theory. For now we get ourselves into *logical inconsistencies* if we try to think of things in the microscopic domain in the same way that we think of the objects of ordinary experience.

Suppose, for example, that I have a box with a partition in the middle and one electron on each side of the partition. I remove the partition for a moment, so that the electrons have an opportunity to exchange positions. I now find when I replace the partition that I again have one electron on each side of the partition. It now involves me in logical contradiction to ask whether the electron that is on the right side of the partition is the same electron that in the beginning was on the right side, or vice versa. Neither can I ask exactly how fast is the right-hand electron moving. Knowing that the electron is on the right of the partition makes it logically contradictory to know how fast it is moving. These are indeed revolutionary restrictions. Not to be able to ask which electron is which means that the electron does not have identity, and not being able to ask how fast it is moving means that the common-sense categories of space and time do not completely apply to it.

Consider another example. It is possible to make a so-called electron gun with which a stream of electrons may be fired at a target. If we start with a comparatively crude gun firing a coarse stream of electrons, we find the stream of electrons behaves much like a stream of water from a hose, so that we cannot hit with it a single sharp point of the target, but there is more or less scattering. Now common sense might lead us to expect that our marksmanship would become better as we refined the apparatus by making it more and more delicate and capable of dealing with a finer and finer stream of electrons. Experiment shows, however, that our common-sense expectations are entirely wrong, and that matters get worse instead of better as we refine the apparatus. In the end, when we have, at great pains, constructed a gun capable of firing single electrons, we find that we have almost completely lost control of the situation. No two shots ever come alike despite the best we can do, and we might as well spin a roulette wheel to find what part of the target any electron will hit.

The electron gun illustrates the general principle that, in the microscopic domain, events cannot be made to repeat. The situation thus disclosed is bad enough from the practical point of view, but I believe that it is even more upsetting from the conceptual point of view. For the one intellectual lesson that science has perhaps most insistently underlined is that our mental machinery is capable of making mistakes and that we continually have to verify and check what we are doing. The fundamental method of verification is repetition; the repeatable experiment has come to occupy such a position that the very definition of truth is often framed in terms of verification by repetition. It looks as though it does not mean anything in the quantum domain to ask for the truth about any specific event, yet how can I get along without the concept of truth? You may try to extricate yourself from the dilemma by saying that, although *I* may not verify the occurrence of some event by repeating the experiment, I *can* verify it by getting confirmation from some other observer who has also witnessed it. But this, unfortunately, is not a way out, because here we encounter another of those baffling properties of the microscopic world, namely, that an elementary event may be observed by only one observer. Confirmation by public report thus becomes impossible. To many, it might seem that thereby science is made impossible, science sometimes being defined in terms of publicity. However, if you are willing to grant that quantum theory is part of science, you see that matters are at least not quite as bad as this. Whatever the method by which eventually we get intellectual order into this situation, I think you can see that the observer must play a quite different role in the quantum domain than in the world of everyday life.

All these considerations mean that the conventional forms of thought are no longer applicable in the realm of the very small. I think you will agree that my foregoing statement is justified, namely, that the failure of common sense disclosed by quantum theory is more drastic than that disclosed by relativity theory. For, when in relativity theory we go to very high velocities, we merely encounter properties of matter that are strange to common experience, whereas when we go far enough in the direction of the very small, quantum theory says that our forms of thought fail, so that it is questionable whether we can properly think at all. One can imagine the consternation of our old philosophical friend Immanuel Kant who declared that space and time are *necessary* forms of thought.

What is the answer to the dilemma with which quantum theory confronts us, and where do the roots of the difficulty lie? Are we faced with the necessity of devising new ways of thinking? It does seem to me that eventually we shall have to find better ways of thinking, but I suspect that any improved method of thinking that we are capable of devising will eventually come up against essential limitations of some sort that will prevent its unlimited application. In the meantime, no agreement can be discerned at present among the experts with regard to the details of any way in which we might reform our thinking. As an example, there is the irreconcilable schism between the views of Einstein and Bohr on quantum phenomena. Whatever the eventual solution, I think we can at least be sure that it will be outside the realm of common sense. Furthermore, I believe the experts would at present agree that whatever new way we devise to think about the microscopic universe, the meaning of our new concepts will have to be found back at the level of the large-scale events of daily life, because this is the scale on which we live our lives, and it is we who are formulating the new concepts. This recognition and agreement entails, I believe, a consequence that is not commonly appreciated, namely, that the seeds and sources of the ineptness of our thinking in the microscopic range are already contained in our present thinking in the large-scale region and should have been capable of discovery by sufficiently acute analysis of our ordinary common-sense thinking.

I would now like to direct your attention to some qualities of our ordinary everyday thinking that are commonly overlooked but seem to be beginning to attract more attention and, I believe, may eventually give us truer understanding of the nature of our thinking process and its limitations. What I shall now say must be taken as strictly my own opinions. I have no professional philosophical competence to speak on these matters, and it is even probable that many of my fellow-physicists would not agree with me, if indeed they have any opinion on these matters at all.

You have all doubtless had some acquaintance with cybernetics, a subject named and largely created by Professor Norbert Wiener at Massachusetts Institute of Technology and you know how much attention this subject is attracting and how many people are working at it. Apart from any specific results that may come out of all this activity, such for example as discovering how to make bigger and better robots that will continually usurp more and more of the functions of human intelligence, it seems to me that the mere fact that so many people are concerning themselves with this subject is going to have important repercussions. For when so many people try so hard to make a machine that functions like the human brain, the point of view will gradually spread that the human brain is itself a machine of sorts. It will also be recognized that this machine must have limitations inherent in its structure, and that the things which the machine can do, including in particular thinking, is in consequence also subject to limitations. Thinking is done by the brain, and the presumption is that thought has characteristics imposed by the character of the brain. At any rate, we will come to see that we may not expect to understand the nature of thought at least until we understand the nature of the brain. If you ask why we should be concerned with the nature of thought, I would reply: the realization that the nature of thought is something which cannot be merely taken for granted is a realization that seems to be gradually dawning on us as we ponder the significance of our failures in the fields of relativity and quantum theory.

You will not, I think, ponder for long what limitations are imposed on thought by the structure of the brain until it will suddenly strike you that what is really happening here is that the brain is trying to understand itself. But is not this a brash thing for the brain to try to do, for how can the brain analyze its own action, when any conclusions at which it arrives are themselves activities of the very brain that was the original problem to understand? At the very best, the situation would seem to be somewhat strained and artificial, and you may perhaps anticipate that any conclusions at which we may arrive cannot have as simple and straightforward a significance as we had perhaps hoped. This does indeed seem to be the case. What we are encountering here is a special case of a system trying to deal with itself. Such situations occur not infrequently, and it seems to be the general rule that such situations present special difficulties and infelicities.

Many of the well-known paradoxes of logic arise when a system tries to deal with itself. A stock example is the ostensibly complete map of the city in which the map itself is located. If the map is complete, it must contain a map of itself; that is, the map must have a map of the map, and this in turn demands a map of the map of the map, and you are off on a chase that has no end. Within the last few years, a theorem with regard to such a system has been proved, a theorem that has been hailed among logicians as a truly epoch-making discovery in logic. This theorem was enunciated by Gödel, now in the Institute for Advanced Study at Princeton. In very crude language the theorem states that no logical system can ever prove that it itself is a perfect system in the sense that it may not contain concealed self-contradictions. This theorem, at one stroke, stultified the endeavors of some of the ablest mathematicians, just as earlier the discovery of new mathematical theorems had stultified the efforts of the circle-squarers and the angle-trisectors. Mathematicians had long been trying to prove by the principles of mathematics that mathematics contains no hidden inconsistencies, inconsistencies that some day might be discovered and bring down the whole imposing mathematical edifice in ruins. But Gödel's theorem showed that this is an impossible sort of thing to prove. The conclusion is that, if one wants to prove that mathematics is free from concealed self-contradictions, one has to use principles outside mathematics to prove it. If one then wants to prove that the new principles are free from contradiction, one must use other principles beyond and over those in question. We here encounter a regress that has no logical end and, humanly, ends in human weariness and the finite length of human life. This means that the human intelligence can never be sure of itself; it is not a tool capable of unlimited perfectibility, as is so often fondly imagined. All we can ever say is that, up to the present, we have found no inconsistencies where we have looked.

There is one other recent development that tends to make us more self-conscious of our intellectual limitations. In Hanover, New Hampshire, Adelbert Ames, Jr., with a number of collaborators, especially A. Hadley Cantril, of the department of psychology of Princeton University, has been studying in recent years how the perceptions of different people adapt themselves to situations that have been purposely devised to differ from the situations ordinarily encountered in daily life. For example, one can play tricks with perception by making lines converge or diverge which ordinary experience leads one to expect must be parallel. By combining various kinds of motion with curiosities of perspective, one can produce sensations completely foreign to ordinary experience, which the unaccustomed brain fits into its perceptual scheme in forced and unnatural ways. A striking example is the so-called trapezoidal window. A wooden frame like an ordinary window frame, except that the top and bottom sashes are not parallel, is rotated uniformly about a vertical axis. When the narrower end of the frame approaches the observer, the converging lines, associated ordinarily with greater distance, present the observer with an unaccustomed dilemma. Most observers resolve the dilemma by seeing the window frame in oscillating motion, back and forth, rather than in uniform rotation. In general, the way in which the observer perceives this and other strange situations varies with different persons and even varies with the same person, depending on what has been happening to him in the immediate past. This means that what a person sees in a given situation may, to a certain extent, be manipulated and controlled by another person.

Of course, there is nothing new in illusions. At Hanover, however, the study of such effects is being elaborated into a systematic technique for finding out about the nature of our perceptual processes. I think that most people, once they have seen the demonstrations, would be convinced that such studies cannot help being of great value in revealing details of the ways in which our perceptual machinery works.

Personally, however, I find these studies tremendously suggestive and stimulating from a point of view of greater generality, namely, in emphasizing the significance of the mere fact that we perceive at all. This is one of those things that are so universal we never think of them unless our attention is forced by some dramatic situation. Perception we have always had with us and we take it completely for granted. We *see things* out there in space moving about, and that is all there is to it. We accept these perceptions at their face value and, on them as a foundation, we build the pattern of our "reality." To this reality, we ascribe an absolute existence transcending its origin and ask ourselves how it is that the human brain can be capable of apprehending the absolute. By asking this question, we disclose our hazy feeling that what a brain can do is probably limited in some way. But except for this hazy feeling, it seems to me that the question is improperly put, and the fact that we ask it discloses an improper attitude on our part. Instead of asking how human brains can apprehend "reality," we should ask what sort of thing it is that the human brain can fashion to call reality. It was, I believe, Suzanne Langer who remarked that philosophy advances, not by finding the answers to the questions of preceding generations, but by finding that those questions were improperly put. Here it seems to me is obviously a question that has been improperly put. The perceptions of time and space have been furnished to us by the machinery of our nervous systems. This machinery is a terribly complicated thing, which in spite of its complication does not give rise to perception until it has received a long course of preparation and education. Anyone who has watched a small infant trying to coordinate its visual and tactual sensations recognizes that we acquire our perceptual abilities only by arduous practice. Yet we take our space and time with a deadly seriousness. Even so great a scientist as Sir Isaac Newton could say that space is the sensorium of God, and nearly every philosopher treats thought as in some way transcending the machine that thinks. It will doubtless be disturbing to many to give up our transcendentally fundamental time and space, but I think there is perhaps something to be gained also. Perhaps when we learn to take them less seriously we will not be so bedeviled by the logical contradictions in which they sometimes now involve us, as when we ask questions about the beginning or end of time or the boundaries of space.

There is another respect in which I have found the experiments of Ames most stimulating, namely, in disclosing details of our mental processes of which we are ordinarily completely unaware. For example, as one watches the rotating trapezoidal window, one's perceptions are in a continual state of flux, melting and forming and metamorphosing into one another in a way quite unfamiliar. How can one find words to describe such unfamiliar happenings, or how can one catch and hold such things? How can one even store in memory what he has experienced so that he may be sure that the manner of fusion of two perceptions which he has just experienced is the same as the manner of fusion which he experienced yesterday?

Of course, ever since psychoanalysis started, we have known that there are processes occurring in the brain that never get to the level of consciousness, but here it seems to me that we have something different, because here we are encountering new sorts of conscious experience. Among these, there are *transient* mental phenomena, accessible to sufficiently acute introspection. For example, as we listen to our fellow, the meaning that he is trying to convey grows before it is complete. Meanings do not spring full grown into our minds but pass through a stage of development that is seldom, if ever, the subject of analysis. It seems to be a general characteristic of our mental processes that we like to operate with static and complete things—we want our words to have fixed meanings and we analyze space into points and time into instants. But to sufficiently acute analysis, the fixed and static does not occur—it is something that we have constructed, and in so doing we have constructed away a whole world of mental phenomena.

It would seem not impossible that this world of transient phenomena and fine structure could be recovered and opened to us by deliberate cultivation and invention. What is needed is the invention of an introspectional microscope. Not until we have amassed a considerable experience of this world will we be able to talk about it or even remember our experiences. Gaining mastery of the microscopic world of introspection will involve much the same sort of thing that happens to a baby or to a kitten when its eyes are opened. Study of the process of gaining mastery of the new introspectional world may help us to reconstruct imaginatively what happened to us in our own babyhood.

It does not yet appear what the final method will be for dealing with all these considerations. I believe that the final solution will have to carry further the consequences of the insight that quantum theory has partially glimpsed, namely, that the observer must somehow be included in the system. The point of view of classical physics, and I believe also of all orthodox human thinking up to the present, was that the observer is a passive spectator, expressed sometimes by saying that what he observes would be the same whether he were watching or not. Quantum theory points out that this is only an approximation valid in the realm of large objects. The very act of observing a small object involves a reaction between the object and the observer, a reaction that must be allowed for in reconstructing the system from observation. To which we now add the insight that the relationship between the observed and the observer is a much more intimate relationship than these quantum considerations would suggest, and that it is in fact meaningless to try to separate observer and observed, or to speak of an object independent of an observer or, for that matter, of an observer in the absence of objects of observation.

It seems to me that our eyes are gradually opening. We are coming to recognize that it is a simple matter of observation that the observer is part of what he observes and that the thinker is part of what he thinks. We do not passively observe the universe from the outside, but we are all in it up to our necks, and there is no escape. It would be difficult to imagine anything more contrary to the tenets of common sense or to the attitude of the human race since it has begun to think. The common-sense way of handling our minds has, without doubt, been of decisive importance, and the discovery of the common-sense way of thinking was, doubtless, in the beginning a bit of an invention, perhaps the most important invention ever made. One of the things that we are in fact doing in accepting the common-sense way of thinking is to declare that, for our purposes, we do not need to complicate our thinking by continually holding ourselves to an awareness that the thinker cannot be divorced from what he thinks. We have thus brought about a tremendous simplification in our intellectual processes, and in the history of the human race the common-sense attitude has been more than justified. It seems to me, however, that we are approaching a position where we can recognize the limit of usefulness of this way of thinking. Common sense evolved in the comparatively simple situations of the primitive experiences of the human race, and although it may have been an invention, we may be sure that it was an unconscious invention, adopted with no due consideration of its limitations or possible alternatives.

The world with which common sense was evolved to cope was simple with respect to the range of physical phenomena that it embraced, and simple also with respect to the social organization of the communities in which common sense was practiced. In the last fifty years, we have drastically extended our physical range toward high velocities and toward the microscopic and have been able to retain our command of the situation only by discarding those common-sense methods of thinking about physical things which had served the human race from the beginning. We may well ask ourselves whether something analogous may not be expected to occur, or is not in fact already occurring, when we pass from the simple to the complex in phenomena other than those of the physical world, using *physical* in its narrower sense. There are at least two other classes of nonphysical situations. These are social situations and the situations presented by the creation of abstractions or by abstract thinking. Consider first the social situations.

There will be, I suppose, no disagreement with the contention that, in the last few generations, the complexity of our social environment has tremendously increased. With modern methods of communication with the speed of light and of transportation with more than the speed of sound, the social environment of each person is becoming effectively the whole world. Plain analogy with what has happened in physics suggests the question of whether we are not here encountering an extension of range in our social experience that will demand an analogous abandonment of common-sense methods of social thinking. By common-sense methods of social thinking, I mean those methods that developed in small communities and are fitted to deal with nothing more complex than the social situations presented by small communities. From this point of view, most of our social thinking would seem to be of the common-sense variety. One characteristic social attitude springing from such an origin is the conviction that there is one and only one "correct" or "right" social philosophy or world-view, or one line of conduct that one "ought" to follow. Such a point of view could be pretty well maintained in a community small enough to offer a background of uniform social experience to all its members and able to enforce conformity on all dissenters. But the impossibility of any such view has become amply apparent when the community has become the whole world, and we are forced to revise the very meanings that we attach to *truth* or *right* or *ought*. It would appear that there is a moral perception analogous to our physical perception of objects in space and time and, like our physical perceptions, dependent on our past experience. We may suppose that the savage, who has never seen a civilized window frame, when confronted for the first time with the rotating trapezoidal window, will see it, not in oscillating motion as we do, but in uniform rotation. Analogously, the Hindu, brought up in the religious traditions of his group, perceives as a moral imperative that he must not kill the mosquito that annoys him. The realization of this is not new; the anthropologist has been dinning it into our ears for some time. The anthropologist, however, could point his moral only in somewhat academic terms and mostly from the record of the past by presenting us with the divergent practices of different peoples in different epochs. The lesson is now pointed with incomparably more dramatic force in our endeavors to find a basis for the harmonious living together of the entire world, a problem that demands the simultaneous reconciliation of so many divergent outlooks. At the very least, we shall have to evolve a new social philosophy and discover some method of getting rid of the provincialism that seems so right to common sense.

In addition to the social situations, a second nonphysical factor in our lives is afforded by our abstract thinking. How long the human race has been thinking and talking abstractly I suppose even the anthropologist cannot tell us, but it appeals to me as a good guess that we developed our common-sense method of handling the situations of daily life before we began abstracting. It is known that there are primitive peoples that have not yet formed as simple abstractions as "tree." The extension of thinking from concrete objects to abstractions constituted an extension of range sufficiently great to suggest the question, inspired by our experience with relativity and quantum theory, of whether the methods adequate to deal with the world of concrete objects continue to be adequate to deal with abstractions. To put the question is to suggest the answer. In the answer, I believe we can glimpse the solution to a riddle that has long baffled us. There is a class of people whose profession is to deal with abstractions—that is, the philosophers. By long tradition, philosophical thinking has come to be regarded by most people as the most exalted of all thinking, and the philosopher is often regarded with an approach to veneration. But along with this veneration most people are disillusioned

when he took his present professorship at the University of Moscow.
He has been the director of the important Institute of Chemical
Physics of the U.S.S.R. Academy of Sciences, and has published sev-
eral textbooks and monographs, notably Chain Reactions (1934) *and*
Some Problems of Chemical Kinetics and Reactivity (1954). *The*
following article is based upon a lecture given in 1958 at the Brussels
Exposition. Semenov—whose experiments led the way to improve-
ments in the efficiency of the internal combustion engine—was hon-
ored in Stockholm for his research in clarifying the mechanism of
chemical reaction in gases.

To make man free from hard physical work, as well as
from automatic work not requiring any mental effort; to
assure all men an adequate provision of food, clothing, and
shelter, so that they will not be oppressed by hunger, cold, and
homelessness, thus making them truly free; using this freedom to
make everyone share, to the full extent of his abilities, the enjoyment of cultural and spiritual values: is this not the fundamental
idea of humanitarianism, common to all decent people, whatever
their beliefs?

Science and technology started their triumphant advance early
in the nineteenth century. In the last twenty or thirty years, this
progress has acquired exceptional speed, and a previously unheard-of breadth. It is hard to imagine at what breathtaking speed
the capacity of men to master the forces of nature may advance in
future. A very real scientific and technological base is being laid
for the achievement of any reasonable level of well-being for all
mankind. Limitations on this progress will be set in the future not
by restricted scientific and technical possibilities, or insufficient
manpower and economic means, but by the structure of society.

If nations consciously decide to strive for this humanitarian
ideal—then, irrespective of the specific path any one of them may
choose, they will have to create rationally directed forms of society
—forms allowing men to be masters of their fates. They will have
to use their social organization for the achievement of rationally
formulated social aims, putting an end to the state of affairs in
which uncontrolled conditions of life are the masters of men, as

if these conditions were made inescapable by nature or history. The distribution of wealth must be such as to assure the greatest prosperity of all; and the social system must be such as to make impossible crises due to overproduction, when many people need many things, but cannot buy them. Mechanization and automation must not be permitted to threaten men with unemployment. I personally am firmly convinced that, without abolishing the exploitation of man by man, this well-being of all people cannot be achieved.

A society setting itself this humanitarian aim must present to mankind new ideals which could inspire men, develop their creativity, and lead to the blossoming of the individual—and at the same time strengthen mutual cooperation and increase mutual respect and aid. An end must be put to aimlessness, pessimism, nihilism, and unlimited pursuit of egotistic interests. Different nations, while going their own way toward the great aim of assuring the prosperity of all men, must establish wide international cooperation, founded on mutual respect and consciousness of their common interests.

In my country, on the basis of the new system of society which it has chosen—a system that has opened wide possibilities for the rapid development of science, technology, and education—the solution of this human problem, by government and people, had already become the order of the day forty years ago. Our entire people, and our scientists in particular, are working with great enthusiasm to bring about the time when the material and spiritual needs of everybody will be fulfilled as completely as possible. We would like to enter into competition with all other nations in the noble task of realizing the great humanitarian dream of mankind: to secure the well-being of all, a dream made realizable by the recently acquired, previously unheard-of possibilities of putting the forces of nature into the service of man.

Each year brings new wonderful achievements of science, making possible plans which would have appeared fantastic only yesterday. A year and a half ago, the first artificial satellite was created, inaugurating the era of man's conquest of cosmic space. Interplanetary travel is becoming the subject of realistic study.

This achievement seems symbolic of the creative potential of science.

What are the scientific, technological, and economic factors that determine the prosperity of mankind? One such factor of decisive importance for the development of industry, the level of agricultural production, and the way of life of men is the availability of energy, particularly of electrical energy. If it were possible to provide any desired amount of electrical energy at any point on earth to serve the needs of men there, then, given an adequate organization of society, the well-being of everybody everywhere could be raised to any reasonable level. At present, the average energy available on earth corresponds to only 0.1 kilowatt installed capacity per capita. This is very little. With such a small supply of electrical energy, heavy physical work remains inevitable, particularly in economically underdeveloped countries. Furthermore, the majority of electric power stations still use coal, whose production necessitates heavy underground work. Hydroelectric stations, power stations using natural gas, and atomic power installations do not have this disadvantage, and their rapid development could lead to a vast increase in the generation of electric energy, and to improved working conditions.

However, the potentialities of all these ways of producing electric energy are nothing in comparison with what will be possible when controlled liberation of thermonuclear energy becomes a reality.

Soviet physicists, and subsequently also English and American physicists, have demonstrated, by discovering the principle of magnetic heat insulation, that, in principle, the thermonuclear problem is soluble. I personally have no doubt that in ten or twenty years the problem of controlled thermonuclear reaction will have been solved, and that, before this century is over, thermonuclear generation of electricity will be in wide use.

The unlimited availability of the raw material (water) needed for the production of thermonuclear fuel, the simplicity and safety of its production, its fantastic energy content, the likely possibility of direct conversion of thermonuclear into electrical energy, the absence of dangerous radioactive by-products in the exhaust gases from thermonuclear power generation—all these advantages promise to make thermonuclear energy generation something truly wonderful. Its development will make real the hope of supplying any desired amount of electrical energy in any chosen point on the globe—and, if needed, also outside it.

It would be therefore by no means utopian to say that, by the end of this century, or early in the next one, the world's capacity to supply electric energy may be increased, say, by a factor of 100, reaching ten kilowatts installed generating capacity per head. This is quite a lot. The supply of such amounts of energy will permit the electrification and mechanization of industry, agriculture, and housework everywhere. A further increase in the supply of electric power from thermonuclear sources, say by another factor of ten, would make legitimate the hope for rational control of climate, since the production of thermonuclear energy would then equal about 5 per cent of the total amount of sun energy taken up by the earth in the same time.

To provide everybody with housing, home equipment, and clothing; to build enough farms, greenhouses, and hotbeds; to construct all needed water mains, sewers, and irrigation canals; to build and equip factories, power stations, electric grids, transportation systems, etc., will require enormous amounts of construction materials. The generation of vast amounts of electrical energy resulting from the use of thermonuclear processes will permit practically unlimited production of metals, particularly aluminum and magnesium, whose natural reserves on earth are virtually inexhaustible.

However, the most characteristic materials of the future will be new synthetic polymers: plastics, fibers, synthetic rubber, leather, fur, and similar products. There is no doubt that before the present century is over, such materials, created by chemistry in the last few decades, will become predominant in industry, as well as in the construction trade and in the home. In the next few decades, synthetic polymers will not only displace the corresponding materials, but will also largely replace metals, since they equal metals in stability but are more resistant to corrosion and more easily shaped. In future, they may even exceed metals in heat resistance.

The volume of polymer production is determined by the availability of raw materials. Among these are, above all, mineral oil and gas, but also coal, cellulose, straw, etc. At present, oil is used mainly for the production of fuel, particularly for ground, air, and water transportation; to a lesser extent, for the operation of thermoelectric power stations, and for heating. If, through wide utilization of thermonuclear energy, the generation of electric energy will cease to depend largely on fossil fuels, all these forms of oil consumption could be reduced to a minimum. Electrification of transportation, agriculture, and construction machinery would be particularly important in this respect. Oil would then be used mainly for the production of synthetic polymers, in amounts reaching many hundreds of millions of tons annually—or 200-300 kilograms per head of world population. To understand what this would mean, it may be mentioned that the present world production of natural and artificial polymers (not counting paper) amounts to about 20-25 million tons, or about 10 kilograms per person per year. Increasing this production 20-30 times will mean that all clothing needs of mankind will be amply fulfilled, as well as other needs for fabrics, home furnishings, industry, and building trades.

Vast possibilities for saving labor arise from the development of telemechanics and electronics, leading to new methods of automatization of industrial production. This should shorten the workday to 3-4 hours, assuring leisure for creative activities, rest, and sports.

Especially significant are the perspectives opened to mankind by the rapid development of mathematical logic, and the construction of electronic calculating machines. Ordinary machines, which carry out mechanical work, liberate men from heavy physical labor; electronic calculating devices could liberate them also from mental work of the kind that requires no creative thinking and is largely automatic. This includes, for example, the control of automatic production lines, the regulation of transportation and also many kinds of office work. This is not all. Electronic machines are built so that in the more or less narrow fields of their specialization, their "memory," and the speed and precision with which they can analyze data, vastly exceed man's own capabilities. The calculating machine of the future will be able to provide information from an enormous store of material, sort out, and even partially analyze it. This will increase the possibilities of man's creative work by liberating the human brain from the need to memorize large amounts of factual material, and by taking over the first steps of the analysis of this material. In our time, taking account of vast amounts of information has become essential for scientific creativity.

The continuous growth of scientific information, resulting from the precipitous progress of science, hampers broadly generalizing scientific thought, makes more difficult comprehensive consideration of phenomena, and converts scientists into narrow specialists. Electronic machines can be expected to do away with this predicament and permit man to concentrate his mental powers on truly creative activities.

Much of mankind is not eating enough; in large areas of the earth hunger is a familiar guest. Yet, simply improving the methods of cultivation, fertilization, and irrigation of all now existing cultivated areas so as to equal the highest contemporary levels— not to speak of an increase in these areas—could assure high quality and sufficient quantity of food, not merely for the present world population, but apparently also for twice as many people. This level could be easily reached if nations would combine their organized efforts. What is needed is not charity, but assistance to underdeveloped countries, permitting them to become technically independent.

With the clearly foreseeable progress of energetics and the consequent growth of irrigation systems, increased production of transparent and moistureproof polymeric films, the development of new species of cultivated plants, and the increased availability of fertilizers and insecticides, broad possibilities of increasing the cultivated area (including the transformation of deserts, jungles, and the Arctic into fertile lands) and of rapid rise in agricultural productivity, are bound to open, thus providing food for many more people.

All this will be merely a logical development of already existing methods of agricultural science and practice. It seems certain, however, that in the next few decades the advance of science will lead to new and more efficient methods of producing food, still using solar energy—the most abundant source of energy on the surface of the earth. For example, in the last few years, it has become known that minute quantities of gibberellic acids can strikingly increase the formation of plant material, and sometimes reduce sharply the time needed for plant development. When science discovers the mechanism of such compounds, it may well open the way to a fundamental revolution in agriculture. Or, to quote another example: already the question of utilizing unicellular algae, such as Chlorella, has been posed. These organisms contain a large proportion of proteins; they can utilize solar energy with an efficiency of up to 10 per cent. Using the proteins and carbohydrates of these algae, and the green leaf mass of other species of plants, chemists may find methods of cheap and profitable transformation of such abundant raw materials into different directly utilizable foodstuffs—proteins, fats, and carbohydrates; in other words, they may learn how to carry out biosynthetic processes outside the living organism. The presently known methods of chemistry are of little use for the solution of these problems; we will have to uncover the mechanisms of biocatalytic processes in living organisms, and to develop from this knowledge new, more narrowly specific—but also more effective—catalysts for biosynthesis *in vitro*.

This applies not only to food. I believe that the future development of our technology will be largely dependent on successful utilization of the working principles of living organisms. We must discover the mechanisms of the physical and chemical processes taking place in living nature and develop from them new and more specialized chemical methods, meeting fewer requirements than in the living organism, but doing this in a more efficient way. This may lead to the discovery of new catalysts, analogous to enzymes and possessing an unheard-of activity and specificity, and thus bring about a far-reaching revolution in chemical industry. One can envisage the construction, from artificial materials, of machines of an entirely new kind, permitting direct conversion of chemical into mechanical energy, as in the contraction and relaxation of the muscle. Such machines should prove better adapted to carrying out special kinds of precision work than the existing ones; and could have much higher coefficients of efficiency. In the development of the unique structures of living organisms, allowing the immensely complex processes of life to be carried out, nature has had only a very small selection of starting materials. The same building stones, such as pirymidine and purine bases, have been utilized by nature to develop structures assuring the mechanism of heredity, and those permitting energy to be stored for metabolism and muscular contraction. Armed by modern chemistry, men have a much richer choice.

Speaking in general, it can be said that the transformation of biology from a descriptive into an exact, quantitative science, which goes on before our eyes, the permeation of biology by physical chemistry, is bound to lead in the future to magnificent results —a scientific and technological revolution of no less importance than that caused by the discovery of atomic energy. The time will come when men will be able to obtain in the laboratory new proteins and nucleic acids of various desirable structures. With the mechanism of heredity fully understood, we will learn how to direct it, and how to create new species of animals and plants by mutations.

Everybody knows what spectacular successes have been achieved in the last few years in chemotherapy, particularly by the discovery of antibiotics. Many terrible, mortal diseases already have been eliminated, and the danger of others reduced. Surgery, too, has made great progress in recent years.

I believe that accelerated, systematic work in combatting disease will free men, before this century is over, from their most terrible predicament—the disease which so often carries men off at the height of their strength. The problem of long, full life will be solved.

By enumerating here the various achievements of science and technology already made or which we have the right to expect in the near future, I wanted to illustrate the vast possibilities which are now open to improve human existence. The fate of man in the atomic age can be wonderful, if mankind can succeed in turning science and technology to the benefit of all men.

We are on the threshold of a new era in history. For many thousands of years, life was hard and brought more suffering than happiness. First, men were dominated by the forces of nature, which they did not know how to command. Then forms of society developed, which could not be directed by men, leading to the domination of society by elemental forces similar to those of nature and giving rise to wars, exploitation, economic crises, and unemployment. This early era in human existence will inevitably yield place to an era of reason and justice. Man, having explored the laws of nature, has subordinated her forces to his will. By studying the laws of society, man should be able to subordinate to his will also its forces, converting the organization of society into a powerful instrument for the achievement of clearly formulated aims, assuring the happiness of all men. My nation is now going forward on such a path.

The modern development of science and technology gives mankind the full possibility of creating satisfactory life for all in the present century. Is it conceivable that we will not be able to utilize it? Is it possible that the inheritance of the unhappy past will prevent nations from beginning to build this happy future at once, in a reasonable way, and by common efforts?

Unfortunately, the same force—the enormous development of science and technology—which makes these hopes possible, is also capable of making the fate of mankind in the atomic age truly horrible, so that the sufferings of the past will be dimmed by the horrors of the future. This will happen if the peoples of the world permit an atomic war to break out, a war that would lead to the destruction of a large part of mankind, and would threaten the health of later generations. On our good will, our efforts, our determination and unity, will depend which of the two alternatives will be realized.

All of us, men of the twentieth century, carry an enormous

responsibility, not only to ourselves but also to future generations. All the disagreements between states are dwarfed by the great danger of the atomic war. We must push these conflicts back, stabilize the *status quo*, and concentrate our efforts on the one basic aim to make war impossible.

If we succeed in banishing this dark shadow, and directing our efforts at the creation of a new, radiant era for mankind, then the fate—a happy fate—of mankind in the atomic age will be secure.

NOONDAY PAPERBACKS
available at your bookstore